TOWARDS JAPAN

Audrey and Arthur, Oxford, Summer 1959

Towards Japan

A Personal Journey

▲

by

Arthur Stockwin

Oxford University

Routledge
Taylor & Francis Group

LONDON AND NEW YORK

TOWARDS JAPAN
A PERSONAL JOURNEY

First published in 2020 by RENAISSANCE BOOKS

Published 2025 by Routledge
4 Park Square, Milton Park, Abingdon, Oxon OX14 4RN
605 Third Avenue, New York, NY 10158

Routledge is an imprint of the Taylor & Francis Group, an informa business

British Library Cataloguing in Publication Data
A catalogue record for this book is available from the British Library

ISBN: 9781912961108 (hbk)
ISBN: 9781041189688 (pbk)
ISBN: 9781003708438 (ebk)

For Product Safety Concerns and Information please contact our EU representative: GPSR@taylorandfrancis.com
Taylor & Francis Verlag GmbH, Kaufingerstraße 24, 80331 München, Germany

To my remarkable family

'Life is a brief and frenetic interlude between two periods of eternal idleness'

J. A. A.

CONTENTS

‣

1

Origins

人

I WAS BORN on 28 November 1935. On that day Adolf Hitler placed all German males between the ages of eighteen and forty-five on the military reserve list, and the Italian Ministry of Propaganda banned musical performances originating from any country that had voted in the League of Nations for sanctions against Italy, following the Abyssinian crisis. Also in the same month Japan proclaimed the puppet state of East Hebei Autonomous Council in northern China. This preceded the outbreak of the Japan-China War in July 1937 by some two years and four months.

In other words, I was born into a world already careering downhill towards an unlimited military conflict that would cause over fifty million deaths worldwide and initiate nuclear war. Needless to say, I had no knowledge of any of this, and my parents, though they followed international events through the newspapers and by listening to the nine o'clock wireless (radio) news every evening, had more personal matters to deal with. My appearance in their lives had followed their marriage by nearly a year and a half, but my mother was already thirty-seven, and her labour was prolonged and difficult. My mother was a doctor, who had been pursuing a busy life working in hospitals for the Birmingham City Council. She had to give this up on marriage in April 1934 to my father, six years her junior, a practising dental surgeon, but in later life she resumed medical work on a part-time basis working in child welfare and ante-natal clinics. She also took over part of her father's medical practice in Birmingham during the war after he became ill with cancer of the throat late in 1942.

After my parents' marriage they had spent a belated honeymoon over Christmas and New Year in the Italian ski resort of Sestrières in a cylindrical hotel with a continuous ramp spiralling down from top to bottom affording an entertaining track for children who would launch tennis balls at the top, allowing their friends to capture them at the bottom. During this holiday they learned to ski on skis that today would be reserved for cross-country trekking (the heels were not fixed to the skis), and they were also able to observe gloomy members of the Mussolini clan staying at the hotel. At the New Year's dinner to welcome in 1936 my mother was placed next to an Englishman who entertained her in a cut-glass accent with stories of 'pig-sticking in India, my dear'. She wished she had been sitting next to somebody else.

My father practised dentistry in a large house on the main road between Birmingham and Sutton Coldfield (separate entities in those days), where he had built an extra room upstairs as one of two surgeries. It was in this house that I spent nearly all my childhood, except for two years in the Shropshire countryside between August 1940 and late in 1942. The address was 152 Birmingham Road, often shortened to '152'.

Building of the house began sometime in 1899 and was completed in 1900, so that it was indelibly late-Victorian, including cellars under most of the house, where we kept ancient washing machines and mangles (and slept under the stairs there for a while during the blitz), and under the roof two small attics for servants, where I occasionally slept in later years. When my parents first saw over the house, they noted an electric wiring system activating bells to summon the servants. The vendor, a solicitor, asked whether my parents would like to pay extra for it. They declined, but when they took possession they found that all the wiring had been crudely ripped out, causing no small damage to the plaster in various rooms. I imagine that the prospect of taking a solicitor to court for this act of vandalism was too daunting, and they fixed the damage themselves.

At the outbreak of war, when the horrors of the First World War were still an intensely lived experience for most of the adult population, the expectation of even worse challenges caused huge apprehension. After all, had not the former Prime Minister, Stanley Baldwin, in 1932 publicly uttered the phrase, 'The bomber will always get through'. My father once told me that preparations had been made in Birmingham hospitals to treat more casualties from bombing in the first week of the war than were treated in the whole duration of the war. No less a military expert than Basil Liddell Hart speculated that in the first week of the war 250,000 people across the UK would be killed or injured by bombing (this from Wikipedia but with no date given for his statement).

So in this general atmosphere of acute alarm, as soon as war was declared my mother took me away from the Birmingham area to friends living in Stroud, Gloucestershire. I was a little short of three months off my fourth birthday. I still retain a single memory of adults playing bowls on a well-manicured lawn in the sunshine. I am sure it was bowls and not croquet. But my mother wrote letters to my father describing scenes of disruption in the family, with the cook having left and other domestics disgruntled. This was of course still an era when having servants was normal among upper middle-class families. But the war was suddenly providing more lucrative sources of employment in factories, particularly those manufacturing munitions, and domestic servants left in droves for these new opportunities. I am not sure how long we stayed in Stroud, but it could hardly have been longer than a couple of weeks, and I also don't know how my mother was persuaded to return home so soon. The later months of 1939 and the early months of 1940 were a period referred to at the time as 'the phoney war', where rather little seemed to be happening. But for me that time was more a question of 'what if?', or more precisely, 'what if I had spent the war in Omaha, Nebraska, USA?'

Let me explain. In 1940, the American consul in Liverpool contacted my maternal grandfather, a Birmingham GP, informing him that a family having the same rather unusual surname as his was interested, for the duration of the war, in harbouring children, were any to be found in Great Britain, with the same surname or closely related to a family with that surname. My grandfather's surname was Ainscow, a name originating in Lancashire, where he also came from. A variant of the same surname is Ainscough, which today may be seen displayed on heavy digging equipment.

Even though I came to be placed squarely in the frame of transatlantic evacuation, I was never shipped off to Omaha, for the simple reason that my mother would not let me go. Nevertheless, a correspondence between the two families linked by the mere chance of having the same surname, followed this act of American altruism. The Omaha correspondent in the early years from 1940 was Betty Ainscow, who informed my grandfather that her husband's father, James Ainscow, was a schoolmaster who left Preston, Lancashire, for the United States in 1880. Betty's husband was also called James. Strangely enough, my grandfather's name too was James Ainscow. But, between them, they never managed to establish a genealogical link between the two families. We nevertheless continued to receive food parcels from them throughout the war.

In a letter to Betty dated 17 August 1940, my grandfather expressed his appreciation of the action of 'American citizens in making the offer to take British children out of harm's way', and continued:

> We have had two pretty bad raids in Birmingham this week and, although nobody is frightened or greatly worried, we all feel that children would be better out of harm's way.

In a long letter dated 19 March 1941, my grandfather gave a detailed account of the progress of the war, including the earnest hope that the US, which at that stage was participating with all the forces at its command 'short of war', would take the plunge and join the war in the full sense. He ended the letter with the following extraordinary statement:

> If, by the aid of America, we can secure victory, Britain and America must then join together to make a world of which we have all dreamed. Indeed, for the life of me, I can't see why Britain and American should not be joined in one vast Commonwealth. But that is, of course, utopian at the moment, although I feel that some kind of fusion of America and Britain would lead to the salvation of the world in which Hitlers would cease from troubling and Mussolinis would be at rest.

Such advocacy of fused sovereignty, written some seventy-eight years ago, stands in sharp contrast to the vandalising of international institutions and initiatives that is damaging the world at the present time.

For a while there was discussion between the two families of my mother accompanying me to the United States, but it was concluded that the complications would be too great.

My grandfather died early in 1943, after which my mother took up the correspondence with Betty, and this continued for many years. My parents met James and Betty in Birmingham sometime in the 1960s, but by that time I was living in Australia. Much later, I met their daughter, Sally (Sara), who kindly gave me all the letters that her family had received from my grandfather and later my mother. In them I found an invaluable family archive.

Some years ago, I told this story to an American friend and perceptive writer on Japan, T.J. Pempel, who responded, 'Arthur, if you had been brought up in Omaha, you would have weighed one hundred pounds heavier than you now do'. While that is an interesting observation on the diet of the good people of Omaha, I am more acutely aware of a more sinister aspect of my personal 'what if?' Travelling by ship across the Atlantic in 1940 and 1941 would have been through U-boat-infested waters, and I am happy never to have made the acquaintance of those sharks of the ocean. My oldest friend John (of whom more later), together with his elder brother, were similarly earmarked for trans-Atlantic trans-shipment, but mercifully that was put a stop to in their case as well.

So rather than musing too obsessively about 'what ifs?' perhaps I should focus rather on what went right in my world.

So let us re-enter the real world of what actually happened.

The village of Edgmond lies on the eastern side of Shropshire, and to the north of the West Midlands conurbation. It is two miles from the town of Newport, and eight miles from what is now Telford New Town, which was developed from the 1960s, incorporating the villages of Wellington and Oakengates. Edgmond today has about two thousand inhabitants, which in present-day terms makes it a large village, with a school, shops, post office, two pubs and other facilities. It houses the Harper Adams Agricultural College, with some 5,000 students. In 1986, it is said to have held 1,486 inhabitants, so that by reverse extrapolation it is likely to have had a population of less than one thousand in the early 1940s. That makes sense in terms of my memories of the village.

On 26 August 1940, my mother and I left Sutton Coldfield to escape the bombing in the Birmingham area, travelling to Edgmond where our friends, the Maddock family, had invited us to stay. I know the precise date of our departure from the laconic diary my father kept throughout 1940. His entry for that day reads:

No rain. Edith and Arthur gone to Maddocks, slept in shelter. Very windy night.
    9.45 – 5.

The next day he recorded:

No rain. Phoned Edith – quieter night – 9.45 – 5.05

The times refer to air raid warnings, first the alert signal, then the all clear. This was, to my knowledge, the only time that he kept a diary for a full year, and despite the momentous events of 1940, the two topics that predominated were the weather (1939-40 was a harsh winter, and the summer of 1940 hot and dry), and gardening. Even though he recorded the various bombing raids, detailing their starting and finishing times, the only wartime event that he noted was on 10 May, when he wrote, 'Germany invades Holland and Belgium'. He did not record the German invasion of France a few weeks later.

My father remained at home to run his dental practice, but often visited us at weekends, especially when we were new to Edgmond. In the event, the only damage our house sustained during the bombing, if I remember correctly, was one broken window from the effects of blast, possibly from a bomb that demolished a house about half a mile away. We had nevertheless been sleeping during nights, when the bombing of Birmingham was bad, in a substantial concrete shelter he had had constructed in the garden. I vaguely remember a conversation in which my father – or possibly somebody else – stated that in the shelter we should be safe in all circumstances except for a direct hit.

In the months before my mother and I decamped to Edgmond, I had amused myself counting barrage balloons, designed to prevent enemy aircraft flying at low altitudes, with increased targeting accuracy. I could see thirty or forty of them at one time. Also at that time (but not now) I enjoyed exceptionally acute hearing, and could detect the sound of an approaching aircraft minutes before adults could hear it. I could not distinguish friendly from enemy aircraft, and in any case the latter arrived for their nefarious missions at night.

Another thing I remember about those months before our departure was the sound of an air-raid siren, and indeed one was located down Highbridge Road, across the railway bridge and near to my paternal grandparents' home on Western Road. The alert was sounded with a series of rising and falling tones, whereas the all-clear was a single prolonged note. It is a strange fact that even today, more than three quarters of a century later, if I hear a factory siren alternating rising and falling notes, I experience a quickening of the heart beat.

When we left for Edgmond, I was four years and eight months old. When we returned to Sutton Coldfield, towards the end of 1942, I was just seven. For a small child, this was a major portion of life. I had become used to an idyllic rural environment, and was far from happy at having to return to an urban existence. Sometime after we returned, my parents showed signs of anxiety at my apparent difficulties in adjusting to city (more accurately suburban) life, and noticed that I was writing essays saying how much I disliked the city and loved the countryside. Much later, it was a thoughtful schoolmaster, Mr Burgess, who made an effort to persuade me that cities were centres of culture and variety of experience, thus helping me towards greater balance in my preferences before the two.

When we arrived at Edgmond, we stayed for about three months with Enid and Noel Maddock, whose house, Horn Cottage, was modern for its time, light and airy, though a passageway from the front door was piled high with Wellington boots. They had had two children, John and Vicky – John of about my age and Vicky two or three years younger. John was a physical boy and a bit of a tough guy. I heard somebody (possibly his mother) telling others that 'John can run up walls', and with a small child's credulity I took this literally, watching out for him to perform this feat in practice. One day, while we were staying at Horn Cottage, I went for a walk up the road with my mother in a fierce wind. When we returned by the same route, we found that a tree had fallen across the road. Its trunk was probably thinner than I remember, but we were happy about the timing of our walk. Other perils that concerned my mother as a doctor were childhood illnesses, particularly whooping cough.

In November, my mother rented a couple of rooms, with use of the kitchen, at No. 10 Shrewsbury Road, Edgmond, in a house owned by Mr and Mrs Green. According to my father's diary, this was on 25 November 1940. His entry for the same day noted, 'Clinic out of action: no gas and water. Went to meeting re evacuation "standing by".'

Mr Green was a plumber, and perhaps also a general builder. At any rate, my first career ambition was to become a plumber after his example. I became fascinated by where pipes ran in bathrooms and was sometimes able to watch him at work. The Greens had one (or was it two?) daughters. The one I remember lived in a semi-detached house with a septic tank, somewhere on the road leading into the village from Newport. They had twin daughters, named Daphne and Denise, slightly younger than me, but we played on bikes in the road outside the Greens' house with traffic no threat, because there was no traffic.

Shortly after our arrival in Edgmond, I learned from another boy that an old lady, Miss Leek, had just died at the age of ninety-nine. At the time such longevity was rare. She must have been born in 1841, or now 178 years ago, in a year when New Zealand became a British colony, the United Kingdom finally occupied Hong Kong, the Manchester to Leeds railway was opened, Robert Peel became prime minister, the first edition of *Punch* was published, the Royal Botanical Gardens at Kew were opened to the public, and the penny red postage stamp replaced the penny black.

The Greens' house was next to the village hall, a wooden structure housing various local events, and down the road on the other side was a chapel, whose denomination, according to Wikipedia, was primitive Methodist, if that is indeed the same chapel.

My memories of Edgmond are fragmentary, but a few of them quite vivid. My parents were seriously concerned with my education, since I was nearly five when my mother and I first arrived, and she took me to see the local school, which I remember as bright and cheerful. But rather than sending me to an ordinary school, my parents decided that I should be given private tuition, as well as lessons given me by my mother. So every day I walked or cycled to the other side of the village, to a large house in extensive grounds just beyond the village church. The house was owned by a lady who in my eyes fell into the category of 'ancient', but also 'formidable', called Mrs Goodbody (I think she may have been a Quaker). She had three grandchildren, Janet, aged about ten, Jerome (pronounced 'Jerrum'), probably seven or eight when the classes began, and Paddy, who was about my age. From my perspective, Janet was far too old, Jerrum was too rough but with Paddy I got along reasonably well. We formed a small class from two, or perhaps three families, and our tutor was Mrs Reynolds. I am almost certain that Paddy Goodbody was in the class, and the name 'Leadbeater' stays in the memory. We took classes in a room with a magnificent view of the Wrekin, a mountain rising from the surrounding country-side to the height of 407 metres above sea level, giving rise to the local expression common even today in parts of the West Midlands, 'I had to go all round the Wrekin to get there.'

In retrospect, I have long believed that it was a mistake not to send me to the local school in Edgmond. When I did finally go to school, after we were back in Sutton Coldfield and I was already seven, I was unused to interacting with large numbers of other boys, and took a long time to adjust. I remember my paternal grandfather telling me, soon after we returned from Edgmond, 'It really is time for you to go to school.' As an only child, I probably lacked interaction in Edgmond with other children and became somewhat solitary. My mother was a strong personality. I was in her company for much of the time and needed to establish my own individuality. But in Edgmond I never made a close friend of my own age, which would have helped me in this essential task. On the positive side, I suppose I read a lot, and enjoyed a carefree existence growing up in the countryside. My parents bought me *The Children's Encyclopaedia*, edited by Arthur Mee, a multi-volume work which I read from on many occasions, and still retain. It is imbued with Victorian religious values (though it was first published in 1908), but the religious bits did not much interest me, and instead I was entranced by abridged stories such as that of Tartarin de Tarascon, about a French eccentric living in the Pyrenees, obsessed with baobab trees, and *The Count of Monte Christo*, who was held captive by criminals for many years, but in the end managed an ingenious escape (they are both in volume 7). When my parents were giving me its eight volumes they discovered that volume 8 was missing, and it appeared that somebody had stolen it. There was quite a row about this, but it was never found, and to this day I only have the first seven volumes.

Mentioning religion reminds me that at Edgmond, for the only time in my childhood, I attended Sunday school regularly. My parents were not religious, but I suppose they sent me to Sunday school supposing that it would 'do me some good', or just to give me something to do on a Sunday. I retain three memories of that experience. One was when we were taken to 'beat the bounds of the church', which I found enjoyable, if a bit hard to understand. The second must have been shortly after our arrival, when I was still very small. The vicar, presumably referring to the story of the Magi, asked us 'Where is the Far East?' I stuck up my hand and replied, 'It's Australia, and my Auntie lives in Australia.' Everybody laughed, much to my embarrassment. A more serious memory was when the vicar recounted the story of the Good Samaritan, and the moral message of that story has stayed with me.

There were some occasions that brought the village together. One of the most enjoyable was gleaning. Opposite 10 Shrewsbury Road was a wheat field, which we could enter over a style. After harvest in midsummer, villagers would gather carrying sacks, and collect ears of wheat and other grains that had been left on the ground after the harvest. It was back-breaking work, but a convivial occasion, and I think we supplemented the harvest to some small extent. All sorts of agricultural activity were encouraged during the war, in 'Dig for Britain' campaigns. I have a photograph of a village gathering, including the vicar, with myself and other children in the foreground, next to a huge pile of potatoes. The potato harvest has escaped my memory, but the photo is there to prove it.

I also retain an old cine film, which shows me and the Dowding twins cycling in circles on the road outside the Greens' house, with not a vehicle in sight. Few vehicles were allowed on the roads during the war, so that we were wonderfully safe. Daphne and Denise were a little younger than I was, but I played with them quite often. On one occasion, probably soon after our arrival in the village, I caused hilarity among the adults, by telling the twins, 'I will marry you', without specifying which of these two delightful young ladies I was targeting. I remember also playing with other children in hay barns, which were a child's paradise.

Quite often we went for cycle rides in the surrounding countryside, including one occasion at a weekend when my father was visiting. I had a bicycle with a wicker basket attached to the handlebars, which attracted critical comments from other children. My parents were not particularly sensitive to the culture of children, who regarded some things as trendy and others as unfashionable, though I doubt that the word 'trendy' had been invented at that point in history. But on this particular weekend the weather was fine and we were enjoying our cycle ride, until I went too fast down a steep hill, was unable to control the bike (which was probably too big for me), skidded on gravel, came off and cut a gash on my knee. The scar remained for many years.

On one occasion, I attended my first ever political event. There was a by-election in the local constituency, and one of the candidates was holding a rally on a local square. I forget (if I ever knew) to which party he belonged, and I doubt that I understood much of what he was saying. I think John Maddock was with me, and he purported to know more about what this was all about than I did.

On 8 December 1941, my mother woke me up in my bedroom and told me that the Japanese had bombed Pearl Harbor, and that the Japanese were 'very naughty'. She could hardly have imagined, in those dark days of the war, that I was to spend most of my career studying that extraordinary country and its people.

One memorable event was a trip to Lilleshall, only a short distance from Edgmond. There we climbed up to 'The Monument', at the top of a substantial hill. For the first time in my life I could look down from the top of a mountain (in my terms) at the landscape below. There were occasional cars and lorries travelling along the road that looked like toys. This was a lesson in perspective, perhaps, and an anticipation of many mountains to come, though to this day I have never climbed the Wrekin. We also sometimes fished for minnows in a stream just out of Edgmond on the way to Lilleshall.

Edgmond in those years was a haven of peace in a world at war. My mother would sometimes receive letters from friends in London and elsewhere telling how they had been bombed out, or other families had been bombed out in the same street. She was careful not inflict on me these tales of violence and destruction. But I do remember some people visiting one evening and describing vividly air raids that they had experienced. I think my reaction was one of excitement rather than of anxiety.

This was the era of rations and ration books, but my main memory of those was after we were back in Sutton Coldfield. I suppose that in the Shropshire countryside the situation for families was easier because of the availability of local produce.

When we paid a visit to Edgmond perhaps four or five years after we had left, No.10 Shrewsbury Road had become the village Post Office, with the front room taken up by the Post Office and a large red post box outside. Sometime in the 1960s, my parents attended the wedding of one of the twins (I think it was Denise), who married an RAF officer. Mrs Green lived to a great age, but spent her declining years in Yorkshire, where she had relatives. Her husband had predeceased her. I am not sure what happened to the Goodbody children. I believe John Maddock married locally, but Vicky married a Frenchman and went to live in Paris.

One day, the war was brought close to our doorsteps in this rural haven. A German plane came down in a field close to the village. The military police were quickly on the scene and arrested the pilot. I have only the haziest memory of this episode, but my mother talked to me about it much later.

Writing this in our French hideout in the Monts de Forez, with the other side of the valley hazy in the spring sunshine, all dark green forest and smaller areas of light green fields, and closer by, a line of red tiled roofs on a low rise in the middle distance, I think of Edgmond, that quiet village that aroused in me a love of the countryside in my early years, as well as of reading, and remains an indelible part of my life.

By the end of 1942, the bombing in Birmingham had eased off, and some time towards winter we returned to Sutton Coldfield. My maternal grandfather (Grandpa Ainscow), a GP but (incredible as it may seem today) a heavy smoker, had contracted cancer of the throat. He came to stay with us at 152, where my mother cared for him, but died in January 1943. From all I heard about him later, I know that he was a powerful personality, intellectually gifted and to some extent politically engaged. He ran a working-class practice in Birmingham, and although I am ignorant of the extent of his commitment, he became involved with left-wing or left-liberal ideas. But when I was a five or six year-old boy, having met him only occasionally, I found him a rather forbidding authority figure. On one occasion when he was visiting us, and I was playing around with a typewriter, my grandfather said I should use all of my fingers on my keys, instead of simply tapping with the first finger of my right hand. I found this unhelpful, having no idea how to put the advice into practice. But a decade or so later, I taught myself to type with all fingers, using a typists' manual – an absolutely invaluable skill for life. This was over one Christmas and I was so absorbed in the task that my mother upbraided me for being unsociable.

The other reason for returning from Edgmond was to send me to school. When, in January 1943, I was enrolled at Wylde Green College, a private establishment a few minutes' walk from 152 along the main Birmingham Road, I faced serious difficulties fitting in. As a new boy, arriving already one term into the school year, and not having been to a real school before, I found myself isolated and to some extent bullied. At the time there was a radio comedian called Arthur Askey. I hardly remember him. But I retain an acute memory of having to stand in the middle of a circle of boys in the playground, all of whom were chanting 'Arthur Askey, Arthur Askey'. Eventually, this kind of treatment triggered an angry reaction in me, and I lashed out at one of the boys, causing him minor injury. My parents were contacted and interviewed, my tormentors were given a detention, and although I was told that what I had done was wrong, I was actually advised to use my fists if taunted in future. The school authorities worked to defuse the situation, to good effect.

Gradually, I adjusted to the rough and tumble of the school and became much happier, but the first few weeks (perhaps more) were a shock and a challenge. I feel sure that all this could have been avoided had I been sent to a proper school in Edgmond.

There was another reason why my life at school took a turn for the better. Every week the marks we had accumulated in the various subjects (everything marked out of ten) were totalled, we ourselves had to write out, in our best handwriting, a table in a standard format giving our scores, this was endorsed with a comment by the form master, signed by the headmaster, Mr Oscar J. Cotton, then taken home for a parent's signature. There was no attempt to conceal how everybody else had done, our total score was given a ranking (e.g. 4th out of 25), and the winning score was also stated. So the competitive principle was given full rein.

One of the other boys in the class, whose name was John Buckler, very frequently topped the class. He was bright, worked hard and consistently, whereas I tended to work in bursts, after which I tended to slacken off, finding it hard to maintain consistency of effort. This meant that most weeks John's overall performance was ahead of mine, but just occasionally, perhaps one time in ten, I would dethrone him from his exalted position.

One day, we had a conversation, in which John gave me to understand that he regarded me as serious competition. From this conversation began a lifelong friendship, which at this time of writing in 2019 has lasted some seventy-six years. We have taken very different professional paths; for over two decades we were living in different countries, and in some respects our fundamental systems of belief are discrepant, but we have remained firm friends. I have known John for many more years than I have known anybody else, and I believe that he can say the same thing about me. Quite often, when I am trying to sort out my own mind on some issue or other, I think to myself, 'What would John's opinion be about this?'

2

Schooldays

ᴧ

MY LIFE AFTER we returned to Sutton Coldfield was stable, disruptions caused by the war largely came to an end, we remained in the same house throughout my schooldays, had very much the same circle of friends, and I followed a course of education from primary school to secondary school without interruption. My father practised dentistry at home, my mother worked part time in various clinics, and also, being trained in anaesthesia, put my father's patients into temporary sleep when a difficult extraction had to be made. My father tended my teeth until I was living in Australia many years later.

Even though the number of domestic servants throughout the country had plummeted dramatically as they found more lucrative employment opportunities during the war, my mother retained a maid called Rene, inherited, I believe from her mother-in-law, and Rene was almost a second mother to me in my very early years. My mother once told me that her mother-in-law had told her when they married that she did not want her son to be involved in domestic chores, and I can only imagine how my mother – professionally trained and a liberated woman – may have responded to that. Rene, however, in effect became part of the family, and even accompanied us on holidays to the coast. She was with us until her fiancé, Albert, came back from the war in 1945, they married and went to live in Stoke-on-Trent, where Albert worked in a ceramics factory painting decorations on pottery. My father made it clear that he didn't want me making a lot of noise in the house while he was treating patients, so that Rene told me that if I continued to be noisy, she would close my mouth with sticking plaster. I am sure she would not have done that in practice, but I took her threat seriously and was wary of her for some time after that. I doubt that it made any difference to the decibel count.

After Rene left, we had a succession of cleaning ladies. There was one, whose name I forget, who gave (sold?) us a collection of poems she had written about life during the war. There was a young woman called Linda, whom I identified as a misery-box. If I remember rightly, her favourite expression was 'darn it!'. This had nothing to do with darning socks (a favourite occupation of the time), but was a corruption of 'damn it'. But Linda was replaced by Jean, in my eyes cheerful and lively where Linda had been miserable and resentful. I liked Jean, and was inclined to support her. On one occasion, in Jean's absence, I heard my parents criticising her and I retorted 'I think you underestimate Jean'. My parents then explained that they had received her from a Catholic home for delinquent children and young adults, that she had problems and that she had been seen kissing a soldier on the street. Reflecting on this last point, I thought that for a girl to kiss a soldier on the street was a slightly odd thing to do, but why make such a meal of it? I still had life lessons to learn. But I still hope that Jean was able to make something of her life.

But eventually, the family attained a stable condition in domestic help. And then there was Elsie, daughter of old Mr Smith, the gardener, who came from rural north Oxfordshire. For some reason we knew her as Flossie. She stayed for many years, she was intelligent and in a later generation might well have received high level education and entered one of the professions. She had one daughter, but her husband died young. She looked after my parents in their declining years.

My father employed a dental mechanic, who worked in what had originally been the stables in the back yard. The first occupant of that post was Jim Orme, and when I was very young I assumed that anybody with the name 'Jim' was a reincarnation of Mr Orme. His successor was Mr Mackenzie, whom everybody called 'Mac'. I got on with Mac, who was a happy-go-lucky character, driving a succession of clapped-out cars, including a Singer of dubious reliability. These cars, however, proved his downfall, because he was so often late for work that my father sacked him. And he once sacked a gardener for reasons I thought unjustified. I was really cross with my father for getting rid of Mac. His successor, however, was Arnold

Skeates (Mr Skeates to me), who later on exercised a curious influence on the intellectual development of me as a confused teenager, as I will describe later.

Finally, we normally had a gardener. At the beginning of the war the gardener was a Mr Clark, who had a wonderful way of murdering the English language with such questions as, 'What do you want me to do with your high geraniums?', and 'Can I clean the gilt on your wife's car?' But Mr Clark, like so many others at the time, went off to work in a munitions factory. And then there was Mr Baldwin, a much older man. Our garden had thirteen elm trees down one side of it. One day, my father asked Mr Baldwin to cut back the upper branches of the trees, in order to bring them down to a manageable height. I watched him near the top of a long ladder against an elm, using an ordinary saw to cut back some substantial branches. One branch fell in a way he had not anticipated, and he was lucky not to have been thrown to the ground many feet below.

One gardener, who was not with us for long, lived in a terrace house on the way to the Boldmere shops where my father did his banking, so he sometimes gave this man a lift back to his home. Once having dropped him off, he saw him come straight out of the house again in an agitated state exclaiming, 'Mr Stockwin, just come and look what's happened.' When my father entered the house, he found that all its contents had been removed, including the beds and the stove. The gardener's wife and daughter had emptied the whole house during the morning while he had been working in our garden. I have no memory of any sequel to this story, but I have a feeling that my father did something to help him.

But our most memorable gardener was old Mr Smith. As I have mentioned, he was brought up in the northern part of Oxfordshire, I think somewhere near Aynho. In fact, his early life must have been spent close in place and time to the events recounted in *Lark Rise to Candleford*. He once told me how his father could afford 'one pint of beer a week', but 'we never wanted for nothing', and I think he sang in a local choir. Sometimes he would reminisce about 'drunken Deddington', a village not far from where my family and I eventually made our home.

So I was growing up as an only child, but in a household that was also a business, employing a number of people over the years. In terms of the English class system, our family was incontrovertibly

middle class, in a leafy outer suburb of a big city, where middle class
values predominated. Even now, Sutton Coldfield has never voted
into Parliament any candidate who did not belong to the Conservative Party. The English middle class, however, was then, and is now,
very far from uniform. Our family was comfortably off, but hardly
wealthy, professional, but not in touch with captains of industry or
people of influence in other spheres. Indeed my father, as a dentist
practising on his own and in effect running his own small business,
identified himself most closely with small businesses. Although he
served on various local dental committees, he was not comfortable
with bureaucracy, thought local councillors were mostly hopeless,
and was happiest chatting with his mates at the golf club about
camera equipment or grafting plants. Once, when my exchange
friend François was staying with us, my father with a bowl of fruit
in front of him, listed the various NHS and other dental committees of which he was a member and commented, 'And all that adds
up to nothing more than that orange'. François responded, 'Ah oui,
j'ai compris ça.'

My father was also intensely provincial, having spent all his life in
the Birmingham area, and rarely visited London. I was twelve years
old the first time I was taken to London; of course, the war prevented it in the earlier years. For me the highlight of that visit was
eating a glorious 'knickerbocker glory' at a Lyons Corner House.
I think we also saw No 10, Downing Street, with hardly any security in those days.

One organisation that my father cordially disliked was the Freemasons. His dislike stemmed from an encounter with somebody
who had advised him to join the Masons 'so that you can attract
more patients, since we Masons work together'. I think it was the
exclusiveness or 'secret society' element he identified with the Freemasons that upset him, showing that he valued equality (of opportunity at least).

Politically, my father was a straight-down-the-line Conservative,
but not extreme. In contemporary terms, he would probably be
seen as a 'one-nation Tory'. He didn't much like the Attlee Labour
Government of the post-war years, and especially criticised 'Aneu-
rin Bevan and all his works'. When Bevan introduced the National
Health Service in 1948, my father and many of his fellow dentists
held back from it, though eventually they nearly all joined (there

was probably no financially viable alternative), and in later years I believe he was well reconciled to it. I am fairly certain that my mother voted Conservative, and spoke sometimes about 'my comfortable standard of living', but her political views were also affected by her father's experiences of running a working class medical practice in some of the most deprived parts of Birmingham. She told me once of a conversation her father had had with a friend of his, Mr Riley. Whereas Mr Riley was impressed with Mussolini for draining the Pontine marshes – a malarial swamp south of Rome – and 'making the trains run on time', my grandfather deplored his anti-democratic methods.

Another organisation some of whose practices and attitudes my parents found hard to accept was the Roman Catholic Church. This was particularly true of my mother and of her family, most of whom had also become doctors. While working in public health for the Birmingham City Council, my mother had encountered Catholic priests who she believed were encouraging women in the slums of Birmingham to have more children in order to boost the number of Catholics in the population. How far this was true I am not sure, but the anti-Catholicism of her and other members of her family (including those in Australia) was intense. She believed that many Catholic businesspeople tried so far as possible to deal with others of their faith to the exclusion of others. I myself was sceptical of this until, as a university student looking after English tourists in northern Italy during the summer vacation in 1957, I had in my group a Catholic couple from Birmingham – wife Irish, husband English – who told me that whenever possible they would do business with fellow Catholics. I think I made no adverse comment, but much later looked back on that conversation with deep sadness that people should discriminate in this way. The wife also told me that the idea of married clergy, normal in non-Catholic denominations, disgusted her. I suppose that what they saw as the exclusivity common to Freemasons and Roman Catholics was a common factor influencing my parents' attitudes.

But, people, circumstances and practices may change. Many years later, when my Great Aunt Winnie was old and ill, my parents found her in a distressed state alone in her house. While they were there the local Church of England vicar called, in search of a collection box for his church, but showing scant interest in her welfare. Later, some Catholic nuns came round, 'and could not have been more helpful', according to my parents. So, on occasion, humanity trumps ideology, perhaps.

One of my principal themes in this book is to discover how it was that the son of a Sutton Coldfield dentist should have become an academic researching the politics of Japan. In other words, why did a young man brought up in the environment I have been describing tread a path towards a life and career so distant from his parents' assumptions, environment and horizons. Having been clear from an early age that medicine and dentistry were not for me, I had little idea what I really wanted to do as a career. Curiously enough, my closest friend, John Buckler, with whom I shared so many experiences throughout childhood from seven onwards, was almost the opposite. He had no medical tradition in his family (except for his elder brother later), but I cannot remember a time when he did not know that what he wanted to do was medicine.

One thing for which I am eternally grateful to my father is that he took great pains to interest me in what was going on in the war. It was from the battle of El Alamein in 1942 that I began to show interest in the war, so my specific war memories were confined to the period in which the Allies were winning, This was around the time that we returned from Edgmond. At our house in Sutton Coldfield I had a large map of Europe stuck onto the kitchen wall, and on it I marked every day the current position of the front on both sides of Germany with pins. This meant that I had to find where the front was by locating it in the morning newspaper. With my interest in geography and place names I was particularly interested in the eastern front, with the exotic names in the area such as Dneprozherzhinsk. Some of my school friends at primary school wore pullovers with 'Red Army' embroidered on them. We knew little or nothing about the realities of life in the Soviet Union, but the Russians were our brave allies in the war against the Nazis and that was what mattered. This was a view shared widely also by adults, and my parents took me to see the 'Sword of Stalingrad' exhibited in a public building in Birmingham. I was eight at the time. It had been presented by Churchill to Stalin in November 1943.

The main building of Wylde Green College consisted of three classrooms divided from each other by retractable partitions, so that at morning assembly and prayers the headmaster could address the whole school. Mr Cotton was a big man with an imposing presence and powerful voice. I believe that he himself had attended Harrow School, which probably explained why *Forty Years On* was not only the song of Harrow, but also of Wylde Green College:

Forty years on, growing older and older, shorter in wind, as in memory long,
    Feeble of foot and rheumatic of shoulder, what will it help you that once you were strong?

This strikes me as too pessimistic a message. Why inform enthusiastic youngsters that in a few decades they must expect to be old and decrepit?

The majority of teachers in the school were women, no doubt because many of their male counterparts were away fighting for King and Country. Of the men, Mr Muir taught maths, and insisted on calling me J.A² Stockwin. (Many years later I encountered an old school friend, who greeted me with, 'Ah yes, J.A².') Knowing also that my father was a dentist, Mr Muir would also occasionally refer to me as 'the molar man'. Of course, we had nicknames for the teachers, but experiencing the process in reverse was unusual. Then there was Mr Howard, in charge of games, who must have been close to retirement. When summer began, he sang the praises of cricket as the greatest among sports (unfortunately, I did not shine at cricket). Among the women, I remember Miss Holden, who also taught maths. She was a starchy lady, who insisted that all exercises be written out in full, with no abbreviations permitted. This annoyed my Grandpa Stockwin, a retired schoolmaster who was giving me informal tuition. In the family he referred to her scornfully as 'Miss Hogben'.

There was also Miss Bixby, whom we generally disliked. I am not entirely sure why we disliked her, but I suppose, using contemporary language, she was not empathetic. One day the teacher of French told us that she would be away and would have to miss her next lesson, but that Miss Bixby would stand in for her. Now we happened to know that Miss Bixby knew no French. We arrived at the lesson in heightened anticipation of what was to come, and itching to point out any mistakes she might make. Miss Bixby arrived at the class well briefed by the regular French teacher, and proceeded to write French vocabulary on the blackboard. She didn't try to pronounce any of it, as that would have given her away. She gave us no target to aim at until she came to the word 'vieille' (feminine of 'vieux' = 'old'). This she spelled 'veille', omitting the first 'i'.

'Please Miss, you haven't spelled that right: it is "v i e i l l e".' The poor woman grimly corrected her mistake and doggedly continued the lesson to the end.

And then there was a wonderful Welsh teacher called Miss Brooks-Evans, to savour the magic of whose name you had to pronounce it with a Welsh lilt. When she deigned to address me, she would preface her remarks by, 'You're a nuisance, Stockwin.'

> 'Please Miss, can you help me tie my tie?'
> 'You're a nuisance, Stockwin.'
> 'Please Miss, I've forgotten to bring my homework.'
> 'You're a nuisance, Stockwin.'

Well, I was so much in love with Miss Brooks-Evans that I have worked hard at being a nuisance ever since.

I know that my parents had the expectation that I would eventually specialise in science subjects, but they also wanted me to learn languages. Ultimately, the second of these objectives was achieved, but not the first. Not long after we returned from Edgmond, they arranged for me to have private lessons in French with an elderly French language teacher called M. Ledoyen. He inhabited a basement flat on Easy Row, right in the centre of Birmingham. The lessons were held at a large table facing shelves of books in French and German – the latter in Gothic script, which intrigued me. Not much light penetrated the room from the outside, and his eyesight was failing. The place was gloomy in the extreme, but he taught me some of the basics of French. The contact had come through my Grandma Ainscow, whom he had also taught before the war, as she and my grandfather used to go on continental holidays. I retain a guide to French grammar written by him, from the pre-war period.

My Grandpa Stockwin and his wife, my grandmother, lived within easy walking distance of our house, so I often went there after school. His name was Arthur Samuel Stockwin, and he never admitted to having a second name because of the initials. If my grandmother wanted to tease him, she would call him 'Sammy'. He was a science teacher, between 1900 (also the year of his marriage) and his retirement in 1939, in the Higher Elementary School in Aston (an inner

Birmingham suburb), which in 1915 became Aston Commercial School. I enjoyed inspecting leaves and other natural items through his microscope. But he also gave me extra tuition in maths (which I struggled with) and even in Latin. He, like my father, had spent all his life in the Birmingham area, so far as I know he had never been abroad, although he and his wife went on holiday to Ireland (still part of Great Britain) in the summer of 1903, and I have inherited a photograph of an isolated house in the Irish countryside where they stayed. Since my father was born in March 1904, he pointed out to me many years later an upstairs window on the photo, beyond which was 'definitely the room where I was conceived'.

In those years just after the war, my hobby was collecting and breeding butterflies. I had a green butterfly net (to blend with the landscape), a bottle of chloroform, a collection cabinet, and boxes of pins. In these ecological times collecting butterflies by killing them is no longer acceptable, but in those days that was not the case. One Christmas, my father gave me a retractable glass fronted box that he had made himself, in which I could place caterpillars (larvae), together with their favourite plants, where I could watch them go through the stages of chrysalis (pupa) and butterfly (imago). I read obsessively through Richard South, *The Butterflies of the British Isles* and his *The Moths of the British Isles*, and meticulously recorded every specimen I added to my collection.

Over forty years later, when I came to clear my parents' house in 1990, I rediscovered my butterfly collection in the loft. But nothing of it was left, apart from a few bits of butterfly wing. Ironically, all my precious butterflies and moths had been eaten by their own relatives – other insects.

In 1944 and 1945 we went on holiday to Nefyn (in those days anglicised as 'Nevin', but with the same pronunciation), on the coast of the Lleyn peninsula in North Wales. On the first occasion we caught a train from Birmingham in the middle of the night, eventually arriving at Pwlleli on the southern side of the peninsula and taking a wheezy old taxi across the peninsula to Nefyn. We stirred cups of tea on the station at Ruabon, on the Welsh border, with a spoon that was chained to the counter, having 'stirred ten thousand cups'. During the second holiday we stayed at a house called 'Ty Cerrig' (Stone House), owned by a Mrs Jones, an interesting and intelligent lady with a fund of knowledge about Welsh culture. I remember watching farmers arriving from the hills for a cattle market, and was fascinated by the sound of the Welsh language. I was now a practised swimmer and was able to swim from one side of the bay to the other, as well as exploring rock pools for hermit crabs. Most evenings I joined a queue at the local fish-and-chip shop, buying fish and chips wrapped in newspaper. I saw this as a step towards independence.

Back home in Sutton Coldfield, I would now walk down to the local shops every Tuesday to buy comics: specifically the *Wizard* and the *Dandy*. The *Wizard* specialised in boys' adventure stories, including 'Has Wilson come back?' concerning an athlete of extraordinary powers, appearing to be semi-immortal, who conquers Mount Everest, but is posted as missing in the Battle of Britain. I am astounded to find that there is today at least one website devoted to his fictitious memory. There was also a story about a massive waterspout that devours everything in its path off the western coast of Scotland and up to Iceland, and at one point actually straddles the Mull of Kintyre. The *Dandy* contained comic strips with the adventures of the muscle-bound Desperate Dan, and the ingenious Corky the Cat. Some adults at the time decried comics as debasing children's reading abilities, but I learned a great deal from them, including what made a good storyline, and how to construct coherent and grammatical sentences.

In the summer of 1945, my mother spent a month or so ill in bed. I am not sure what was wrong with her medically, but I suspect that part of the reason was severe overwork. The morning after 6 August she told me dramatically from her bed that 'they have split the atom'. The concept of 'atom' was probably new to me, so in the ensuing days and weeks were partly spent in learning some of the science behind an atom bomb, and the same would have been true of my friends. We went a short trip into Wales, where I was trying to envisage, using a Welsh valley as reference, the spatial extent of destruction affecting two Japanese cities. On the morality of what had been done, my parents, whom I do not remember criticising the 'conventional' bombing of German cities in the later stages of the war, expressed serious reservations about using the atom bomb against Japan. But my memory is vague about the nature of their reasoning.

My later years at Wylde Green College were dominated by the need to prepare for entrance to King Edward's School, Birmingham. This involved some tough examinations, covering all the main school subjects studied to that point, followed by an interview with the Headmaster. I worked extremely hard for the exams, coached as before by my Grandpa Stockwin. One interest of mine, going back to early childhood, was the study of maps. I have a curious memory, soon after we arrived in in Edgmond, of being shown a map, and told that 'this is a map of Europe'. Now I knew that Europe was a large area of land, but I could not understand how a piece of paper infinitely smaller than that area of land could also be 'Europe'. I must, however, have figured out eventually that a map is a drastically reduced representation of an area of land on the earth's surface, because I obtained an atlas, from which I set about learning where all the countries of the world were located relative to each other, what their shape looked like, and the names of their capital cities. One of the tasks in the geography exam for King Edward's was to indicate where specific countries were located on a map of the world where boundaries were marked but not country names. One of these was Mexico, which I correctly located on the southern border of the United States. But as I left the room I caught sight momentarily of another candidate's script with Mexico occupying the whole of South America. That put a spring into my step.

Before I presented myself for an interview with the headmaster, my parents told me firmly that I must address him as 'Sir'. I knew that he was far, far above my station in age, rank, experience, understanding and height, so it was not difficult to accept my parents' advice, which indeed I took all too literally:

'What is your favourite school subject and why do you like it?'

'My favourite subject, Sir, is geography, and I like it, Sir, because, Sir, I enjoy looking at maps and learning, Sir, the names of countries and their capitals, Sir, and I want to be able to visit them some day, Sir.'

But what saved me in the interview was a curious ocular phenomenon caused, I am told, by flexibility in a child's eye. Around that time in my life I would be sitting in a chair looking at some scene of people or objects, and I would gradually see these recede into the distance. On this particular occasion, when I was about half way through the interview, I realised that this eminent headmaster (who would go on to be Vice-Chancellor of the University of Leeds as Sir Charles Morris) was becoming smaller and smaller, and I gained in confidence as our relative size began to alter in my favour. I may have been a little worried that the receding headmaster would disappear altogether, but that did not happen, so that I was able to finish the interview feeling more confident than when it started (and I was accepted into the school, as was John Buckler). This may well have been the last time that I experienced receding vision, which disappeared with the arrival of adolescence. Whether I had read *Alice in Wonderland* by that time I do not remember, but in any case it was a physical phenomenon and not related to the imagination.

Life at King Edward's was more challenging than at Wylde Green College. For one thing, instead of walking to and from school (and also back and forth for lunch – called dinner in those days), we caught a train around eight o-clock in the morning to steamy, sooty Birmingham New Street, then a tram (in later years a bus) to school in Edgbaston. And then I would be back home at five or six in the evening for supper, followed by often demanding homework. The train journeys stimulated an interest in engine numbers, like several of our school-friends. We desperately wanted to see the 'Lickey Banker', an engine whose sole purpose was to push trains with inadequate power up the track over the Lickey Hills south of Birmingham, but I don't think we ever got to see it.

My form master in the first year was Captain Power, a man of advanced years, known to his pupils as 'Codger'. He seems to have been a controversial figure, but I got on with him quite well. He taught us Latin and devised Latin names for all members of the class. I was 'Ditesce' (grow rich!), a boy called North was 'Boreas' (north wind) and Oliphant was 'Olea Formica' (olive ant).

We had different masters for different subjects – too many to list. But I will mention Mr Street, an elderly master who taught us French. He spoke in a rasping voice and indicated his displeasure with the phrase, often repeated, 'Boy, you have the brains of a wasp!' He had taught my father when the school was still in New Street, central Birmingham. During the First World War the school employed a number of women teachers with so many male teachers away at the war. Mr Street had the habit of answering any knock on the classroom door with 'Entrez!' One day, there was a timid tap at the door prompting Mr Street to respond in his usual way. The door did not open. This happened more than once. Eventually Mr Street exploded with 'Come in, you blithering idiot!', and in walked one of the women teachers. He had to apologise and the class strove to suppress its collective mirth.

In my second year at King Edwards, I was in a class whose form master was the larger than life figure of M.A. Porter, M.A. At the end of term we took internal exams in the subjects we were studying. A group of us conducted a post-mortem on the exams once they were over (or perhaps after we knew the results). Most of my friends expressed the opinion that they preferred exams involving calculation, in other words maths and science. I had never really thought about this before, but it suddenly entered my consciousness that, no, the exams I most enjoy were those on history and languages. I had always found maths difficult, except perhaps for geometry, which was spatial, so that I could envisage the problem as a set of linear relationships. After all, the solution to Pythagoras' theorem, 'The square on the hypotenuse is equal to the sum of the squares on the other two sides' was pure poetry to my ears. But numbers lacked the kind of immediacy, the kind of familiarity, that attached to words or to drawings. The Indian mathematician Ramanojan famously regarded numbers as 'my friends', but I had never managed to make social contact with their exclusive community.

In the classroom used by Mr Porter and his class, there was a small library of popular fiction, available for us to borrow, 'so as to broaden the range of our reading'. My parents noticed that I had brought home a novel titled *To the Gallows I must Go*, whose fictional narrator had murdered his wife and was facing execution. The writing was lurid, and there was another book even more lurid than that (but of course no explicit sex in those days). My parents became concerned about the turn my reading had apparently taken, and wrote to Mr Porter, who replied apologising for not checking more carefully what was in his class library. At that time the death penalty was still applied, and widely taken as normal.

Between second and third years a crucial decision had to be made – whether to specialise in science or in arts and humanities. Based on my performance in the various subjects so far, the school put me down for arts and humanities, and more specifically, for classics. My parents were concerned about this and asked for an interview with the newly arrived headmaster, Thomas Howarth. The letter my father wrote to him specified that they had expected I would be on the science side, with languages as a supplement. Mr Howarth managed to persuade them that classics was a good intellectual option, although he could see that these scientifically trained parents found the idea that their son would concentrate on the study of Latin, Greek and ancient history decidedly exotic and felt they were stepping into uncharted territory. According to their account of the interview, he treated the issue with some light-hearted humour and was able to win them round.

There was a further demarche that might just possibly have sent me in a different direction from Greek and Latin classics. One of the history masters, Mr Osborne, whom I liked and respected for his teaching and for the sense that I could talk with him easily with little sense of hierarchy, tried to persuade me to move to history as my main focus. I considered this with due care and was tempted to follow his advice. In a diary I have only just rediscovered, I noted that Mr Osborne regarded my essays as quite different from those of my colleagues. This was probably because I once wrote an essay on 'Revolution', in which I recorded the things that happened in one of the earth's 'revolutions'. Other teachers would probably have found this entirely out of order, but Mr Osborne seems to have taken it as a sign of originality. But in the end I decided to stick with classics. History was a favourite subject of mine, but so were languages, and since classics combined the two, that was the direction I took.

In those days, the examination regime of O-levels (later GCEs, later GCSEs), followed two years later by A-levels, was like walking along a path gradually narrowing into a bottleneck. Pupils were expected to specialise to an extraordinary extent, though our school tried various means to ensure we learned at least something about other areas of knowledge. One subject we took for O-levels was 'general science', but quite frankly it was a Micky Mouse subject that the teachers found difficult to take seriously. On the other hand, in the sixth form we participated in a not-for examination course on modern English literature taught by an inspiring teacher called Tony Trott, whose teaching has had a strong influence on my approach to literature. But my science-trained mother once discovered to her surprise that I didn't know plastics were derived from hydrocarbons.

I am getting ahead of myself here, because I was still only in the third year of secondary school, and external exams were still some years ahead. In the school year that began in the autumn of 1948

I joined the weirdly named 'classical upper middle', abbreviated to 'CLUM'. The form master was a soft spoken man with a sharp mind and a firm will, Mr Williams, whose surely undeserved school nickname was 'Stuffer'. Several years later he was ordained into the Church of England. It was under his tuition that I began to study ancient Greek, to consolidate my knowledge of Latin begun in the earlier two years, and to read Greek and Roman history through textbooks such as *A History of Greece to the Death of Alexander the Great*, by J.B. Bury, whose first edition had been published in 1900. This was a scholarly work, but in places Bury (pronounced 'Bew-ree') tended to equate Greek and Roman civilisation with the fortunes of the British Empire of his day – a point that was not lost on our post-imperial teachers. We were never given any formal sex education at school, but I recall Mr Williams uttering the gnomic statement that 'men and women are complementary'. My friend John, studying biology on his path towards medicine, kindly shared with me the relevant section of his biology textbook.

My graduation to membership of CLUM marked a crucial stage in my school career and intellectual development, and I embarked on the path thus laid out for me with some enthusiasm and commitment. I had a sense of starting off on my own, in a different direction from the scientific path that had dominated my parents' careers. It was becoming increasingly important for me to branch out on my own, to establish my own identity – no doubt a common ambition among teenagers. This was ironic in the sense that for them, and indeed for their respective fathers (one a science teacher, one a GP), embarking on training in the natural sciences probably seemed like liberation from old fashioned educational norms based on the classics and other humanities subjects. So was this not a reactionary step on my part?

Whatever my parents' feelings might have been, I didn't see it in that light at all. For me, this was a venture into a new and exciting (also challenging) intellectual world. I was sometimes asked 'What is the point of studying a dead language so as to spend a career teaching a dead language?' That sort of criticism I easily dismissed, to my own satisfaction at any rate. What was less easy to dismiss was my own occasional feeling that in spending so much time wrestling with the grammatical complexities of Greek and Latin, I was in danger of missing out on contemporary intellectual (and increasingly as my interest developed, political) developments going on in the wider world.

Indeed, what was going on in my world might be seen as a kind of class transition. But it was a completely different class transition from the 'working class to middle class' transition that is the subject of so much modern British literature. My family was indisputably middle class. Each of my parents owned a car, in both cases used both for work and for pleasure. I once stood outside my school gates and did a rough calculation (on the basis of who was being met by parents in cars) of what proportion of boys had parents that owned cars. My unreliable conclusion was that it was about fifty per cent. King Edward's was a direct grant school (a category later abolished), which meant that a comparable proportion of the parents paid fees for their sons as were supported by scholarships.

But my class transition was from a small business, conservative, provincial kind of middle class to a middle class that was more intellectual, progressive, internationalist, academic, than that of my parents and their immediate friends. And yet even that needs to be modified by the fact that both my parents were open to new ideas, so that my transition was complex.

3

A Long Wide Road

ᛣ

THE BRISTOL ROAD is the main artery out of Birmingham from the city centre to the Longbridge car works, Bromsgrove and the south. During my days at secondary school I travelled along it every day on my way to school and back again after school had finished. In the earlier years I went by tram, until the City Council, in its unwisdom, replaced the electric trams with polluting, gas-guzzling buses. The last trams ran in 1953, though some sleek modern trams were reintroduced to Birmingham in 2015. Whether by tram or by bus, I would alight at Edgbaston Park Road, which led off the Bristol Road to the right, up a hill to the main school entrance.

As the 1950s began, my eyesight, which up to that point had been perfect, began to deteriorate as I became more and more short-sighted. It was some time before I had my eyes tested, even though by the middle of 1951 the landscape was seriously indistinct. Eventually the condition was recognised and I was able to wear glasses. But the first morning that I wore them at breakfast, I had the fright of my life. When I started to drink a cup of tea, the steam from the cup clouded my glasses. This was a wholly new experience for me, and momentarily I wondered if I was losing my sight.

One of the voluntary extra-curricular activities at the school was the CCF (Combined Cadet Force). I never joined it, despite some of my friends trying to persuade me that since after leaving school I would have to do national service for two years, I should have some preliminary military training to make national service easier. My response to this was that if I was subjected to military training at school as well as in national service, I should merely be doubling the agony. I was happy belonging instead to the school scout troop, which enabled me to go camping in Wales, the Lake District, various parts of England within reach of Birmingham, and in 1950 the French Alps at La Grave. We were not allowed to join both the scouts and the CCF, so I opted to remain in the former.

One of the activities permitted to those older boys who joined the CCF was motorcycle training within the school grounds. So far as I am aware they were given instruction both in riding and maintenance. The geography of the school grounds was such that whereas the main entrance to the school was up Edgbaston Park Road, there was also a back entrance opening directly onto the Bristol Road itself. My friends and I would often enter and leave the school by this back entrance as an alternative route to the school buildings, since it was closer to the tram (later bus) stop.

Where it passed the capacious school grounds, the Bristol Road was divided into two lanes between a central reservation wide enough to accommodate tram tracks between two rows of trees. This gave the road a spacious aspect, though this was not the case throughout its length. For a period in 1951, however, the lane which, seen from the school grounds, was on the far side of the tram tracks, was closed for major road works. This meant that the near lane temporarily had two streams of traffic travelling in opposite directions.

One day, during that period, I was waiting with other boys at the tram stop for a tram to take us northwards to the city centre. Between the tram stop and the school back entrance was a distance of perhaps seventy-five yards. Standing at the tram stop I was facing south, that is, away from the school entrance.

There was a loud bang, at which I twisted round in a reflex action. I was in time to see two blurred objects flying through the air. On the road, exactly at the spot where the school back entrance met the Bristol Road, a lorry and a hearse were passing each other in opposite directions, the lorry going north, the hearse travelling south. Both came to a halt. As we soon learned, two boys riding one of the CCF motorbikes in the school grounds had failed to stop and impacted at speed one of the two passing vehicles. What I saw with my impaired vision as blurred objects flying through the air were two boys a year or two ahead of me, John Pickworth and Bob Moseley. I had not known John well, but with Bob I had been on scout camps in previous years. Bob Moseley was an extremely colourful character whose pranks put him at odds with the school authorities quite often.

A geography master, Mr Whalley, told two of the boys at the tram stop to go up to the porter's lodge so that the porter could contact the emergency services. The distance I estimate from memory as about 300-400 yards. The boys began walking so he shouted at them to get moving and run as fast as they possibly could. Mobile phones, had they existed, would have done the job quicker.

The accident had closed the road in both directions, and a number of stranded motorists were trying to help. Not long afterwards we boarded a tram towards the city centre, taking us slowly past the scene of the accident. A woman on the tram helpfully blurted out, 'It looks as if there's been an accident.' But curiously, I retain no memory of what I saw as we passed the scene of the accident.

When I arrived home on the other side of town I told my parents what had happened and immediately left again, taking a bus to Chester Road tram terminus where I knew there was a newsagent. There I tried to find out what state John and Bob were in, but of course it was much too early for any reporting to have been published in a paper in those pre-digital days.

Next morning when a number of us left the tram at the usual stop, one of the porters met us. I asked him what was their condition following the accident. He replied, 'Well, as you know, Moseley has been killed, and Pickworth may be losing his leg.' But I didn't know, even though I had tried my hardest to find out the previous evening.

As the facts gradually emerged, we learned that John Pickworth had been in control of the bike, but somehow had failed to find the brake as he approached the road. It is normal for motorcycles to have two brakes, one manually operated and the other operated with the foot, so the failure to stop is hard to understand. Bob Moseley had been riding pillion. They were unbelievably unlucky, firstly that the near lane was carrying twice its normal traffic, and secondly that they entered the road just at the moment when two vehicles were passing in opposite directions.

That was the end of CCF motorcycle training in the school grounds.

I am almost certain that it was Bob Moseley, with others perhaps, who had advised me to leave the Scouts and join the CCF, as he himself had done. But his decision was to cost him his life.

John Pickworth returned to school after he was discharged from
hospital, with a prosthetic leg, and went on to have a distinguished
career as a doctor.

At the next school assembly, the Headmaster, Tom Howarth,
referred to Bob Moseley as 'as spirit so gay [1950s gay] that he
would not have wanted people to be gloomy at his death'.

As for my own reactions, I don't think I experienced grief, but
I certainly suffered from shock. Some weeks later, my mother
remarked on my reactions as she had observed them, 'You went
very silent'.

During my middle years at King Edward's I was still free of worries about external exams, so that I could develop other interests.
With one exception, I was incompetent at sports, and although I
played as a rugby forward, I had no talent for it. Moreover, having become myopic, I found that both team-mates and opponents
presented blurred features. The exception was swimming. I had
learned to swim when I was four or five, and became adept at the
'crawl' (now known in the UK as 'freestyle', as I think it was always
known in Australia). My father swam a stroke that was known as
the 'trudgen', defined by the OED as 'a kind of hand-over-hand or
double over-arm breast stroke... with leg action resembling that of
walking', and discovered by a Mr Trudgen in Argentina in 1863.
Certainly it was not very pretty. The key to fluency in freestyle was
getting the breathing right, and once I had mastered that I progressed fast. I also practised the 'dead man's drop', whereby I would
stand on the highest diving board with my hands stretched verti-
cally above my head, and simply fall forward with my body held
rigid, entering the water hands first, feet last. In my final year at
primary school I managed to win both the senior and junior swimming prizes.

But I never made it as a swimmer, for two main reasons. The
first was that once I was at secondary school I went to public swimming classes in Birmingham, where I was taught by a singularly
unsympathetic instructor, who more or less told me that I was no
good. The second reason was that over one winter my mother very
sensibly would not let me swim in local baths because of a polio
epidemic. Later I swam for my house at school, but that was the
limit of my ambition. I also went in for the annual half-mile swim
in a lake not far from the centre of Birmingham, usually in freezing

conditions in the month of May under polluted skies. We coated our bodies with vaseline to keep out the cold. Ever since that time I have enjoyed non-competitive swimming, whether in a swimming pool, a lake or the sea.

On one occasion when we were on holiday at Salcombe, I was given a rather different kind of swimming lesson from ones I had experienced before. Aged about twelve, I took part in a swimming carnival, entering for a race from a jetty out in the harbour to a wooden structure marking the shore line. The distance was maybe 100 yards, though it may have been a bit more. The course certainly did not conform to Olympic standards of precise length.

When the competitors lined up, I was standing next to a local Salcombe boy of about my age, quite a beefy character if I recall. Together we watched competitors in the previous race swim the same course. These may have been separate heats preliminary to a final. I remarked innocently to my companion that the swimmers we were watching were quite slow, and I was sure I could beat the lot of them. He nodded but made no reply.

When it came to our turn, the starting whistle was blown, and we dived in for the race, the boy roughly pushed my head under water and shoved me back, propelling himself forward as he did so. I bobbed up again like a plastic duck in a bath, but by now he was well ahead and I was unable to overtake him. He won the race and I came second.

My parents and grandmother, standing in a crowd of spectators behind the finishing line, witnessed the episode. They talked with me of informing the organisers about what had happened, and speculated on antagonism between locals and holidaymakers. But my embarrassment at the idea of complaining was stronger than my anger at having lost the race by unfair means, and I managed to prevail on them not to complain. At any rate, they let the matter lie.

The episode, however, provided me with a lesson for life, and over six decades later I now thank that boy, whoever he was, for teaching me that lesson. And this is what my swimming lesson taught me: don't put all your cards on the table before you compete; leave some things to test your competitors' imagination and keep them guessing.

Around that period I took with enthusiasm to small dinghy sailing, tutored by my father who had joined the Sutton Sailing Club shortly after its foundation in the early 1930s. The club sailed small dinghies on Powell's Pool in Sutton Park. At the club we raced in a succession of one-design craft, including the Cooper, the International 14 footer, the 505 and the Firefly – all wooden boats of course. During one winter my father and I built a Yachting World Cadet from a kit in our cellar at home. It was, however, too small and we did not keep it for long. Every summer we took whatever boat we were sailing at that time on a trailer down to Salcombe in South Devon, and sailed – sometime raced – on that wonderful harbour. In the hot summer of 1947 (after the coldest winter for a generation), my parents and I sailed our International Fourteen Footer out of the harbour into the open sea and for a distance along the coast and back. Dinghies of that class had no built-in buoyancy, so we should have been in trouble had we capsized. During that summer large numbers of clouded yellow and pale clouded yellow butterflies arrived from France, and we sailed through swarms of those beautiful creatures. Many years later my mother would reminisce about that summer, and describe it as one of the happiest times of her life.

During the next summer at Salcombe, 1948, the weather was poor and I got into trouble with my parents for allowing our boat to be stranded at high tide on a sandbank in the harbour. My parents had worries about older family members, including Grandpa Stockwin who died that year, and perhaps the tension affected their mood.

As I grew older with aspirations to greater independence, I came to enjoy scout camps with their opportunities for new experiences, and accompanied my parents to Salcombe more rarely. I was once part of a small scouting group camping in the Lake District at Easter in very cold weather. When we woke up in the morning our tent seemed surprisingly warm given the external conditions. The reason was evident when we ventured outside. A fall of snow in the night had covered the tent giving it a thick layer of insulation. I learned to cook on campfires and to combine camping with trekking through hills in Wales and elsewhere. And then in the summer of 1950 I went abroad for the first time, to a scout camp that we set up near La Grave in the French Alps, with La Meije, one of the highest and most impressive mountains in the French Alps, towering above us. Somewhere around that time also, I was at a scout camp on the island of Arran in southern Scotland. John was also at the camp and the two of us on our own spent several days crossing from Glen Rosa, near the main town of Brodick, in heavy rain through wild country to the western side of the island, through the village of Lochranza, where we bought provisions, then walking clockwise round the coast, setting up camp on the shore, watching gannets diving headlong into the sea in their search for fish, until we found our way back to the base camp at Glen Rosa, within sight of precipitous Goat Fell, the highest point on the island.

John and I did cycling trips over New Year during two successive winters in the early 1950s, staying at youth hostels. On the second occasion we went into central Wales, and on the way stayed at the magnificent Wilderhope Manor on Wenlock Edge in Shropshire, which remains a youth hostel more than 65 years after we were there. Youth hostellers were expected to be tough in those days, and the vast halls of Wilderhope Manor were virtually unheated in the middle of winter. Our first cycle tour was to the West Country. We negotiated precipitous roads along the north coast of Devon between Minehead and Ilfracombe, passing Exmoor along the way, aiming for a youth hostel near the village of Parracombe a day or two before New Year. To reach it, we had to fight our way through heavy drifting snow, and when we finally reached the youth hostel, there was nobody there. Some two hours later the proprietor and his wife returned from a shopping expedition, and told us that we were the first youth hostellers to visit during the whole of December.

Around that time, or perhaps a year or two later, the two of us were the youngest members of a scouting expedition walking about a hundred miles from Cirencester in Gloucestershire to Rhayader in Wales, near the Elan Valley reservoir that supplied Birmingham with water. No scoutmasters accompanied us on this trip. Somebody had had the bright idea of loading all our camping gear onto a trek cart, which we took in turns to push the length of the journey. But the trek cart was seriously overloaded, so that the spindles of its bicycle wheels kept snapping. Some of our number had to make detours to find cycle shops in nearby towns to buy spare spindles.

In the summer of 1951, I experienced one of the formative periods of my life, participating in an exchange with a French family living in the town of Nérac in the Département of Lot-et-Garonne in the south-west of France. The visit was organised through an arrangement between my school and a local school near Nérac. It began with an exchange of letters between me and a boy called Jean-Louis Magniont. The two of us shared an interest in the sea and sailing, even though we both lived many miles inland, and exchanged information about the pre-war French sailor Alain Gerbault, the first person in modern times to sail single-handed across the Atlantic from Europe to America. But Jean-Louis was an orphan, whose parents had died in a road accident near Savannakhet in the southern part of Laos, in those days a region in the colony of French Indo-China. I think we wrote to each other mainly in French, and I remember Jean-Louis' entirely justified reaction to some phrase I had used, 'C'est un barbarisme!' He was looked after by his uncle, who in the end sadly refused to allow Jean-Louis to participate in the exchange scheme.

This meant that I was paired with a new exchange partner, whose name was François Lignac. Before our school year was over, François came and stayed for six weeks with our family, and accompanied me to school most days. In French classes he was used as a valuable linguistic resource. The school also organised joint activities for the various French exchange students that had come on the scheme.

François was the second son in a family of four children (three boys and a girl, who was number three), though another daughter was born sometime after I returned to England at the end of the summer holidays. His father was a doctor, who was a GP (to use the UK equivalent) and ran a laboratory carrying out medical tests. Dr Lignac, a big man and seriously overweight, took pains to stimulate me intellectually, and taught me some classic poems, including one by the nineteenth-century poet Théophile Gautier, titled 'Le Pin des Landes'. He referred to a region of endless pine forest in the nearby Département des Landes, where we regularly swam in local lakes of immense depth.

One day, a woman visited the house and talked at some length with François' parents. Some way into the conversation, to my surprise, Dr Lignac turned to me and started speaking to me in English. I had hardly heard him speak English before, and was surprised, both at his level of fluency and that he should suddenly break his rule of only speaking to me in French. After the woman had left he explained that she was a well-known local Communist and that he was wary of expressing any political opinions that she would understand. Dr Lignac and his wife, much like my own parents, were moderate conservatives, and in the still turbulent political atmosphere of France and Europe only six years after the end of the war, he expressed anxiety about the prospect of the United States abandoning its European allies.

Again, like my parents, they were not particularly religious, and I have no memory of them going to church. But well into the twenty-first century, when François, now living near Toulouse, took me back to Nérac and the nearby town where he had attended school, he reminisced about his first communion, which was an experience of his childhood that still clearly affected him emotionally.

During my stay we spent about a week staying with some friends of the Lignacs at a large house called 'Le Chancet' near the town of Guéret in the Creuse, well to the north of Nérac. The father of the family was a well-known surgeon and pioneer of hip replacement, Dr Judet. When François was himself training to be a surgeon as a young man, Dr Judet gave him much of his training. Whereas Nérac was surrounded by rich agricultural land, the Creuse was far less prosperous, much of its countryside having poor soil, good only for rough scrub. The Judets had five children, all younger than François, except for the eldest, Henri. I have a memory of being in an attic room, surrounded by young children, when somebody spotted a rat. Absolute hysteria broke out, with everybody attempting to climb onto furniture and escape the 'dangerous, rat-infested' floor. With what I imagine was self-identification as a phlegmatic Englishman, I suggested that with all this racket the rat must be at the other end of the house by now, or out in the fields, so why not just calm down? The rat was actually killed by their dog, Miquette.

During our stay Drs Judet and Lignac did the rounds of sick people in that extremely rural area and returned with sad stories of people stricken with polio and other terrible diseases.

Staying with the Lignacs, and more briefly with the Judets, gave me some valuable lessons. One was that the French I had learned at school was at best an imperfect guide to the way people actually spoke in ordinary life. I picked up a certain amount of dubious slang: on one occasion François infuriated his father by saying to one of his siblings 't'accouche!', by which he meant 'hurry up'. But the literal meaning of 't'accouche!' is 'give birth!', implying that

since giving birth is generally a slow process, it would be a good idea
to hurry it up. When, many years later, we returned from Australia
to the UK and began to take holidays in France, it was pointed out
to me that I was still speaking adolescent French, and this occasionally elicited a critical reaction, 'Il était vachement soul, ce type-là'
– 'Il ne faut pas dire ça'. ('That bloke was pissed out of his mind' –
'You mustn't say that'.)

Another lesson was simply the experience of living in a family consisting of several children. This was not something I found
entirely easy, and my problem was compounded by having an
allergic reaction to mosquito bites, which came up in great wheals.
Sometimes I just wanted to be on my own, but this was not looked
on very kindly. Mealtime conversations could be disputatious, as
indeed they should be in a lively family, but it was difficult for me
to be entirely part of that scene. Nevertheless, I remember thinking,
towards the end of my stay in Nérac, that I wished I could stay a lot
longer, and I even said that to Dr Lignac, who responded with an
invitation to return (sadly, I never did).

Summer holidays were a time for travel. In 1952, John and I
hitchhiked as far as Chamonix in the French Alps, camping along
the way, and sometimes spending much of the day vainly trying to
get a lift. John lost his passport in a forest near Chamonix, which
meant that he had to obtain a new one at the British Embassy in
Paris on the return. We managed on extraordinarily little money,
but returned home safe and sound, to the comfort of our parents,
who had responded to news of the lost passport with relief that we
had not suffered some kind of accident.

But the next summer, that of 1953, I embarked, very much at
my father's prompting, on a quite different kind of expedition.
The British Schools Exploration Society sent schoolboys on camping expeditions to wilderness areas in various parts of the world.
It had originally been the Public Schools Exploration Society, but
the changing structure of British society after the war resulted in a
widening of the pool from which candidates were selected. Secretly,
I had wanted to make another sally into Europe, on my own, or
with a companion. But my father persuaded me that the BSES was
a wonderful organisation and that I would have a great adventure.

And so, I embarked in Liverpool on the *Empress of Scotland*, bound
for Montreal, and then by rail across the continent into the wilds of

British Columbia. The railway carriages that were our home for several days were known as 'colonist cars'. At the end of each of them was a coke stove, on which we cooked our food. The principal and allegedly most nutritious part of our diet was a high energy substance consisting of fat and protein known as 'pemmican', originally developed by native peoples of North America, which became our staple throughout our time in Canada. After our return the *Birminghan Mail* published a piece under the headline 'Arthur eats Moose in the Wilderness'.

Our journey took us through Winnipeg (where we visited the zoo!), Edmonton, Calgary, spectacular Banff in the Rockies, Jasper National Park, and we left the train at a small settlement called Vanderhoof, where everybody's surname appeared to be Frazer. From there we were conveyed by bus or car (I forget which) to Fort St James at the southern end of Lake Stuart, a lake that was to be main feature of our landscape for several weeks. Boats then ferried us to the stretch of shore on which we were to set up our base camp, about half way along the lake – essentially a naturally flooded river valley. I was assigned to a survey group, tasked to make a map based on accurate measurements of the general area. A major problem facing us was that the whole landscape was covered with totally unmanaged deciduous forest. When a tree came to the end of its life or was brought down in a storm or its branches felled with the weight of snow in winter, it would remain on the ground, gradually rotting. This made travel within the forest extremely problematic. We lit fires to signal to each other from one side of the lake to the other. Of course, being 1953, we had no electronic means of communication. There was hardly any boat traffic on the lake (apart from our own), though we once encountered a canoe of native peoples, who sold local produce to some of our number. We were issued with bush hats from which hung netting covering our faces to protect us from the ubiquitous blackfly, a biting insect that caused any non-protected human face to swell up alarmingly..

The organisation was rather too military for my taste. The armistice ending the fighting in Korea had recently been signed, two or three of our 'officers' (if that is the right word) had fought in Korea, and all or nearly all the rest were officers in the services. We were also accompanied by two doctors. The man directly in charge of the survey group was a young officer, whom we knew as 'the General Rule'. Frequently, he would begin a sentence with 'as a general rule'. One suspected that he might have struggled with more precise analysis. He was twenty-one at the time, and had just graduated with a third class engineering degree from the University of Cambridge. He explained that his principal motivation for going to university had been the social life. Such an attitude was still, I believe, quite common in Oxford and Cambridge at that time. It is less common today, reflecting a more competitive academic environment.

Another problem I had with the expedition was that even though 'British Schools' had been substituted for 'Public schools', some of the less attractive aspects of traditional public schools were still in evidence. I remember travelling in a small boat on the lake, with two or three others, one of whom was an Etonian, who spent this brief voyage sneering at pupils he had encountered from Slough grammar school. On the other hand I got on well with a boy called Neil Grant, who was at the Nautical College, Pangbourne (today Pangbourne College), on the Thames. We were very different, but had enough in common to hit it off. On the survey team we were allowed to name a small lake 'Lake Grockwin'.

When we left Lake Stuart we once again stopped at Vanderhoof, where we were invited to participate in square dancing with the local population. And here we witnessed an extraordinary, indeed "educational" phenomenon. One of our colleagues, named Beverly Columbin, could hardly be described as handsome, but he was stunningly and inexplicably attractive to women. We witnessed several of the young ladies at the dance actually fighting each other to get close to him, behaving like bees round a honey pot. We watched in wonder and in the vain hope that we might learn something from his technique.

We returned to eastern Canada via Edmonton, not Calgary, and left the train at Quebec City, which seemed even more French than Montreal, and returned home on the Franconia, a much less grand vessel than the Empress of Scotland. A few of my colleagues expressed interest in Canada as a place to settle, and although I was not one of them, the huge distances, wild country and white water rivers of Canada made a lasting impression that might be seen as a kind of taster for the admittedly far drier and hotter Australian outback, a decade or so later.

The final two or three years at school were years of increasing pressure of work. I was now in the Classical Sixth, preparing for university entrance. It was my form master of those years, Mr Roger Dunt, who advised me to seek entry to the University of Oxford. Mr Dunt in some ways was the epitome of an old-fashioned schoolmaster. He greatly admired Gilbert Murray, a popular classicist of the inter-war period, who had gone out of fashion by the 1950s. Roger, if I may call him that (since I owe a huge amount to him), was baffled by most modern developments in art and literature. But that didn't matter, since he know the gamut of classical literature like the back of his hand and was good at teaching it at sixth form level. And he was well informed about strategy for university entrance. It was he who pressed ne to apply for Oxford.

In those days Oxford or Cambridge entrance required high level passes in A-levels followed by excellent results in special entrance examinations for either of the two universities. For both A-levels and Oxford entrance (my choice) we were examined in Greek and Latin Prose, as well as Greek and Latin poetry. Incredible as it now seems to me, we were expected to compose poems in Greek and Latin, following the rules of poetic composition of those languages during the classical period. By my final year at school I had achieved reasonable proficiency in those skills, and seemed ready to take Oxford entrance. This was the result of an incredible amount of hard work, meaning that I had more or less overcome the hit-and-miss approach that marred my performance in primary school. Even when I was in the lower forms of King Edward's, my term reports could be patchy. My parents would not let me forget the comment of one subject master, 'He has horrible lapses'.

But now I seemed to have learned how to work consistently and had gained in self-confidence. In those days Oxford colleges grouped together to run common entrance exams, so that it was possible to sit a succession of exams run by separate groups of colleges. Taking advantage of this system, I put myself down for three successive clusters of exams, the first in the autumn (spring?) of 1953, the second in January 1954, and the third around Easter of that same year. In applying for a particular cluster, you had to designate a particular college as your preferred destination. I aimed high and put down Christ Church as my first preference. Staying over the period of the exams in rooms at Christ Church was an experience in itself, and I think I may have chosen it because I was overawed by the architecture. Every day I swopped notes on the previous day's exams with another classicist,

Graeme Watson, who became a good friend. His family later invited me to stay at their house at Walton-on-Thames in London. For me as a provincial, just to travel to London on my own was still an adventure. Graeme eventually became a vicar in the Church of England, like a number of classicists I knew along the way.

I was offered a place by Christ Church, but without a scholarship, so I decided to try again, sitting the second exam cluster, in January of the following year. This time the less prestigious Exeter College was my main choice. I went to Oxford in the middle of a great freeze up, and remember writing exam scripts in the great hall of New College, an enormous space heated only by a large log fire in the middle of one of the walls. Those candidates seated at huge dining tables close to the fire were able to thaw out, but those further away were swathed in thick coats, mufflers and mittens, desperately trying both to keep their bodies warm and to prevent the freezing temperatures from dulling their brains.

I was also interviewed by the Rector of Exeter College and three or four other fellows of the College. The Rector was Eric Barber, a classicist (like most of his predecessors), who had been in post since 1943 and was coming towards the end of his term. He had been working for several years revising Liddell and Scott, *A Greek-English Lexicon*. This was a book with which I was closely familiar from constant use in my work, and I still retain a copy of the fifth edition, 'revised and augmented', dated MDCCCLXIV (or to put it in another context, four years before the Meiji Restoration in Japan). It has 1644 pages of text. Its authors, Henry George Liddell, DD, and Robert Scott, DD, were respectively Dean of Christ Church and Master of Balliol. But at the time I was applying for Oxford, what had been the dominance of classics (and with it the prominence of theology) was approaching its end.

At the interview, the following exchange occurred:

Rector Barber: 'Well, Mr Stockwin, what do you contemplate doing as a career after you graduate?'
    Candidate Stockwin: 'Well, Sir, I think I would like to write.'
    College Fellow (Mr Raitt, the French tutor?): 'But if you want to write, you will have to find somebody to pay you.'
    Candidate Stockwin: 'Yes Sir, I understand that.'

When I retailed this exchange to my parents later, they found it hilariously funny. And when I look back on it, I realise just how wet behind the ears I still was at that time, when I was eighteen years of age.

But my life was about to change, in a dramatic and unexpected fashion. In those days a sword of Damocles hanging over the heads of most young men was the prospect of national (military) service. Had I accepted the offer from Christ Church, I would have begun my course in the autumn of 1954 in classics. Mods and Greats (classics) being a four year course, I would presumably have graduated in 1958, and given that national service itself was approaching its end at that time, I might have been able to postpone it 'until the Greek calends' (that is, permanently, since the calends figured in the Roman calendar but not the Greek calendar) by enrolling in a postgraduate course of study.

When I opened the letter from Exeter College at the breakfast table sometime after returning home, I was delighted to read that the College was offering me a place, and that I would be awarded the 'Waugh Scholarship' for the duration of my course. Apparently this scholarship was named, not after Evelyn Waugh, author of *Brideshead Revisited*, but after his brother Alec – also a novelist – of whom Evelyn's son Auberon is said to have commented, 'Alec has written innumerable novels, each one worse than the last.'

And then I read the final sentence of the letter, stating that I would be required to enter national service *before* beginning my course in Oxford, and that I should therefore take up the College's offer from the autumn of 1956.

That final sentence changed the direction of my life in a multitude of ways, but since an alternative personal history based on the proposition that I might have transitioned seamlessly from school to university is unknowable, all I can write about is what actually happened.

From childhood I had been travelling a long wide road of home life and education until I finished school, used to a high level of predictability. But then I had to follow a fork in the road, with the predictable direction blocked. This was not remotely the kind of catastrophic event that I had witnessed on the Bristol Road outside the back entrance to the school. But while blocking off expected directions of travel, it meant that after an interval I had new opportunities with which to shape my life, new influences, new interests and a different life path.

4

From One Life to Another

入

WHEN I LOOK back on my life between the ages of about eighteen and twenty-four, I am astounded to realise just how many things changed, not only in my circumstances (from school to national service, to university, to marriage and to Australia), but also in how I thought about fundamental questions of life, philosophy, religion and politics. No doubt many people go through significant transitions around that period of their lives, but in my case it seems to have been particularly extreme. Obviously, it was a time of exploration, but I seemed to be picking up things and dropping them again in quick succession. My mother said to me more than once, 'You never stick at anything.' This was not entirely accurate, because I was determined to develop intellectual abilities, and getting into Oxford through classics was both a strategy towards that end and based on genuine interest in languages, history, literature and increasingly politics. But while I seemed to know which way I wanted to go in broad terms, there was a certain will o' the wisp character in my tendency to sample new things briefly, and also to reject abruptly ideas or activities that I had been involved in for a long time. I dropped sailing, which had been a long-term passion, and when my parents and I revisited Nefyn and the mountains of North Wales, and indeed Salcombe, I indicated rather too clearly to them that I was bored with those places. I think at times they were hurt, and I regret that.

In fact, the origins of these changes go back well before my fateful discovery that I was required to follow school with military training. Specialising in classics as I had been, I was in the company of school friends some of whom were taking classics as a step on the road to a theological degree and ordination. Such was the case with Brian Coleman, a classicist whom I knew at school and later at Oxford, and also with Michael Counsell, who switched from science to arts subjects (not, I think classics). Both of them were ultimately ordained in the Church of England. Both urged me to think about religion. So did my long-term friend John Buckler, who came from a devoutly religious family.

To understand my rather uncertain and convoluted reaction to this advice from my colleagues, I need to take account of two factors: the role of religion at the school I was attending, and the history of religion (or non-religion) in my family.

At King Edward's, and no doubt in most schools of a similar kind at the time, religion (specifically Christianity and even more specifically the Church of England) were part of the scenery. Morning assembly always began with prayers, led by the Headmaster, from which Catholics and Jews were excused. I am almost certain that there were no Muslims at the school, although there was one boy of Indian ethnicity called Sankarayya. I knew one or two boys whose families adhered to more or less heterodox Christian sects, but they kept a low profile. We had lessons on the Bible, which if I remember correctly were called 'scripture' at primary school but 'divinity' at King Edward's. We were taken through St Mark's Gospel in considerable detail at one stage. We also read *The Man Born to be King*, originally a wartime BBC radio drama written by the crime writer Dorothy L. Sayers, which had caused a storm of controversy, being attacked both by devout Christians for 'impersonating Jesus' and by atheists for distorting history. I had also acted in *Murder in the Cathedral* by T.S. Eliot about the assassination of Thomas à Becket, Archbishop of Canterbury, with the late charismatic John Grimley Evans (later Professor of geratology at the University of Oxford, but then known to us as plain J.G. Evans) in the role of Becket: The King's alleged challenge, 'Will nobody rid me of this troublesome priest?', may be a figment of later writers, but it provided a compelling theme for the play. So religion was certainly in the air, and prompted explorations – sometimes into the remoter reaches of sectarianism – by adolescents seeking to make sense of their lives.

The other important influence was my own family, whose religious tradition was thin, to say the least. My paternal grandparents were married in 1900, aged about twenty-seven, and my father, an

only child, was born on 18 March 1904. So, I am the only son
of an only son. More than four decades later, my father told me
that his parents decided after their marriage that they would no
longer attend church since both of them had had more religion
than they wished forced upon them in their childhood. But since it
remained socially necessary to know how religious services worked,
they would make sure that they knew 'when to stand up and when
to sit down', so as not to embarrass themselves and others when
they were obliged to attend church for a funeral or a wedding.
I remember that when I first heard this story, probably in early adolescence, I was more than a little shocked at what seemed to me its
unprincipled nature.

On my mother's side of the family, there was similarly, so far
as I know, very little churchgoing, but my grandfather, a general
practitioner, certainly understood much about the culture of Christianity, even if he did not consider himself a believer. In his lengthy
and fascinating account of a cruise to the Caribbean undertaken by
him and my grandmother in 1925, when they were in their fifties,
he describes a discussion with a Roman Catholic priest on board
ship, in which the priest gave 'the religious position' and he gave 'the
medical position'. Their views fundamentally differed but he liked
the priest as a cultured individual.

I never had any discussion with my Ainscow grandparents about
any aspect of religion, since Grandpa Ainscow died when I was
seven and my grandmother three or four years later.

But I remember clearly a discussion I had with Grandpa Stockwin
when I was probably about eight. It must have been not long after
we had returned from Edgmond to Sutton Coldfield. While we were
walking in our garden he told me the story of the crucifixion and
resurrection of Jesus. I don't think he presented this either as gospel
truth or as fiction, but when he had finished he said to me: 'remember this story'. I think I was puzzled by what he told me because it
did not seem to fit in with what I had learned of the world and the
way it worked in my life to that point. I may also have been surprised
to hear it from him of all people, since he was a science teacher, and
what he normally told me was based on clear rationality. At the time,
I had little idea how to process this information.

My Grandpa Stockwin was a favourite of mine, and I remember
him with enormous affection. He was gentle and decisive, rational

and compassionate, serious and humorous – a great teacher and the ideal grandfather. Let me diverge from my theme for a moment to relate a story my father once told about him. It was in 1919, soon after the ending of the Great War. My father, then fifteen, came down to breakfast to find his parents already sitting at the table. His father had just opened a bill for a delivery of coal (yes, the post was delivered in time for breakfast in those days). He said, with a dramatic gesture, 'Laura, the country's finished: coal's a pound a ton' (from that baseline of ninety-nine years ago, the price of coal has now risen well over three hundred times, depending on quality). It is also worth recording a phrase he used quite frequently. He would make a factual statement, and then he would seek to establish causality, with the phrase, 'and I'll tell you for why'. To my surprise, I find that this phase is now attacked on the Internet by some who see the 'for' as redundant, and regard it as an American import, polluting the English language. It is nothing of the kind, but rather an example of local dialect, probably centred on the Midlands of England.

So what of my parents' attitudes to religion? For my father religion was something he found difficult to take seriously. He regarded it as extraordinary that otherwise rational people who accepted religious belief could believe such things as they apparently did. He accepted the existence of religious institutions and practices as part of the scenery of everyday life, and was generally too polite to contest views of a religious nature that might be put to him, though in any case that rarely happened. My father was certainly not any kind of militant. Once, however, in the 1980s, I drove from Oxfordshire to visit him at home in the West Midlands, when he was already old and infirm. The first thing that he told me, with great glee, that he had 'despatched with my arguments' a missionary who had called at his door. I think their argument concerned the differences between atheism and agnosticism.

It would be difficult to call my mother religious, but her approach was subtly different from that of my father. I am sure that she did not accept the literal truth of miraculous events associated with Jesus and recorded in the Gospels, nor indeed do I think that she had any real belief in God. But she valued the insights she saw embedded in Christian teachings (although I cannot remember her spelling these out as specifically derived from Christianity). I also think that she retained some affinity with Christian culture, though she would not have put in in quite those terms. Once, when I must have been in my early twenties and she had seen me go through a couple of years 'trying out' Christianity but in the end abandoning it, she suggested to me that I should not abandon everything that Christianity stood for. In those days I tended to be a bit sharp in my answers to her advice, so I breezily replied, 'Yes, it's part of the culture.' She paused a full ten seconds before replying in a low voice, 'Yes, it's part of the culture.'

One boy, whom I knew through the school's Scout troop, was a Welshman called David Davies. At least, you would not have realised he had a Welsh background until you heard him talking with his parents, when he gallicised his accent. At school he was known as Dai Davies, but here I will refer to him as David. David and I organised camps together, one in the countryside south of Solihull, close to a field near a monument close to what is now the intersection of the M40 and M42 motorways, and another in North Wales, under Cader Idris and up the valley from Tal-y-Llyn (lake).

With David I had often discussed religion, at a time when both of us were trying to establish a world view for ourselves, and Christianity was a powerful candidate for that. David's family was in the Baptist tradition, but he was becoming uneasy with it. He also had pacifist inclinations. I was quite genuinely 'trying out' Christianity, never having experienced it as part my family's culture. At the time we were both idealistic young adults barely out of adolescence, and contemplating a future that was both exciting and also impossible to forecast. We were also quite adventurous, one evening at the Tal-y-Llyn camp climbing up the steep wooded hill behind the camp and being overtaken by the dark. Even though we had torches with us, it was fiendishly difficult finding our way down again and back to the camp. We arrived back covered with scratches from the undergrowth after everybody else was asleep, and we told nobody what we had done.

Another evening at the camp, David and I walked the three miles or so up a steep road to the village of Corris, where we enquired about services at the Methodist chapel (one of three in the small village) on the coming Sunday, suggesting that we might bring our colleagues from the camp. The local people we spoke with were incredibly hospitable, and agreed to arrange for the service to be given in English, not Welsh, so that we could understand it, though some hymns would be sung in Welsh. The conversation (and it was already quite late in the evening) was complicated by the presence of a loquacious Englishman from Wolverhampton, who among other things referred to Welsh as 'a growth, not a language'. After we left I expressed to David my irritation with the man, but David, true to his ideals of tolerance, took his part, emphasising what he saw as his intelligence.

At the service on the following Sunday, to which we brought the troop from our camp, I was immensely moved by the following, as recorded in my diary:

> There were only a few English hymns in the Welsh hymn book, and the singing had very great volume. The address took as text 'The Peace of God which passeth all understanding', and dealt with the circumstances of its being written. Mr Jones drew attention to the circumstances of its being written – 'one of the most beautiful phrases in a letter' – with a very Welsh intonation on [the first syllable of] the word 'beautiful' .

Dr Mayor, one of our scoutmasters, who taught science at King Edwards, also attended the service, and was asked to speak to the congregation towards the end of it. But it was David and I that had organised the initiative.

Readers of these words may well find it difficult to understand that even though my 'experiment' with Christianity was ultimately doomed to failure, that day and the events surrounding it remain, sixty-four years later, one of the most memorable of my life.

Unlike me, David had an easy relationship with girls. I was with him on several occasions when he went up to a girl he had never met before and began a conversation with her. I lacked that kind of confidence or skill. From school David went on to Cambridge, married Gill from our school's sister school, embarked on a career in materials technology and other areas, had children and in 1992 set up a small software development business. In 1998, I discovered he was living in Henley-on-Thames, made contact and we met in Oxford. But although we met a few times later, it seemed that life had taken us on paths too divergent to re-establish a close friendship.

I met David and Gill again, however, in the spring of 2019, and suddenly found that we had a great deal in common.

At this point, I need to back-track a small number of years and introduce Arnold Skeates, whom I have mentioned before as my father's dental mechanic. Mr Skeates (as I knew him) was a Christadelphian. The Christadelphians (brothers in Christ), are a Unitarian sect of Christianity founded in the early nineteenth century, with members in many countries, but particularly strong in Birmingham. They believe in the literal truth of the Bible, that the return of Jesus to set up the Kingdom of God on earth is 'imminent' (Mr Skeates' word), will not participate in military service or the police, and do not vote in political elections. They also differ on various aspects of theological doctrine from more mainstream branches of Christianity (rejecting 'Hell' for instance), and worship in 'ecclesias' that are run independently according to rather democratic principles. In some ways they are comparable with the better known and far more numerous Jehovah's Witnesses, but my impression is that their attitudes are generally softer than those of the latter (some of this information comes from Wikipedia and other websites). During the Second World War they helped evacuate Jews from Nazi Germany in the Kindertransport scheme, and in turn their German members were savagely persecuted by the Nazis.

I had several conversations with Mr Skeates when I was in my early to mid-teens, and was both astonished by his ideas and to an extent excited by meeting a world view that differed so radically from the notions I had been brought up with. Despite the refusal of the Christadelphians to engage in politics by voting or other kinds of participation, I found that he was well informed on broad political issues. He effectively disabused me of the then still prevalent British view that Great Britain and the British Empire remained a powerful (central?) part of the international system, by telling me that power essentially now lay with the United States of America.

Since at school I was also encountering theological views no less difficult to credit than those of the Christadelphians – such as the notion of the Trinity, for instance, which incidentally the Christadelphians rejected – I went through a period of radical intellectual confusion, reflected at least once in bizarre performances at the school debating society, though I have forgotten the details. There is also a curious link here with my friend David Davies, since we were both acquainted (he much better than I) with a boy called Mark Sawyer, who adhered to the sect. Mark was extremely low-key and did not broadcast his beliefs, but David had heard his views.

A very different character involved in non-mainstream religious observance was John Haseler. John belonged to something called the New Church, based on the writings of the Swedish theologian Emanuel Swedenborg, an eighteenth century scientist turned mystic. I never hear John talk seriously about his church or its beliefs, and knowing him I doubted how far he took them seriously. John was passionate about science and I identified him as a committed rationalist. He was another person I knew mainly through the Scouts, whose ethos he took more seriously than I did. On one occasion a group of us were at a Scout camp at Lea Hill in Northfield (in the absence of scoutmasters), it was after dark and we were having an animated discussion about something or other, illuminated by a light bulb powered by some kind of hand generator that we activated by taking turns continuously pulling a length of sisal. Gradually we became aware that an extra voice was quietly contributing to the discussion. John, who was not supposed to be at the camp, had turned up unannounced and seamlessly merged with the rest of us without our realising it.

But John made a splash in a different context. After the headmaster Tom Howarth left in 1952, he was replaced by the utterly unique Canon Ronald Lunt, who was to remain at the school for the next twenty-two years. He was an intensely controversial figure, and spoke in the accents of at least fifty years before. I remember him seeking to illustrate some point of pronunciation, 'You say it like the French do: - laaar tayte.'

I once heard him comment on a slide show presented by the art master to show the relationship between some modern artists and their classical predecessors. A juxtaposition between Leonardo and Picasso elicited the remark, 'Oh, how have the mighty fallen!'

Lunt was domineering, often scathing in his criticisms but worked for the school all hours that came. In his history of King Edward's, titled *No Place for Fop or Idler* (a phrase from the school song), Tony Trott commented, 'Life with Canon Lunt ...was often bumpy and seat belts needed to be permanently fastened' (p. 119). He was referring to relations between the 'Chief Master' – the term Lunt had coined for his position – and the teaching staff. I personally did not care for him that much, as he was so pompous and overbearing, but he was also a contradictory figure, being an effective teacher despite his pomposity. I think of him, even so, as one of the most peculiar men I have ever met. I never felt I understood him.

During our final year at school the Chief Master ran a weekly class for senior students, in which each of us had to choose a substantial book, read it, and write a review of it to be delivered orally to the class. When it came to John Haseler's turn to say which book he proposed to review, the conversation went as follows:

Lunt: 'Well Haseler, which book have you chosen?'
Haseler: 'The Kinsey Report, Sir' [this was shortly after it was published].
Lunt: 'Kinsey on the male, or Kinsey on the female?'
Haseler: 'Kinsey on the male, Sir.'

When I told them about it, my parents appeared quite shocked by this exchange, but my father commented that for a schoolmaster how to respond in circumstances like that was very difficult. Canon Lunt, on the contrary, took it in his stride.

John Haseler went on to describe and analyse the substance of the book in a meticulously scientific fashion, with not a hint of prurience or double-entendre. And the class, after a moment or two of heightened anticipation perhaps, accepted it as such. This seems to me something of an achievement in those buttoned up days, with both teacher and pupil brushing aside contemporary prejudices.

I had another friend called John Rivers, whom I knew at school and later at Oxford. This takes me to an episode at Exeter College, in my first year.

I am standing on a carpet in the middle of a college room- or is it a rug placed on top of a carpet? A party had just finished and my friends are trying to put the room to rights. To accomplish this task they need to remove the rug – or is it the carpet? But the problem is that I am standing on the carpet – or is it the rug? – and refuse to move away. Being a raw undergraduate in Oxford, I have had too much to drink, am relatively unused to dealing with the effects of alcohol, which means that I stubbornly refuse to move. Expostulations directed against me have no effect, but eventually John Rivers, an old friend from school who is reading English at my College, gently persuades me to step off the rug and leave the building.

John sees the state I am in and realises that I might not make it back to my digs if left to myself, so he accompanies me there and sees me back safely back into the house. I had not realised how kind he is, and was not used to having people take pity on me in this way. I had become used to attitudes in national service, which I had recently completed, where you were more likely to be shouted at than spoken to kindly.

John himself, both at school and university, seemed not entirely together and at times I saw that he was grappling with difficult life-problems that clearly affected his work. In the end he gets a rather poor university degree. One day, a bunch of us are walking in a group somewhere near the Backs in Cambridge (why were we in Cambridge?). John is with his girlfriend Monica, a startlingly attractive young lady who, unconsciously perhaps, though critics thought otherwise, frequently flashes her eyes (or perhaps raises her eyebrows) at people who approach and pass us. I am walking along just a few paces behind the two of them, and I see man after man (perhaps women too) approach Monica, pass her and then turn their heads in her direction to have another look.

But John is not really in love with Monica. He has another girl, from Birmingham, whom he is really fond of, but whose name, six decades later, evades me. Once, probably earlier, we are at my parents' house in Sutton Coldfield, John talks about this Birmingham girl and indicates that things are not going as well as he would like, and he doesn't know how to handle the situation. My mother – ever the down-to-earth doctor – tells him that women are by temperament more practical creatures than men, and less given to romantic flights of fancy, so he should descend a little closer to the earth himself.

I remember John Rivers especially from Mr Burgess's class at school, when we were perhaps fourteen or fifteen. Mr Burgess was one of the best teachers I ever experienced, and it was a great loss when he was appointed headmaster of one of the other schools in the King Edward's Foundation in Birmingham. On one occasion he asked John what he wanted to do in life. John replied that he wanted to be a farmer, and for a while it seemed that he meant if, as he often talked with his friends about farming. But he had been living an ordinary suburban existence in a big city and it was unclear where his interest came from. Mr Burgess also asked him during a class which political party he preferred. 'Conservative, Sir', replied John, at which Mr Burgess (who was hardly left wing) suggested he should carefully consider the various alternatives. I suppose we were all vaguely conservative on those days, since we were mainly from middle class families.

I visited John's home once, and remember John's father as a warm and generous man, and for that reason he remains in my memory as a breath of fresh air in those conformist times. He had an early tape recorder, recorded and played back our conversation. It was the first time I had listened to my own voice. John's sense of humour resonated with mine. He wrote to me from a holiday in Scotland, telling me that he had encountered 'two lemurs and a wombat' on some mountain that he named.

During one summer vacation John spent a while in Italy, and told us about his adventures on his return. He had met an Italian girl, and their relationship had evidently progressed well beyond mere friendship, even though she told him she admired Mussolini and what might be seen today as his Trump-like extreme right wing radicalism, on the grounds that he 'got things done'. But so far as I know the relationship soon ended. A year or two after we graduated from Oxford John wrote to me from northern Italy, where he was part of a scheme to teach Italian students creative writing in English. But he complained about inadequate funding for the project, and then I heard no more.

For years I received no communication from him, and despite my occasional efforts to get back in touch, I drew a complete blank. We of course were in Australia throughout the sixties and seventies and into the eighties, and memories of those days in Birmingham and Oxford were receding. Even when we returned to the UK at the end of 1981, I suppose I was too busy to give much thought to long lost friends, though in John's case I did make a few enquiries. But then, probably in the early 1990s, I received a brief letter from him from Australia. He gave no detail of what he was doing, but I think my reply was equally brief, and even a little cold, and I heard no more.

But not knowing what happened to John Rivers, what kind of a life he carved out for himself, is for me a piece of unfinished business that will remain unfinished, barring a miracle. That kind, intelligent, but also strangely troubled individual may well have done wonderful things in his life, or he may have crashed somewhere along the way, but all I have to fall back on is speculation. He was another piece in the jigsaw puzzle of my own life as I was growing up.

In this chapter I have discussed events and people from when I was still at school and also afterwards, including at university. I see that whole period as a complex series of transitions, but also as a continuum rather than as a series of discrete experiences. It was not until life in Australia began, from 1960, that one life ended and another started. Even then, significant elements of the old still underlay the new.

I still need to fill in some gaps in developments when I was at school.

The first area is music and art. I had surprisingly little interest in music until, around 1950 my parents bought one of the early LP record players, and we began to acquire a few classical LPs. I knew a few silly pop songs, but the Beetles were still far in the future. My mother had been a competent piano player in her younger years, but it seems that she gave this up completely after her marriage, and we never had a piano in the house until we inherited Grandpa Stockwin's piano after his death in 1948. Even then nobody was allowed to play the piano while my father was working. It is one of my great regrets in life that I never learned to play any musical instrument. The first record to be played on the LP player was *Sylvia* by Delibes, and after that some Chopin. I played these over and over, but eventually realised that they were thin gruel by comparison with the great music also available. I then started collecting myself and became familiar with music that really meant something. By comparison John Buckler had learned to play the piano from early childhood, and knew a great deal of the classical repertoire.

In drawing and painting I was more experienced, even though my talent was exiguous. But I loved sketching out of doors, and my parents encouraged me in this. For some time I attended the 'voluntary art' classes at school, given by the newly arrived art master, Bruce Hurn, and one year actually won the 'voluntary art prize'. This was the context in which I became friends with a brilliant artist called John McCracken. John (most of my close friends at school seem to have been called 'John') came from Northern Ireland, and having been partly brought up in that troubled province, called

himself a 'rebel', though what he was rebelling against was not
entirely clear. His father, who taught philosophy at the University
of Birmingham, was a Marxist – or at least close to Marxism – and
gave a series of university extension lectures that I attended in the
library at Sutton Coldfield. At the end of his final lecture he told
his audience, 'I hope I have not disrupted your society with these
lectures'. One or two in the middle class audience appeared to think
that he had. Apart from this, the only phrase I can recall from his
lectures was, 'It would be stretching the meaning of "religious" to
call Bertrand Russell religious.' Yes indeed.

With John McCracken I had many conversations, about art,
about politics, about life. I doubt if these were terribly sophisticated, but they were enjoyable. John went on to study at the Slade
School of Art. Many years later, when I met up again with Bruce
Hurn, we made some effort to track him down, but without success. There was a rumour that he had taken his own life while at the
Slade, but this turned out to be a different person. We could also
firmly establish that the Californian artist John McCracken was not
the person Bruce had taught. The trail has gone cold. But perhaps
the fact that I was drawn to him indicates again that people outside the mainstream in their personality or opinions were people I
sought out. There were to be more instances of this later on.

Another course of university extension lectures I attended at our
local library was given by a science master at King Edwards, Mr
Matthews, on astronomy. From an early age I had known that light
travels at '186,000 miles per second', and that the earth is 'eight
light minutes from the sun', and that distances between the stars
are immense. I had read some of James Jeans, Fred Hoyle and other
astronomers. Mr Matthews knew his science, was a lucid communi-
cator, but seems to have had little understanding of what underpins
the universe of art. In one of his lectures he criticised a contemporary artist for placing the sun and the moon in a painting in
apparent contravention of astronomical principles. Astronomy is
an interest that has stayed with me, and I follow as best I can, and
despite my lack of competence in maths, the fascinating and bizarre
modern insights into the subject.

Another passion I was developing in my later school years was
poetry. Even though I was not formally studying English literature,
I learned much about modern poetry from Tony Trott's inspired

classes. One day, I was hit by a guided missile in the form of T.S. Eliot's *Waste Land*. At first, reading it meant little to me, it appeared almost to be written in a foreign language (parts of it were), but once I persisted and was guided through its mysteries by Tony Trott and others, it exercised upon me a mesmeric attraction. I read and re-read nearly all the poetry that Eliot had written, and even though eventually I found some of his underlying attitudes unattractive (his anti-semitism, his literary class snobbery, some of the religiosity of the *Four Quartets*), what stayed with me was his astonishing linguistic inventiveness and sensitivity to the subtleties of the English language. Indeed, I must have assimilated some of his principles of style. When, later during national service, I showed a poem I had written to Geoff Thurley (more about him in Chapter 6), he commented, 'this is pure Eliot'. But at home, when I read some passages from the Waste Land to my mother, she gently suggested that I should stick with ancient Greek verse.

I recall Tony Trott taking us through Eliot's *Journey of the Magi*, during one of his classes. He went through Eliot's description of the harrowing journey made by these three eastern potentates, guided by a star to see the new born Christ, uncertain about their mission. But he dwelt on one of the shortest lines in the poem:

'And three trees on the low sky'

Just seven monosyllables, no description of the trees, no description of the landscape, but a powerful image in its absolutely pared down simplicity.

Over many weeks on the bus going home, I read contemporary poems, using in particular *The Faber Book of Modern Verse*, edited by Michael Roberts (1951 edition) but other collections as well. Some thirty years later, Adam Roberts, son of Michael Roberts, poet and mountaineer, who had died young in 1948, was a colleague and friend of mine in Oxford.

Having secured my entry into Oxford in January 1954, I had two terms left at King Edwards with no exam pressure. My father suggested that I should use the time to study for an extra A-level in French. I wish I had done so, but instead I joined the school choir and with Brian Coleman translated a Latin play, *The Rope* (Rudens) by Plautus, which we performed at the school. I suppose also that a little relaxation seemed appropriate after all the hard work I had put in to securing Oxford entry.

In this account so far, girls have not figured significantly, mainly because of my extreme shyness in respect of the fair sex. But in our amateur dramatics initiatives we got together with young ladies from King Edward's High School for Girls, just across the way, and this began to break down my shyness. I also saw quite a lot of Valerie, whose parents were in the sailing club, though it would be stretching things to say that she was my girlfriend. We went to a school dance together, but the ambiance was so unfamiliar and difficult to react to that I can hardly have been good company for her.

Once I had left school the prospect of national service loomed. But I needed to find some work and earn a little money before what would be a radically new phase in my life. So I secured a temporary job with the Birmingham electoral commission, helping to bring the electoral role up to date. Equipped with a street map of the city and a bagful of electoral registration forms, I would take a bus to a strategic location among the streets I was tasked with covering on that particular day, and call at each house in turn. Where possible I would hand a form to somebody in the house, but where I got no answer I would leave a form in the letter box.

This job unexpectedly gave me a valuable education in how other people lived at that time in a large English provincial city. As a middle class youth from an affluent suburb I had visited my friends' houses, but these were mostly also in middle class areas of the city. In my life so far, though I had passed through working class suburbs on the way to school and elsewhere, I had never actually visited people's houses there. The electoral commission job gave me access to the houses of people living in states of poverty that I had never imagined existed, and so close to home. Birmingham still had many 'back-to-back' houses, with no through ventilation and outside toilets in a row along the back wall. In 1954, the backlog of house building caused by the war was far from overcome, and there were many houses in a state of dilapidation.

Two or three examples will suffice. I went into the living room of one house where my immediate impression was that the wallpaper was jet black. This was before I caught sight of a patch of wallpaper behind a photo of some ancient ancestor and understood that the original colour had been cream. The colour had been darkened over the years by a coal fire in the grate. Another small house, built against a factory wall, had partly subsided so that it was almost impossible to shut the front door. At another house a woman assumed I was from social services and wouldn't let me go until she had poured out all her troubles to me. Another, very nice, elderly lady, was obviously getting by on very little money indeed, and said to me, 'Oi've 'ad two 'usbands, an' they was both poob-wallopers. Don't yow get married, young man, it ain't worth it.' I learned that fine class distinctions were made between streets. One middle aged woman told me that inhabitants of Legge Street, about two streets from where she lived, were the lowest of the low. When I knocked at the door of a house in Legge Street, I was in a room almost empty of furniture except for a large wooden table at which was seated a hefty woman peeling potatoes into a huge basin. She had several children around her, who told her she needed to 'talk proper' to the visitor. But she rounded on them with, 'I can't talk no different from the way I talk.' It occurred to me that the future of those, obviously bright and lively children might be a good deal more hopeful than their mother's had been. The names I had on my list for one house were 'Mr and Mrs Bhattacharya'. They were not there so I asked next door if they knew where they were. 'Oh, them Indians?', came the useful reply. Immigration from the sub-continent was still in its early stages and Enoch Powell's famous or notorious intervention was several years off.

5

National Service: Learning Russian

⅄

ON 21 OCTOBER 1954, I stood at the bus stop opposite my parents' house waiting for a Midland Red bus to take me to central Birmingham. I was about to embark on a journey that would take me from the comfortable life of a middle class teenager engrossed in education, to adulthood in the rough environment of the Royal Army Service Corps (RASC). As I stood at that bus stop, I reflected that the day was a turning point in my life, and that whatever difficulties lay ahead, they were likely to be of a different nature from anything I had experienced in my life so far. In particular, I was leaving home – not totally perhaps, that would come later, but I would no longer be permanently resident in the family home. I was excited and apprehensive in more or less equal measure.

My first two weeks in national service were at the Royal Army Service Corps (RASC) barracks in Aldershot, where I was kitted out with uniform and allocated the number 23083284. My school friend Alan Kirkby, like me interested in languages but unlike me a fine musician, joined up at the same time, with the number 23083283. My memory of those two weeks has mostly gone, but when I try to recall it what comes into my mind is the satirical, but also curiously moving, poem by Henry Reed, written during the Second World War, titled *Naming of Parts*. This is its first verse:

Today we have naming of parts. Yesterday
We had daily cleaning. And tomorrow morning
We shall have what to do after firing. But today,
Today we have naming of parts. Japonica

Glistens like coral in all of the neighbouring gardens,
And today we have naming of parts

At Aldershot, I conducted a minor piece of research. One morning, I stood for twenty minutes or so beside the barracks newsagent stall, observing what kind of material the men were buying. I found that seventy-five or eighty per cent of the material that these new recruits – mostly eighteen-year olds – bought were children's comics. I myself had enjoyed comics when I was ten or twelve, but not at age eighteen. Later, I found ample confirmation that the bulk of national service recruits had received a shockingly low level of education. Although I never encountered anyone that could not sign his name, I met many that managed only marginal literacy. In those days anybody who failed the 'eleven-plus' examination for entry into grammar schools was consigned to secondary modern schools, from which many pupils graduated with extremely limited knowledge, skills and qualifications. I had friends in the Education Corps, who were teaching absolutely basic literacy and numeracy. Some men that I knew came from itinerant families and had only attended school sporadically. One man (I think this was later) when we were being taken somewhere in an army vehicle, asked me what was the point of education. I replied as best I could, whereupon he replied, 'I suppose then you have education just to get cunning'.

After two weeks at Aldershot, we were divided into separate sections: drivers and clerks. Alan was assigned to the clerks and later in the army taught secretarial skills, before becoming a language teacher back in civilian life. He was not accepted for the Russian course, but taught himself Russian later. It was determined that I was to be a driver, and (with many others) I was transferred to the RASC camp on a more or less circular plateau some way out of Blandford Forum in leafy Dorset. The RASC shared the complex with the Royal Electrical and Mechanical Engineers (REME). We occupied one half of the circular perimeter of the hill, and REME the other. I should explain that in the Army of that time, the RASC was regarded as the lowest of the low, apart from the Pioneer Corps, whose anthem began:

Run Pioneer, Run Pioneer,
There's dog muck on the square…

I became DVR (Driver) 23083284 Stockwin, A., learning to drive a three-ton truck round Salisbury Plain, coached by a cheerful northerner named 'Geordie' Appleby. Once winter arrived we had to drain the radiator in the evening and fill it again with water before driving off next morning. The army regarded antifreeze as a soft and expensive option. I seem to remember that all gear changes, whether up or down, required the driver to double-declutch. I passed my truck driving test on the second attempt. Luckily in my civilian driving coached by my father, I had already learned how to double-declutch.

The army in that era was famous for 'bull', or the daily routine of applying liquid or powdery 'blanco' to equipment, and inspections took place every morning, requiring meticulous and time-consuming preparation. (Years later, visiting Israel, I was told by an Israeli army officer with a London background 'there's no bull in this army').

One consequence of the daily inspection system was that it institutionalised thievery. Theft was of course an offense, but it was equally an offense to be at inspection without any item of equipment, and punishment could be harsh. It followed that the automatic response of many to the lack of any item was to steal it from somebody else. This of course initiated a chain reaction of theft, and consequent bad blood between individuals. Many of the men I knew were in street gangs in their local towns, so that conflict was instinctive. One saving grace was that the use of drugs was not yet widespread.

We were part of a platoon of about 160 men, divided into squads of around twenty each, according to alphabetical order of surname. One chance result was that nearly all those whose surnames began with Mc or Mac were in the same squad. Most of them were from Scotland, and a few were Irish. I hope Nicola Sturgeon will forgive me for saying that this squad became notorious for its aggressive behaviour. I remember in particular a man called McRitchie, a small bundle of aggression from the Gorbals of Glasgow, who most days would approach outsiders (outside his squad), fists at the ready, with the words 'Ye wanna fight? Ye wanna fight?' It became evident that McRitchie did not know where he was. He knew he was in England, but thought he was about a hundred miles south of London, which would have put him just off the coast of France. I also remember him complaining of his surroundings with the words. 'Och, it's a barren desert round here'.

I forget the exact amount we were paid as national service recruits, but I think it was less than (or not much more than) thirty shillings (£1.50) a week. Even though our board and lodging were provided, this left little reserve even for minor purchases. As a result, some among our number would try to cadge from others, 'Got any change?' One man (English) approached me so persistently with this appeal that I eventually exploded and gave him a well-aimed punch – not my normal style at all. He never badgered me for money again.

While I was at Blandford camp I was still half committed to Christianity, and asked the army chaplain to give me instruction for confirmation into the Church of England. The chaplain was Padre Willis, who took me through the relevant parts of the Bible. He was a pleasant and understated man, who plainly disliked the army and the attitudes prevailing in the camp, and sometimes told me that he would like to move on and take over a parish somewhere. When the time came for the confirmation I was driven with others by army truck to Salisbury Cathedral for the service. I was almost nineteen. While there I talked with a man who had lost his son, and was cementing his relationship with the Church, I suppose, as a means of coming to terms with his loss. I had occasion to remember this meeting some thirty-three years later.

I attended a lecture by a particularly dour and unattractive sergeant-major who I think had fought in the First World War. Apart from telling us not to get involved with 'skirt' in the town of Blandford Forum, he impressed upon us that the Allies had won the Great War 'because we could shoot straight', and that our duty as soldiers was 'to kill the enemy'. On some of his audience he may have had the reverse effect to that he intended. I later heard one or two of my colleagues expressing doubt whether they could kill people, even if the people targeted were on the enemy side.

Once we went to the camp cinema to see a film called *Donovan's Brain*, in which a mad professor invents a brain that eventually manages to control him. I believe it retains something of a cult status even today. The next day, our corporal (who like me came from Birmingham), retailed the whole plot of the film to those who hadn't seen it, his account almost entirely devoid of adjectives except for that ubiquitous one that begins with 'f'. 'And the f****** brain says to the f****** professor...' His account was even funnier than the film itself, and his memory for detail remarkable.

Towards the end of November I was suffering from depression (as I later realised), and although I was coping more or less with the environment I was in, it was clearly taking its toll on my state of mind. By my own stupidity, I fell into a black hole – one of the worst of my life – most of the detail of which I have blanked from my memory. My nineteenth birthday would fall on 28 November, and I was missing my parents. The same corporal who retold the story of 'Donovan's Brain', perhaps sensing that I was not coping well, suggested to me that if I was clever I could leave the camp for the weekend and return undetected. He showed me how this could be done, though I now forget the details. I duly followed his suggestions and was home for my birthday, which fell on a Sunday. My parents were perturbed by my actions, and of course when I returned to camp my absence had been noted. The punishment was two or three days in the guard house, and I have no memory of that period, except for a general memory of darkness.

Some of the men made a habit of going AWOL. I heard a seri-ously delinquent character called Hamilton say more than once, 'I think I'll just f*** off', and for him the prospect of being confined to the guard house on return seemed a normal, if inconvenient, part of life. Of course, he knew perfectly that if he failed to return at all he would picked up by the MPs (military police). But for me a single instance was a trauma in which guilt was mixed with deep anxiety. Hamilton, much like his Scots counterpart McRitchie, claimed he was never happy when out of a fight. My sporadically kept diary, reflecting on events two or three months before, is worth quoting here:

> Driver Clark told us that he had always treated Hamilton as a friend; so when he had to go as escort to bring him back from his London hideout, this friendship stood him in good stead. Hamilton had been in trouble with the police, and was standing trial when Clark and Pannell arrived, armed with handcuffs. He had moreover been offered massive protection from his friends so that he should be able to jump the escort when he came out of the court. But Hamilton forewent this when he saw that 'his pals had come to pick him up' (entry, 17 February 1955).

At the camp the range of accents was astonishing. Some men (from Yorkshire?) used 'thee' and 'thou' with their local mates, there was a man from my home town of Birmingham called Righ Ooptn (Ray Upton, pronounced on a rising tone), and a friend of mine called 'Arold 'Oltby from 'Ooll (Harold Holtby from Hull). 'Arold was a large-boned expansive character whose intelligence belied his lack of education. One night I shared guard duty with a Scotsman called Stobo, who told me everything that was possible to know about Scottish football. Again, I realised that formal education is not the only way to acquire knowledge.

I made friends with two men from a comparable background to my own, both from other platoons. One was Noel Dyrenforth, who in later life became an artist. Years later I met up with him again through the chance of seeing an exhibition of his work in an Oxford gallery. But at the time I knew him in the Army he was deeply uncertain about his future, engaged in boxing and acting in films, but uncertain where either of these might lead. The other was Tony Fielding, in civilian life working at a scientific research institute in Bristol. Tony had political views on the left of the political spectrum that he discussed with me in a low-key fashion. He was also an agnostic. I was still struggling with the idea of religious belief, even though I had recently been confirmed. A diary entry, written in Bodmin but remembering Blandford, included the following revealing passage:

> ...since I was out of a general religious atmosphere, indeed in a highly pagan and anti- or un-Christian set of people, I became very lackadaisical. And Tony was an agnostic. Knowing that I had not strength or resources in myself, I was content to wait until real outside help was at hand. I am not yet prepared to be a Christian all of the time, intellectually or morally. So I borrowed ideas from Tony and did not oppose him as many would have done. Though I have no regrets at this.

At the beginning of national service I had applied to join the Joint Services School of Languages in order to learn Russian. Indeed, before joining the Army I had tried to enter the Russian course via the Navy, this involving a stay in Portsmouth, but been rejected. I had brought a Russian grammar with me to Blandford camp, and occasionally dipped into it. But after five months or so of 'basic (military) training' I fell off the roll for a reason I forget, if I ever knew. Thus for a couple of weeks, like Major Major in *Catch 22*, I did not officially exist, and could stay in my billet studying Russian. This was fine, except that there was no heating and the outside temperature was well below freezing all day. At least, I must have had access to the canteen. And then one Friday I received a movement order to go by train the following Monday to the Walker Lines on Bodmin Moor in Cornwall to join the Joint Services School of Languages (JSSL) for its Russian course.

With 'Arold and some of the others in the billet I had sometimes talked about Russian and my desire to study it. The problem was that my methods of exposition and their ways of thinking meshed together only with difficulty. If I mentioned the Kremlin, 'Arold would say something like, 'Well, we've got gremlins, then', and I had to try another tack. If I said something about vowels and consonants, somebody would ask me what these words meant. The atmosphere of the camp was one of verbal confrontation, and sometimes physical, so that I had become unused to anything that smacked of emotion or kindness. And so it was a surprise to me when I announced my imminent departure and my friends told me they were sorry to see me go. Human sentiments like that were not a normal part of the camp ethos, and I was touched by them. Whatever 'appened to 'Arold, I wonder?

When I reflect on my time at Blandford camp, I am faced with two questions: why was the camp regime so mindless and so many of its activities pointless? Even though I never saw men ordered to whitewash coal or mow a lawn with scissors, such widespread stories symbolised much of the ethos of the place. Secondly, why was the ethos so vindictive and confrontational? One commissioned officer allegedly (and I must stress 'allegedly'), unsatisfied with the state of one man's kit, ordered him to carry his wooden cupboard onto parade with him. As a result he developed a hernia and had to go to hospital. I suspect that a good part of the answer to both these questions was that a decade after the war the Army was not sure that it wanted conscripts any more, and had little idea how to motivate them to work towards specific goals. The wartime impetus towards bravery and dedication to the cause of national salvation had largely disappeared. In its stead an almost wholly negative regime of mindless make-work activities and vindictive punishments became normal.

In addition, the general level of education in the 1950s (except for the top end of the market) was deplorable. And yet many of those with a poor educational background were plainly intelligent and some had amazing memories. At the other end of the spectrum, admittedly, was a man in our billet who spent every evening throwing a ball of rolled up paper at the wall and catching it. Some of our NCOs exhibited sadistic tendencies, though military regulations kept these in check to some extent. But others tempered their bawling out of the men under their control with some crude humour. An NCO stands close behind a man on parade and shouts into his ear, 'Am I hurting you?' 'No Sir.' 'Well I should be, because I'm standing on your hair.' (In other words, 'get a haircut'.)

The Joint Services School of Languages (JSSL) represented a major feat of organisation by the British Army, Navy and Airforce working together. It lasted essentially throughout the 1950s, during which time around 5,000 national servicemen were trained to a high level of Russian language competence. It was taught at several centres around the country, of which I experienced three: successively Bodmin, Cambridge and Crail. It was established during the early stages of the Cold War, when the threat of a new European war, with the Soviet Union as the principal adversary, seemed imminent. Should war break out, the need for Russian linguists for such purposes as interrogating prisoners of war was regarded as urgent. About 5,000 курсанты (kursanty – course students) went through the various centres over the decade) and came out in most cases with an advanced command of the Russian language. A book by Geoffrey Elliott and the late Harold Shukman (later my colleague at St Antony's College, Oxford), titled *Secret Classrooms*, tells how the courses were established and maintained, those organising and teaching the courses, as well as providing vignettes of life for young national servicemen learning Russian. To my taste the book concentrates too much on celebrities (Alan Bennett, Michael Frayn, Denis Potter and others) and too little on those amazing people who were our instructors – men and women who in most cases had endured almost unbelievable experiences through murderous times in the Soviet Union and Eastern Europe. Nevertheless, the book remains the best source on the JSSL. Towards the end of our course, when we understood spoken Russian well, we listened to an hour-long lecture without notes by a youngish man named Ross (presumably he had anglicised his name) who had survived the Nazi siege of Leningrad, during which more than half of its population perished. It was one of the most moving lectures I have ever experienced.

Students at the JSSL (which included several centres, including one in London) were housed in the wooden huts of the Walker Lines on Bodmin Moor with views of slag heaps at Bugle and St Austell, 'looking like the Alps from fifty miles away' (diary), breaking the monotony of the horizon. There were fifty huts, each heated by a coke stove in its centre, with beds arranged around its walls. The classrooms were in rather more substantial buildings. We arrived in the middle of winter, and after our arrival we were cut off from the outside world by deep snow for two or three days. Each of us was allocated a cupboard in which to stow our kit. My colleague John Westwood would interleave his inadequate supplies of blankets with sheets of newspaper, helpful to keep warm but disturbing to the sleep of neighbours as his newspapers rustled in response to any movement. Life was hardly comfortable, but the difference in intellectual atmosphere between Blandford and Bodmin was extreme. I was back among people with similar interests to my own, we had a difficult language to learn, and although we had parades, our main activities were directed towards clear and definable goals.

That is not to say that we were no longer subject to military discipline, but that the character of that discipline was radically different from what had been the norm at Blandford. Instead of nightmarish kit inspections every morning, we were now working towards an examination some ten weeks away that would determine our future. Those who did well would be expected to complete an eighteen months course, leading to a qualification as Russian language interpreters. Those that performed less well would do a year-long translator course, and spend the final six months of their two-year national service stationed in West Germany and elsewhere, listening in to and translating Russian Airforce messages on the other side of the Iron Curtain.

In my hut there were two Scotsmen, the first a classics student from Glasgow with firm opinions, called Bill Train. Naturally the Russian for 'train' – Поезд (Poyezd) became his nickname. I once asked him what he thought of Scottish nationalism, whereupon he replied in emphatic Glaswegian, 'We have our grievances.'

The other Scotsman was Hugh McTurk, cultivated and dapper, a fancy dresser when allowed to wear civvies, from Castle Douglas, who had been a law student. They were both Scots, but very different, and highly critical of each other. There was Willie Ledgard, a graduate of Manchester University whose home was in the Pennines, a man full of fun and off-colour stories, who later worked for the BBC monitoring service at Caversham. He lives in Norwich and I am still in touch with him. There was Michael Ardouin, who I think later went into teaching. Something I once said prompted him to tell me that if I were ever to teach languages, my students would have a rough time.

The resident hut 'nerd' or 'geek' (though I did not hear those words until decades later) was the abovementioned John Westwood – cousin of my school friend Brian Coleman but starkly different from him. He had graduated from Birmingham University in Economics and Russian, and had encyclopaedic knowledge about Russian railways. He knew a lot of Russian but had a tin ear and pronounced it at the end of the course as badly as at the beginning. Later in life he wrote respectable books on the Russo-Japanese War of 1904-5 and other topics.

Finally, we had in our hut Keith Harding, who came from Manchester and had attended Manchester Grammar School. He did more to drive me away from religion than any other individual I ever met. Like me, he was one of the pre-university contingent. In the end, I came to know him reasonably well, both in the Army and later in my college at Oxford. Keith's problem (and a problem for those around him) was that his mind had been captured by extreme religion to an extent I have hardly ever seen in anybody else. He may have been a member of the Plymouth Brethren, though I cannot be sure of that. He was unable to keep his beliefs to himself or refrain from seeking to impose them on others. Once, when he heard me say 'Good Heavens', he intervened and told me that this was a blasphemous expression that I ought not to use. One day at Bodmin we students of Russian were taken to a church service led by an Orthodox priest according to Orthodox rites. Afterwards Keith told all who would listen that the service was entirely heretical. In retrospect I think that it would have been a kindness if I had had a long talk with him, with the aim of persuading him that he should show more tolerance and not impose his beliefs on others in this manner. We did argue, but I never got round to a proper talk with him.

We all had personal cupboards in which to stow our kit. Most people would paste photos of their wives or girlfriends on the inside of the cupboard door. Since these were often left open, others could see and admire them. Willie Ledgard was married and so was Michael Ardouin. They both became so fed up with Keith's sanctimonious moralising that they decided to play a trick on him. I was not involved in this and only heard of it much later. They swopped over the photos of their respective wives and managed to persuade Keith that Michael was having an affair with Willie's wife (or perhaps the other way round). Keith took the bait and sermonised about the sanctity of marriage and importance of monogamy, threatening also to write to the 'wronged' wife. All this came to an abrupt end when they told him he had been fooled. The trick was cruel but most understandable.

In sorting out our affairs at Bodmin, my fellow курсанты and I discovered a bureaucratic anomaly that divided us down the middle. We now had the status of Officer Cadets. All of us had completed basic training in various parts of the armed forces. The nominal length of basic training was six months, but some had served a full six months and others a week or two less. I was in the latter category. This had serious implications for our pay, and the solution arrived at by the authorities was the height of mindless bureaucratic ingenuity: Those whose basic training had already pushed them over the six months threshold would be required to sign on as full (not national service) personnel, for an extra period of a week or two, depending on how far beyond six months they had served. Since the duration of the Russian course was eighteen months, they would receive a written guarantee of release once the year and a half of the course was completed. WITH THIS WENT A DOUBLING OF PAY. Those of us short of the six months would retain the formal status of national servicemen, and our pay would not change. Those in my category found this discriminatory, but knew we had no means of challenging it.

In the weeks I was at Bodmin I worked hard learning Russian, and passed the final examination easily, assuring my entry to the year-long university based course, which we eventually discovered would be at Cambridge for those of us who were in the army.

Indeed, if I remember correctly, I came out second, behind George Craig, a brilliant linguist of Irish origin, married to a French woman and based in Paris. But life was not entirely taken up with Russian grammar and vocabulary. Having been confirmed in Salisbury Cathedral while at Blandford camp, in Bodmin I attended a Christian Union group at a local church. But although I was, as it were, still trying to be a Christian, I was meeting people whose beliefs and attitudes I found increasingly problematic. Keith was merely the most extreme example of these. At the time also I was suffering from bouts of depression, though these, mercifully, were of short duration. In any case, we saw a good many films, including some from the Soviet Union. I remember in particular 'Мать' (Mother), based on a novel by Maxim Gorky, a moving portrayal of resilience amidst extreme poverty. We also saw 'Meeting on the Elbe', a hilarious and outrageous send-up of the Americans when American and Soviet forces met on the river Elbe in 1945.

Given my eventual unexpected intellectual destination in Japan, I will reproduce in full my entry for 15 March 1955:

> The weapons training film this morning was made by the US Army during the war, to show the military power and tenacity of Japan. What emerged was something like an enticement to a five minutes hate. It was difficult to know whether to dislike most the makers of the film or its subjects. No attempt was made to counter the impression that the Japanese were a different and verminous species of animal from ourselves. Indeed, the commentary stated that the two races were totally different in mind: 'Their thinking is 2000 years out of date'. There are two reflections to be made: Is Japan safe now, while we transfer our hatred to China, and how easily could a nation of fanatics like this be turned into something better?

I knew next to nothing about Japan at the time, but with the advantage of hindsight I think that my reaction to the film was spot on. My only reservation concerns its final phrase, since the ethos of wartime Japan was essentially the product of a semi-totalitarian regime imposing its savage will on a people vulnerable to militarist appeals. Pre-war Japan contained strong elements of liberal thinking alongside traditional (but not necessarily extreme) attitudes.

The teaching during our year in Cambridge took place in a large Victorian house rented from one of the colleges, in Station Road.

But we lived in a capacious mansion called Foxton Hall in its own grounds in the village of Foxton, about ten miles south of Cambridge. This was one of two university level branches of the JSSL, the other being in London. The director of the branch was Professor Elizaveta Hill, a woman of Anglo-Russian origin, born at the turn of the century, who had fled Russia with her family after the Bolshevik revolution of October 1917, and later rose to be Professor of Slavonic Studies at the University of Cambridge. She had been a prime mover in persuading the War Office that with relations between the West and the Soviet bloc rapidly deteriorating, the UK needed to train a substantial body of Russian interpreters and translators. She was a strong willed, even imperious lady, whose relations with the late Ronald Hingley, the *de facto* head of the London school, and later a colleague of mine at Oxford, were notoriously bad, with each accusing the other of incompetence. Both, quite frankly, were difficult and egocentric characters. But although Lisa Hill was in Cambridge for our first term there, for the remaining two terms she was away on sabbatical.

Most of our instructors were native Russian speakers, and in nearly all cases refugees from the Soviet Union or from one or other of the Soviet bloc countries. Their task was to familiarise us with the sound of Russian speech and increase our vocabulary through immersion in the language. There were also a small number of British instructors, who mostly took us through the grammar, though some native Russian instructors did this as well. I remember with particular gratitude Courtney Lloyd, a rather shy man who was a talented language teacher and administrator. David Jones was very different character, flamboyant in his own style, driving an enormous clanking 1930s car that we called the 'brone boy', from the Russian for armoured car (or armour plated): 'броневой'. A much more exotic character was George Trapp, again Anglo-Russian, who was in charge of devising vocabulary lists on all imaginable subjects, from musical instruments to shellfish (for a selection, see Elliott and Shukman, p. 140). He was not good on people's names. The name of the French right wing politician Pierre Poujade, prominent in the media at the time, he pronounced as 'Mr Pooh Jayde'. Willie Ledgard recalled that Mr Trapp once addressed me as 'Mr Stukebind'. Westwood became 'Wedgwood'. But he was refreshingly down to earth, and could defuse the often tense atmosphere of Russian and east European refugees interacting with us students, who did not always accept what our instructors told us without argument.

There were several generations of native Russian instructors, ranging from an elderly gentleman who had fought in the Tsarist Army before the Revolution, a Don Cossack who had fought in innumerable wars during his military career but was now a gentle old man, to those who had been educated under the Soviet regime and those who had fought in the Soviet Army during the Second World War. As may be imagined, their political views differed according to 'generation', even though as refugees they were all critical of how things worked in the Soviet Union. The experience of war had shaped nearly all of them.

Of the Russian instructors several retain a sharp presence in my memory. Our class teacher for a considerable period was Andrei Romankiewicz, bilingual in Polish and Russian. He was ferociously anti-Soviet and would counter any dissident views from his class with: 'Я сидел два года в тюрме, Господа' (I sat [spent] two years in prison, Gentlemen). Indeed, his two years in prison were spent at Vorkutà in the Arctic, where little concession was made to the comfort – or even survival – of inmates in the deep freeze of winter.

A very different individual was 'солдат Иванов' ('Soldier Ivanov'), who gave us graphic descriptions of his time fighting as an officer in the Red Army, where, as he breezily expressed it: 'Я сам убил два-три человека' ('I myself killed two or three men'). I imagine what he meant by this was that he killed in close combat, not just firing a rifle at enemy lines. He was strongly critical of the Soviet regime, and would point out blatant distortions and lies in Pravda and Izvestia, but his thought categories were plainly influenced by Soviet education. He was rough in his manner, but I quite liked him. Soviet educational influence was even more evident in a female instructor called Aleksandra Chernyshova, who, according to Elliott and Shukman, had worked in the Soviet Control Commission in Berlin before she defected (p. 135). I heard once heard her talking in pure Marxist terms about the stages of human history, as though this were uncontroversial.

Then there were two ladies, Mrs Hackel and Miss Heiseler, who were stalwarts of the course. Mrs Hackel made no concession to the English pronunciation of the surnames of the students.

A man called Bartholomew was to her Господин Бартоломев (Mr Bartolomyev).

Pressure to make rapid progress in the learning of the Russian language was intense. Every Friday was devoted to a series of examinations. Failure in three successive Friday exams officially meant relegation from the interpreter to the translator course, although nobody on our course suffered that fate, and I wonder how rigidly it was applied. The principal criticism levelled at the Cambridge course by Ronald Hingley in its London counterpart was that the atmosphere at Cambridge was not tough enough. The pressure he imposed on his students was extreme, apparently requiring his students to perfect their Russian almost to the exclusion of any other activity. One former student on the London course, who later became a colleague of mine in Oxford, described Ron Hingley when in charge of the course in London as 'a holy terror'. Our regime was hardly easy, however, and after about nine months from beginning Russian we all passed A-levels in Russian, about half of us with distinction. Admittedly, we had time over some summer weekends for punting on the river, and we saw many films.

During our time at Cambridge we were allowed to wear civilian clothes, and were issued with 'civvies' by the army, though stylistically these were unwearable. But of course we had to wear uniform for parades. We had the status of officer cadets, and appropriately to our status there was a bar at Foxton Hall, where I acted as barman for a while.

We were not, however, freed entirely from military life. In the spring of 1956 we spent a week at the Kitchener Barracks of the Royal Engineers (Sappers) at Chatham, where we were introduced to earth moving 'dozers', interacted with carpenters, bricklayers, smiths and welders, and were shown a film on atomic warfare. At the end of the week we spent the night erecting a Bailey Bridge over a stream close to Canterbury, with the illuminated spire of the cathedral visible above the trees.

We spent a second week attached to the School of Artillery at Larkhill camp near Salisbury. As I commented in a letter to my parents, we were in antiquated accommodation (comparable to that at Bodmin), and 'the view of Stonehenge does not sufficiently compensate for the fact that Salisbury is 12 miles away'. One Sunday morning, a small group of us walked across fields to Stonehenge, where there were no fences, no security and no people.

From Larkhill, we travelled by train to Crail, on the Fife Coast in eastern Scotland. The whole of the Bodmin operation had been transferred to a former Royal Naval Air Station, and we were reunited with some of our instructors of a year before. On arrival I described it to my parents in the following terms:

> Crail is a big camp extending on both sides of a road, virtually next to the sea itself, twenty minutes' walk from the town. In the winter the cold must be Siberian, and even now an unpleasant biting wind comes in from the sea. From the headland a little way along the road you can see both Firths, Tay and Forth, while a couple of islets are out at sea... The C.O. is continually being approached by people proposing to set up cafes, asking if, in his opinion, they will pay. As at Bodmin, a mushroom growth of comforts and entertainments is likely to arise in the next few months.

I added that St Andrews was a shilling bus ride away, though to get there for Saturday evening dances in practice I normally cycled the relatively short distance across the peninsula.

During my time at Cambridge, I had been reading classic Russian literature in the original. As part of our course we had been introduced to Dostoyevsky's *Crime and Punishment*, and on my own I read the whole of *Anna Karenina* by Tolstoy. I remember wondering why anybody bothered with contemporary novels, when they could read gripping thrillers by Dostoyevsky such as *Crime and Punishment* and *The Possessed* (Бесы).

In the next Chapter I shall introduce some of my colleagues at Cambridge and later at Crail, because my interaction with them had a lasting impact on my life and thought. Finally here, however, I want briefly to reflect on the quality of the language teaching that we were given. Having completed the course and on later reflection, I remain convinced that intensive, immersion study of the language is the most efficient, and also satisfying, way of assimilating a foreign language. Even though Ron Hingley's views on the subject were too extreme and his exposition of them almost fascist in their vitriol against rivals like Lisa Hill, I have some sympathy for his view that concentrated language immersion really works. I have seen too many language teachers let students get away with poor pronunciation and inaccurate grammar, almost assuming that a non-native speaker learning a language is like a cat trying to bark like a dog. In fact, and demonstrably, human cats really can bark like dogs, if they are properly trained to do so. I was confirmed in this view later, when involved with Japan and Japanese.

6

Out with Religion, in with Politics

ᴋ

BEING ACCEPTED ONTO the Russian course in the JSSL was a hit and miss business. One of my colleagues on the course, the late Kevin Ruane, told the following story. Being in basic training at Woolwich Barracks as a clerical trainee, he tried to apply for the course through 'normal channels'. This, however, met with uncompromising resistance from his sergeant, who told him he had no right to ask the country to spend 'thousands' on teaching him Russian.

This seemed to be the end of the matter, until about two weeks later the same sergeant was ordered to take Kevin to see the Commanding Officer. The CO told him he had discovered that Kevin, who came from Liverpool, was a Catholic. The CO therefore asked him if he would sell some raffle tickets on behalf of the Children of Mary, since his daughter had become a Catholic. Kevin agreed, and ended up buying most of the raffle tickets himself. When Kevin told the CO that he was keen to join the Russian course, he was given the impression that that would not be too difficult. 'The Brigadier', he said, 'is an old chum of mine.' About a month later, Kevin was posted to Bodmin.

Kevin Ruane was to pursue a distinguished career in later life as BBC correspondent successively in Washington, Warsaw and Moscow. He was in Warsaw at a crucial and fascinating time, able to observe the birth of the Solidarity movement led by Lech Wałęsa and the subsequent crackdown on dissent, under Soviet pressure, by the Communist regime of Wojciech Jaruzelski. His book *To Kill a Priest*, about the murder of Father Jerzy Popiełuszko under the Communist regime, was based on much first-hand information gathered by him in the aftermath of the murder.

So 'spending thousands' on teaching Kevin Russian, agreed over the purchase of three books of raffle tickets, was to give the world a deeper understanding of crucial events in Poland during the 1980s leading eventually to the collapse of the Soviet Empire.

Each separate course of kursanty was designated by a letter of the alphabet. We were 'L' course, in other words the twelfth course since the JSSL was launched. For a while we overlapped with 'K' course, and perhaps also with 'M'. Kevin was one of a small elite group among us, who had already graduated from university. They were mostly three or four years older than we were. To some extent they exercised intellectual leadership over us, but the picture was rather more complicated than that might suggest.

Certainly, apart from Kevin, the most impressive member of the course was George Craig. A brilliant linguist, George was Irish, married to a French woman and living in Paris. Even in 1955 it was possible to travel from Cambridge to Paris and back on a seventy-two-hour (even forty-eight- hour) leave. Politically, he was knowledgeable and articulate, and his political outlook was located on the moderate-to-far left. Being based in France he had clear and detailed opinions about French politics, at the time of Pierre Mendes-France, President of the Council of Ministers from June 1954 to February 1955, and his successors. France at the time was entangled in a sanguinary colonial conflict in Indochina, and Mendes-France, on the political left, worked hard to extricate France from this and other colonial wars. By withdrawing France from the conflict he essentially turned it into an American war. He was fiercely opposed by right wing politicians, including Pierre Poujade, and a young Jean-Marie LePen, who several decades later founded the *Front National*. The fact that Mendes-France was of Portuguese-Jewish origin provided ample ammunition for the right wing to use against him. George expounded all this to us from an anti-colonial perspective, and was not slow to take our instructors to task on political issues.

Also among the graduates was Derek Brooks, a Welshman, who already had a degree in Spanish, and was, one might say, rather more interested in the pleasures of life than in intellectual or political disputation. But I know that he supported the Labour Party.

I have already mentioned the grumpy John Westwood, who perhaps rightly regarded our intellectual discussions as immature. I have little idea what his politics were, but I remember one evening at Foxton Hall, when John was engaged in intensive conversation with David Coleman, who had not yet been to university, throughout most of the evening. All I know about this is that David had relationships problems and John, in effect, was counselling him.

I have already mentioned Willie Ledgard, who kept us all laughing with his stories and light-hearted attitude to life.

Finally, among the graduates was Bill Nicholas, whose background was radically different from that of anybody else, in two senses. First of all, he was born of a Russian father and English mother, and brought up in Finland. Secondly, he was a qualified architect, practising at Louth, in Lincolnshire. He had been put on the course when it was realised that he had a near native fluency in Russian. His name in Russian was Василий Николай (Vasilii Nikolai). Unlike the rest of us, he had never seriously studied languages, but had absorbed Russian naturally at home. This meant that the instructors found it next to impossible to 'correct' a number of non-standard, or dialect, usages that were habitual for him, and he used them about as frequently at the end of the course as at the beginning. Grammatical categories meant little to him, but he did well in conversation classes with our native speaker instructors. And as an architect, he was no doubt better qualified than any of us.

Bill was not particularly interested in politics, except, perhaps, in so far as it might affect his architectural practice. But later, when we were at Crail in Scotland, he became friendly with a Scotsman called Bill Smith, who was politically on the far fringes of the left. Apparently, the two Bills did not discuss politics among themselves, but on one occasion I myself got into an argument with Bill Smith, in which I remember him uttering, in a strong Scots accent, the following statement, 'Ye have to understand, Arthur, that Mr Molotov is a great friend of the working classes'.

Now the old Bolshevik and Stalinist Vyecheslav Molotov may have talked a great deal about the working classes, but he and his regime's policies had led to millions of deaths, including deaths of workers.

Among those of us yet to enter university, I will single out four: John Field, Ivor Samuels, Edward Lewis and Geoffrey Thurley. John Field was probably more mature than the rest of us at the time, was judicious in argument, went to Oxford and pursued a career in the Foreign Service, serving in both Moscow and Tokyo, his final posting being that of Ambassador to Sri Lanka. During his term there the president and another prominent politician were assassinated.

Ivor Samuels was the son of a Jewish tailor in London, knew a lot about classical music and literature, and possibly had some hang-ups resulting from his background. In later life he engaged in various business ventures. Ed Lewis had been to a school in Wales that he disliked, struggled to some extent with Russian, was highly artistic, and was to combine a career in teaching with the life of an inspired and dedicated painter until his death in May 2018. Geoff Thurley had superb understanding of English literature, was a self-described theoretician of literature, an enthusiastic proponent of modern trends in classical music, and was left wing in his political views.

Geoff was an intellectual leader among us, even more so than George Craig or Kevin Ruane, even though he was a good deal younger than them. He came from Harrow in London, had I think attended a local grammar school, and did not seem to have any particularly intellectual family background. But for Ed Lewis and me, the two who were to be most influenced by him, he was a crucial source of intellectual challenge on several fronts at that formative stage in our lives. Some of our colleagues regarded him as a trendy, and at a hop at Foxton Hall a 'special concert' was announced, at which 'music by the celebrated composer Geoffrey Thawpitoff' would be played, and one of our colleagues executed an excruciatingly discordant piece of improvisation on a cello. ('Thawpit' was a contemporary brand of kitchen cleaner). Geoff took it in good part and laughed along with the rest of us.

But the influence that Geoff exercised on my thinking was profound and long-term, even though I never completely accepted all his political views. In fairly recent conversations with Ed Lewis, it was clear that Ed was also strongly influenced by him, though perhaps with somewhat different emphases. Ed told me that, not long after they had first met, Geoff asked him whether he was interested in politics. Ed replied that he was not particularly interested in it. To which Geoff countered, 'Well you'd bloody well better be interested in politics!' And no doubt Ed started to take note of what was going on the political world. So far as I was concerned, I had always had some interest in politics, my father had taught me the essentials of what was what in the political sphere, but always from his own perspective of moderate conservatism. During my final years at school, however, I was listening to a greater variety of views, and to some extent also my involvement with religion at that time may have impacted on my attitudes to politics. In other words, I was starting to think for myself, but never feeling that I was in possession of sufficient information or understanding to be sure of my own position.

When I began to discuss these things with Geoff, I was confronted with a forcefully expressed holistic view, within which everything seemed to fall into place. But I had enough critical sense not to take on board the whole package right away. During a period of leave we travelled to Paris together and stayed in accommodation provided by the Sorbonne. While we were there Geoff asked me, 'Are you now a Socialist?' I don't remember what I replied to that, but I suspect that I managed to avoid a categorical reply. During our week in Paris, Geoff through his literary contacts, managed to arrange a meeting with the widow of Ilf, famous as one half of the satirical writing duo Ilf and Petrov. They had entertained Soviet readers through the late 1920s and into the terrible repression of the 1930s.

Whether my reply to Geoff's question was categorical or not, my politics changed quite radically. I think that part of this was a need to throw off the influences of my childhood, looking with greater understanding at the social reforms put in place in Britain by the Labour Government after the war, coming to prefer 'reform' to 'conservatism', no longer entirely happy with the Churchill cult that was so central to the Conservative Party but now seemed to impede new thinking, trying to see the Cold War in rather less black and white terms, and beginning to think of ways in which the international tensions of the Cold War could be mitigated. Stalin had died in 1953, and there seemed some prospect that the Soviet regime might become less repressive and more liberal. Of course, these hopes were to be dashed by the Soviet suppression of the Hungarian, and much later the Czechoslovak revolts, but in 1955 hope was not yet lost. Geoff was inclined to go much further than this, and defend the Soviets in some at least of their actions and policies. But he specifically ruled out any relationship with the British Communist Party. He also, like my school friend David Davies a year or two earlier, played around with notions of pacifism, but never followed this through to the extent of becoming a conscientious objector. Even though I was not taught by the same Russian course tutors as Geoff, I am sure that he sometimes questioned their deep hostility to the Soviet Union and all that it stood for, based in most cases on their own bitter personal experiences.

While on the Russian course, I was reassessing whether I wanted to go back to Latin and Greek classics when I went on to start my undergraduate course in Oxford from 1956. I discussed this with Geoff, who suggested that I should move to PPE (philosophy, politics and economics) instead. After consulting Exeter College and my school (which tried to dissuade me), I pursued this idea, and PPE was the course I took. So he influenced not only my political orientation, but also my subsequent academic training. In addition he taught me a great deal about music, art and literature.

Between Geoffrey Thurley and Ivor Samuels there was little meeting of minds, and indeed it is clear that each disliked the other. Neither of them was tall, and they had similar interests in music and literature, but Ivor could not stand Geoff's leftist politics (though he admired his literary and cultural sensitivity), while Geoff found Ivor provocative and perhaps also too rough.

After the Russian course Geoff went to Cambridge, where he was taught by F.R. Leavis, celebrated radical critic of English literature and enthusiast for the novels of D.H. Lawrence – an enthusiasm shared by Geoff. Some twenty years later, when we were living in Canberra, I discovered by chance that Geoff was teaching at the University of Adelaide. I contacted him and he had us all to stay for two or three nights. He was married with two daughters, but the family had never fallen in love with Australia as we had. Also, his political views had moved a considerable way to the right, partly perhaps as a result of spending a longish period in Communist Poland. I felt that I had been politically leapfrogged. Sometime after we moved to Oxford from Canberra in 1982, I found that he had also returned to the UK and was teaching at the University of Essex. He wrote several books of literary criticism, including one on Dickens. My informant (a woman I met by chance in the post office) told me that he was a brilliant teacher, but his department wouldn't let him loose on first year students. Being incredibly busy I failed to contact him for a couple of years, but when I did I was told he had died of a heart attack in 1983. This news was a shock that took me some time to get over.

At the end of our year in Cambridge, we moved to a camp near the village of Crail, on the Fife coast in Eastern Scotland, to which the Bodmin establishment had moved, holus bolus. It was there that we spent the summer of 1956. The main difference between language instruction in Cambridge and that in Crail was that at Crail we had to concentrate on military vocabulary and expressions. The main purpose of our training, after all, was to enable us to interrogate Soviet prisoners of war. So, we were drilled in Russian marching orders, military ranks, strategy and tactics, vocabulary relating to tank warfare, and such exotica as the parts of a bren gun.

Although I now forget where this took place (not Crail), there was an occasion where we were drilled in how to *fire* a bren gun. This is an automatic weapon that spits out a stream of lead for as long as you activate the trigger. As I held this object, standing in a row of men, some to my left and some to my right, I suddenly realised that all I had to do was turn round, and I could create a massacre. My reaction was one of sheer terror, but if one of our number had been in some way deranged, how would the army have prevented such a disaster? Official attitudes to security seemed far too casual. The next time I saw a bren gun I was with my parents at the East German border post overlooking Poland across the River Oder. Two or three young soldiers wielding bren guns were surveying the river dividing their Communist homeland from their Communist neighbour through binoculars. More of this in Chapter **7.**

But I have diverged from my main topic, which is the language teaching at Crail. Our main teacher was Mrs Levitskaya, a matronly lady who led us in intensive Russian conversation. Like most of the rest of the instructors, she had experienced a traumatic escape from the Soviet Union around the end of the war. Her attitudes were as anti-Soviet as those of any of them, and backed by the unanswerable argument, 'My husband was shot by the Bolsheviks.' On social issues she was an old- fashioned conservative, and in one of our conversation classes expressed her displeasure that the Queen in her birthday honours had awarded a knighthood to the cricketer Len Hutton, 'Hutton, rytsar (a knight)???!!!' In her mind such a prestigious award should not have been granted to a mere sportsman. She was not without a sense of humour, and once related to us how in Germany, having escaped from the Soviet Union, she had secured a precious interview with an American general, in an effort to normalise her status in the West. When she entered the office, she found the said general lolling back on his chair, in his shirt sleeves, feet on the desk, blowing smoke rings at his secretary. One Sunday morning at Crail our group was invited by Mrs Levitskaya to sample Russian cookery. As I wrote to my parents:

> ... she is so overwhelmingly hospitable that everyone has a job to get away. It is difficult to describe what we ate, because the words are only in Russian and there is no English equivalent. But I expect you have heard of 'kasha', a rich Russian porridge eaten with butter.

Later on in the course at Crail, we were taught by a Latvian, Mr Klavins. Some of my colleagues referred to him as 'Butcher Klavins', since he had fought in the German Army against the Soviets. But one story he told us suggests a good reason, even if not perhaps a total justification, for a Latvian to have fought alongside the Nazis. When the Soviet army invaded Latvia in 1940, a Soviet officer and some of his men visited the house of Mr Klavins' uncle. The officer addressed him in Russian as 'Ty, tolstii svinya' (you, fat pig), as they removed any valuable or usable items from the house. When Mr Klavins' nephew asked the officer not to take his suit, the officer shot him dead. Faced by a choice between the Nazi and Soviet regimes, it could not have been easy to choose, though it was the Soviets that were taking over his country and his family had personally faced Soviet brutality.

In civilian life before the war, Mr Klavins would, I suspect, like most of our other instructors, have been a fairly conventional right wing conservative. One morning he told us rather dramatically that a new dance form had arrived, that was 'unbelievably sexual'. He was referring to Bill Haley and the Comets, and the beginnings of Rock and Roll. He often talked about his own country, telling us how, in 1940, a President had come to power who put an end to the 'chaotic multi-party politics in our little Latvia', essentially by getting rid of political parties altogether. Mr Klavins was not dissatisfied with this presidential coup, as it 'created stability'. More humorously, he told us about a state visit to Latvia by King Zog of Albania, who issued medals stamped with his portrait to the mayor of practically every small town in the country: truly a splendid moment in the history of Albanian-Latvian relations! We may laugh at the Ruritanian character of King Zog's visit, but should not forget that small countries were soon to become easy victims of vicious power politics between great powers. Only a few years later, not only was independent Latvia absorbed into the Soviet Union against its will, but Albania became a colony of Mussolini's Italy, later a satellite of the USSR and later still of China.

Not all our time at Crail was spent learning Russian military terms. One of the instructors was a colourful character and talented theatre director called Dmitri Makaroff. This being Scotland, some of his mail was addressed to 'Dmitri McKaroff Esq'. His parents had fled Russia around the time of the Revolution, settled in Sydney where his father worked as a hairdresser, in the confident expectation that the Soviet Union was a brief episode in Russian history, so that in due course he would be able to return home and resume a prestigious profession for which he had been trained. Dmitri was born in Sydney and read classics at Sydney University, but didn't do much work and eventually drifted into a bohemian life among Russian emigres in the UK. He was gay, as we would say today, a word that in the 1950s had a quite different meaning. This, of course, was at a time when homosexual relationships were still illegal, though he did not appear to be seriously deterred by the legal situation in which he found himself. I described him in a letter to my parents as 'an Australian-born Russian with a store of culture (or kulcher), inseparable from a duffle coat, an out-at-elbows jacket and a pug-dog on a string'.

He was indeed a brilliant theatrical producer, and directed a cast consisting of kursanty and a few instructors in a production, in Russian, of 'The Government Inspector' (*Revizor*), a comedy by Gogol. The point of the story of course, is that the 'government inspector' who arrives amidst great fanfare in a small provincial town, turns out to be an imposter. The lead role was played by Patrick Procktor, who later became a well-known painter, and contributed several illustrations to the Elliott and Shukman book on the JSSL. As I told my parents, 'I will be playing the part of the director of charitable institutions – a nasty old man, as usual'. Dmitry had us all dancing a mazurka as a lead into the final denouement. We put on four successive productions. Some of the instructors helped the audience (mainly local people) as 'living subtitles'.

Dmitri wanted to take our performance to the Edinburgh Festival, but this was vetoed at a high level in the War Office. Dmitri was most upset, and thought that such a polished production should not be allowed to die a natural death. I lost touch with him after the end of national service, but I understand that he did become a director in Covent Garden, and later, most surprisingly, according to Willie Ledgard, an Orthodox priest in Belgrade. He deserves a biography.

In August 1956, my national service was approaching its end. Having had the status of officer cadet throughout the duration of the Russian course, we were required to take WOSB (War Office Selection Board) for promotion to full officer status. I retain hardly any memory of it, but to everybody's surprise including my own, I passed. This was followed by some two weeks of leave, during which I hitchhiked to Italy and back. I had little idea where in Italy I wanted to go, but I accepted a lift (perhaps from somewhere in France) with a French orchestral composer called Francis Miroglio, who took me to Siena, where he was attending a musical conference. Many years later I chanced to hear a piece by him on the radio. Siena was a wonderful introduction to Italy, and in those days it was less overwhelmed by tourists than it is today. While there I met a Canadian artist called Ivan Fainmail, who taught me useful lessons about painting. I commented on the trip in general in a letter to my parents:

> Lorry drivers gave me the most gruelling lessons in Italian and insisted that I write to them on returning home. Some of them knew a few words of English, French and even Russian learnt in POW camps during the war. One man knew two words of English only, both as familiar as they are unrepeatable! … I went round Florence with a Colombian, talked Russian with some Finns, while he talked to them in German and Swedish.

While in Crail I was once asked by a local Scotsman, 'Are you from that there interrupters' school?'

On my return I had a few more weeks at Crail and a final exam, but then we were subjected to a couple of weeks or so at Maresfield in Sussex, where we were set to work translating Soviet military manuals from 1940. It would greatly surprise me to learn that our translations ended up anywhere but the dustbin, but this was fairly typical of the 'make work' approach of the British Army in that period when they had to train huge numbers of conscripts. Rather than employ a group of men newly fluent in Russian on tasks that could use their skills to good effect, you sit them at desks and have them translate redundant documents just because you have to occupy them doing something. Only one memory remains from Maresfield: We were told we could take an afternoon off provided we engaged in a sporting activity of some kind. Bill Nicholas and I therefore went to the local golf club, hired clubs and paid for a round. I had never played golf before (despite my father's golfing talent), and found it difficult even to hit the ball, as distinct from throwing soil up into the air. Somehow, I suppose we finished the round. I doubt if I bothered to keep the score.

When I found that I would have to do national service before, rather than after, studying at Oxford I was horrified and took a long time in the summer of 1954 to adjust to the prospect. But in a letter to my parents in July 1956 I reflected as follows:

> It suddenly came to me to think the other day what a thankful thing it was to do N.S. before university. I am quite sure that, if I had acted as I well might have done [that is, accepted the Christ Church offer and done national service after university], I should not have been mature enough to benefit from univ. until 5th or 6th term. Incredible on what thin threads these decisions hang.

Reading between the lines of this statement, I suspect that I was reflecting on national service as I had experienced it as an intellectual adventure, in a process where I was – at times desperately – trying to make myself literate in a number of fields where those I was with plainly possessed superior knowledge, combined with superior confidence. In several senses, I was a different person at the end of the two years than I had been at the beginning. Oxford, however, was going to present a new set of challenges that would be as hard to meet as those during national service. If my diary entries and other writing in national service give ample evidence of immaturity, linked with lack of confidence, that combination would continue into my first year at Exeter College. It was not until second year that things really began to fall into place.

Let me, therefore, say something about the transition from national service to university.

I enrolled in Exeter College, University of Oxford, in October of 1956. I was most disappointed that of those learning Russian on 'L' course only John Field, reading History and I, reading PPE, were now in Oxford. A much larger number, including Geoff Thurley, had gone to Cambridge. One person I did encounter, however, was Keith Harding, whom I had known at Bodmin and whose religious commitment was extreme. He was now at Exeter College, reading Law. But he did not survive his course beyond the first year, most probably because he spent most of his time and effort seeking to convert people to his brand of Christianity.

In striking contrast to Keith was a French graduate student, Jacques Millet, who was writing a thesis on diplomatic relations between France, Britain and Germany in the years immediately after the Second World War. He entertained all who would listen with lurid tales of his sexual exploits in various parts of the world, '...et la troisième fois, je presque n'arrivait pas'. According to his account, all he had to do while on a bus in Sweden was to open a copy of *Le Monde* and he would shortly experience a female foot stroking his leg. On one occasion Keith was telling everyone about a talk to be given in Oxford by a Russian Christian. The reaction of Jacques was, 'Est ce que c'est un rouge, ou un blanc? Si c'est un blanc il n'y a AUCUN interêt.' When I relayed this response to Keith, he replied, 'But you must understand, Arthur, this is a REALLY interesting young man.'

Five or six years later, while I was preparing a report for the ABC (Australian Broadcasting Commission) on some conference in Tokyo, I noticed the name 'Jacques Millet' on a list of participants, as a representative of UNESCO. But either because I was short of time, or because I remembered his boastful and dismissive attitudes, I failed to contact him.

In those days PPE students had to take courses in the two Ps and the E, though some specialising was possible in the second and third years of the course. For one of the first year philosophy 'papers' (to use the Oxford jargon), I chose symbolic logic, which was a completely new venture for me, and potentially dangerous because I had never been any good at maths. Symbolic logic, with its 'truth tables', propositions and formulae, bore a strong resemblance to algebra. But I had a sympathetic philosophy tutor, William Kneale, and I managed to pass.

For economics, I was farmed out to another college, St John's, where my tutor was George Richardson, who much later directed

Oxford University Press. Since my tutorials with him were early on Monday mornings, I would see him in his carpet slippers, and on occasion he would ring his wine merchant while I was reading out my weekly essay. Nevertheless, he taught me the basics of economics, which I had not studied before.

But it soon became clear to me that my favourite area of study was the second 'P' – Politics. This was partly because of prior interest, but also because I had a first rate tutor, Norman Hunt. Norman was a Yorkshireman, who amused us with his ways of pronouncing some common words. For instance, he said 'gross' to rhyme with 'cross' (and why not? – they are spelled exactly the same except for the initial letter). My tutorials, according to the Oxford system, were normally two to one, so that each of us would read a short essay to the tutor. Norman always came meticulously prepared with copious information to impart about the subject of our essays, and sent us away with much to think about. His politics were left of centre (though far from extreme), and thus attracted some criticism from my colleagues, who were a fairly conformist bunch. But one week we had to write an essay on 'the role of the monarchy in British politics', and arrived at Norman's tutorial expecting a diatribe – or at least strong criticism – directed against the institution of monarchy. Not a bit of it: he spoke at length about the importance of the monarchy in humanising politics. I owe a great deal to the training in political science given me by Norman Hunt, teaching me that politics could and should be studied in a spirit of objectivity but also of conviction. During national service I had come under the exciting influence of people on the left of the political spectrum (especially Geoff Thurley, but also George Craig and others), so that the broad message I received from Norman Hunt was that I should not abandon my convictions, but rather reinforce them both with meticulous collection of information and objectivity in analysing such information.

In 1973, Norman was elevated to the House of Lords by Prime Minister Harold Wilson with the title 'Lord Crowther-Hunt'. He was a member of the Fulton Commission on the home civil service and the Kilbrandon Commission on devolution, and did other tasks for the Wilson Labour Government. In 1982, he became Rector of Exeter College, but sadly died prematurely while he was still in post, in 1987.

One of the papers we had to take for Prelims at the end of the second term was French. This was taught by an elderly man called Mr Struth, who took us through de Tocqueville's *Democracy in America* in the original French. He reminded me of my antique French teacher from school, Mr Street. While I was at home for the Christmas vacation I learned that he had died. His *Times* obituary contained the statement, 'he spoke fluent French'. I read this in disbelief: surely it went without saying that a French tutor in Oxford would speak fluent French? He was replaced by Mr Raitt, a man from a different century.

When I arrived at Exeter College I had more or less completely abandoned any religious commitment, and did not attend church services, even services in the college chapel. But in my first year I shared a study with a man from the Wirral called John Pinnington. John was a student of history, worked extremely hard, was deeply involved in religious issues and was in the process of converting from the Church of England to Roman Catholicism. Some of his friends from his school on the Wirral visited him regularly and when they did I was treated to a great deal of religious argument at a time when this was not something that I particularly wanted to be involved in. John did not much involve himself in college activities, and since we shared a study, to my embarrassment, I tended to become linked with him in the minds of the more sporty and extroverted members of the college. This I found difficult and was relieved when second year began and I had my own room in College.

After we graduated we more or less lost contact, though he came to our wedding a few months later. I occasionally saw articles about him in the press, since he was campaigning within the Catholic Church against the Vatican's ban on artificial methods of contraception. I also knew that sometime in the 1960s he married a woman who had earlier contemplated becoming a nun, that they had had a son together, and John was teaching at a New Zealand university. Sometime in the 1970s, when we were living in Canberra, I was told by a New Zealander, Adrian Chan, that John had undergone a sex change operation and was living as a woman, using the name Judith. In those unenlightened days this effectively meant that she could no longer find employment, even in school teaching. It can hardly have helped that she was over six foot tall, so that living as a woman must have been challenging. She wrote to me asking if I could find her a teaching position in Japan. I tried but was unsuccessful. Fairly recently, I discovered that she was working as a city councillor in Cambridge, but sadly died in 2006. Some lives are indeed complicated.

Not long after I arrived in Oxford I applied to join the Voltaire Society, an intellectual society that Geoff Thurley had recommended. I went to an interview, where I tried to put up a front as an intellectual. Soon afterwards I received a polite letter of rejection (or was I told at the end of the interview?), after which I decided it was ridiculous to keep on pretending to be an intellectual, realising that my efforts over recent years had been characterised by far more pretension than substance. I decided to concentrate on the things that really interested me, and try to get a good degree.

One thing that I did do was to join the University Labour Club. As a spin-off from that I joined the Labour Party – the only time in my life when I have been a member of a political party. I don't remember whether I ever told my parents about that. My membership no doubt lapsed when I left Oxford. I went fairly regularly to the club's meetings on a Sunday morning, and became aware of the differences between the people who edited *Universities and Left Review* (later *New Left Review*) and those further to the right. I also met certain luminaries of the movement including Clement Attlee, already an old man, Douglas Jay on the moderate wing of the party, a far left winger called Konni Zilliacus, whom I found unconvincing, and also the broadly sympathetic chronicler of Soviet history Isaac Deutscher, also very old at that point. For a while I distributed flyers around the colleges about the Club's activities and also liaised with the student newspapers, but frankly, my involvement with Labour politics at Oxford was essentially passive.

Only a short while after my arrival in Oxford the simultaneous crises of Suez and Hungary took place, signalling a key stage towards the ending of British colonialism and a pause (at the very least) in the liberalising of Soviet and Eastern European Communism. In a letter to my parents postmarked 22nd August 1956, when I was still at Crail, I wrote, 'I hope the gov't's not silly enough to commence hostilities over Suez. I also don't think there's much chance of it.'

I give myself zero out of ten for that one (the second sentence at least). I also added that 'in Arab and most Asian eyes Nasser is seen as embodying quite legitimate claims of anti-imperialist Nationalism', that 'within limits he should be given free rein – in spite of the oil at stake', and more in the same vein. I suspect that I was trying to wind up my parents, who were basically conservative, much as I loved them.

Shortly after the Suez crisis began I attended an acrimonious meeting at which two officials of the Soviet Embassy in London had been invited to speak. They gave standard Soviet policy statements on the international situation. But as soon as they finished speaking (perhaps even before), the audience erupted into verbal fisticuffs between Israelis and Arabs, in the course of which the Soviet officials were virtually forgotten. They appeared completely bemused and disoriented by what was going on, and as they were leaving I said a few words to them in Russian to cheer them up. This was an extremely dramatic meeting which anybody present must have remembered for a long time to come.

So far as the Soviet invasion of Hungary was concerned, the media gave sustained attention to a couple of British students who had driven a car into Hungary during the chaos following the Soviet invasion. They were arrested and later released. One of them was Judy Cripps, daughter of Sir Stafford Cripps, Chancellor of the Exchequer in the Attlee Government after the war. She was subsequently a stalwart of the Labour Club, and when I was swotting hard for finals, she tried to persuade me, without success, to devote more time to the Labour Club. The whole Labour Club experience teaches me that fundamentally, I am not a joiner.

7

More Distant Fields

𐤀

IN THE SUMMER vacation of 1957, I took a position as courier
with a Birmingham travel company, the Midland Air Tour Opera-
tors (MATO), which ran tours to northern Italy. My task was to
look after successive groups of tourists from the Midlands, which
changed every fortnight. Each group stayed, as I did, at the Hotel
Ristorante Le Palme (the palm trees), in the village of Laigueglia,
about an hour's walk along the coast to the west of Alassio, in Ligu-
ria, northern Italy. The position was challenging in more senses
than one. First of all, the company brochure assured its clients that
the charter flights would land at Albenga, an Italian town about
three quarter of an hour's drive from Laigueglia. The reserve airport
would be Nice, across the border in France. In fact, however, the
company had not managed to secure the right to land at Albenga,
and all flights landed at Nice as well as taking off from Nice on the
way home. The journey from Nice to Laigueglia took three to four
hours, and in those pre-EU days there was officious bureaucracy
to deal with at the Franco-Italian border. Naturally, I became the
target of complaints to the effect that the company in its publicity
was misleading its clients.

The second problem was that the company representative had
chosen the Hotel Le Palme in mid-winter, at a time when there was
relatively little traffic along the main road along the coast that ran
past the hotel (this was before the invention of the autostrada). In
full summer, however, the main road was choked with traffic well
into the night, and in addition a garage directly opposite the hotel
was testing motor bikes until past midnight. Those whose bedrooms
faced the main road needed earplugs. Those whose bedrooms faced
the courtyard, on the other hand, were spared noise from the road

and garage, but since dancing went on in the courtyard up to one in the morning, needed to find dance music conducive to sleep. Therefore, the next morning after each party arrived, I was faced by disgruntled clients requesting a move, either from the roadside to the courtyard side, or vice versa. I handled these requests as best I could, stressing in each case the advantages of the side they were already on.

My third problem was that the hotel patron, Signor Chiavacci, did not get on with his wife, and they apparently divided up the hotel takings between them into separate accounts. This led to an internally competitive environment in which I faced occasional attempts to squeeze the number of rooms the company had been allocated. The problem was compounded by inefficiency in the Birmingham office, which sent me client lists that were not always accurate. When one particular group arrived, I found that I was one room short. To solve the problem I identified a young man of about twenty who I thought would not be too upset at being allocated a rather small room over the kitchens, which was vacant but not part of our allocation. Unfortunately, I had not reckoned with the fact that he was travelling with his mother, the stern headmistress of a Catholic school in Birmingham, who was not in the least pleased with the room I had earmarked for her son. She threatened dire consequences for my company if the situation wasn't resolved, not realising, perhaps, that I was a mere student doing a vacation job, with no equity in the firm whatsoever. I responded with, 'I am just trying to help you, Mrs H(arris).' This calmed her a little, but the only way I found to solve the dilemma was to give up my own room to her son and move into the sub-standard room myself for the duration of that group's stay.

I had studied a little Italian on my own before going to Italy, but once in Laigueglia I had to immerse myself in the language simply for survival. These were the early years of mass tourism, and a few of my flock roasted themselves on the beach so that I had to take them to the doctor in the village for treatment of sunburn. One elderly man appeared on the beach in a suit. I made friends with Giovanni, who hired out paddle boats, and he in turn introduced me to a watch salesman, who gave me a modest 'commissione' on any watches he sold to members of my flock. One of my group members showed him a sophisticated watch he owned and valued at

£80, a huge sum in those days. The watch salesman examined it and talked at length about 'questo orologio fantastico'. With Giovanni I learned much colloquial Italian, some of it unprintable. I remember him describing in graphic detail a night of passion, ending up, 'si alza la mattina...' (you get up in the morning ...), with the three dots connoting 'and you feel absolutely wonderful'. One day I made an embarrassing error in my Italian. Giovanni, and a young lady I didn't know, were with me on the beach. What I meant to say was 'Vediamo stasera' (Let's see about it this evening – I no longer recall what we would be seeing about). By inadvertence, however, I said 'Ci vediamo stasera', which can be rendered as 'let's get together this evening'. Giovanni howled with laughter at my expense and a spot of pink appeared on the young lady's cheek.

I took my people on excursions, to the city of Genova along the coast to the east, and to a place in the mountains with wonderful fields of lavender. I wondered why some of them bothered to travel to Italy at all. One man told me that, on principle, he would never buy any item not manufactured in the UK. Another, when we were all together in a large café, talked in a loud voice about 'those foreigners over there' (meaning Italians). Throughout July and August, most of the tourists around Laigueglia were Italian, some of them staying in atrocious accommodation, but on 1 September, the hotels put their prices down and Italian tourists were to a great extent replaced by Germans. Some of my Italian friends categorised German tourists as skinflints. This was only twelve years after the end of the war, some members of my flock had fought in the war, and showed signs of wishing to re-fight the Second World War against the Germans they suddenly found in their midst. The Germans naturally responded in kind.

There were lesser problems I had to sort out. One of my people was a seriously overweight woman who managed to break her bed, which meant negotiation with Signor Chiavacci (or 'Mister Chaya vacky', as some of my flock called him). The head of the company I was working for decided to stay at the hotel for a few days with his wife, and I was required to hire a car to pick them up at Nice airport. Later I was told that they found the car too small, but I think that it was the largest available and it seemed fine to me. The owner of a hotel in Leamington Spa and his wife were on one of my two-week parties, they complained about the food, but hired one of the waiters at Le Palme to work in his hotel in Leamington. Unfortunately, however, the hotelkeeper from Leamington had not done the paperwork properly, and when the waiter and his wife (Giuseppino and Giuseppina) arrived at the airport, they were put in the cells until their new employer appeared to bail them out. Since Pino and Pina, as they called themselves, were friends of mine, I was terribly embarrassed at such stupid and unfeeling bureaucracy in my own country. I met them again later in the Midlands, where they still addressed me as 'Signor Arturo'.

In my spare time I went around with a group of young people, the males mostly English, the females nearly all Italian. I enjoyed the company of a young lady called Romana, who came from Forno Canavese in the Italian Alps. But she was twenty-five when I was twenty-one, and that seemed to me an impossible gap in age.

By the end of my stay in Laigueglia I had earned enough money to travel by train to Sicily. Both southern Italy and Sicily showed signs of terrible poverty. I saw many women doing the family wash by hand in local rivers, and some of the housing was dilapidated in the extreme. I saw the local headquarters of the Italian Communist Party. But the Italian government had established the Cassa del Mezzogiorno (Fund for the South), and probably with money from the Fund, had set up a chain of modern youth hostels throughout Sicily, so that it was in those that I stayed. I visited the ghoulish catacombs in Siracusa, and in Catania took a bus to the youth hostel which was on the edge of the town. I was the only person on the bus except for the driver and the conductress, so I got into conversation with them. When we reached the hostel, the driver invited me to visit his family home the next day, which was his day off. I agreed, met his lovely family, including wife and several children, then he took me half way up mount Etna, to the end of the road, on the back of his motor bike. I was experiencing the typical hospitality of people in poor regions of the world.

That was my summer in Italy, a country that made sense for me, despite its manifest problems, including the visible gap in so many ways between the relatively prosperous north and the poverty-stricken south. When, in Laigueglia, I told my friends that I was going to see Sicily, I was met with, 'da Roma in giu, non c'e niente' (Beyond Rome, there is nothing). When I quoted this to people

I met in Sicily, they told me that most institutions in the north were run by southerners. In Italy's most recent elections in 2018, the country was clearly divided between La Lega, a conservative regional party in the north, and the five-star movement, also radical, though whether left or right is obscure, based almost entirely in the south and in Sardinia. Surprisingly, the two parties are now in office together as an anti-immigrant coalition. The old parties are close to extinction as Italy reshapes its politics, and Europe is forced to adapt to narrow nationalist movements as well.

My second year in Oxford was much more satisfactory than the first. I had passed Prelims and it would be two academic years before I had to take 'Schools' (Finals). I had found a congenial friend in the person of Pedro-Pablo Kuczynski, who had Peruvian nationality, a family in Switzerland and was trilingual in Spanish, French and English. His doctor father left Germany in the early 1930s – before Hitler came to power – to found a clinic for tropical diseases in Lima, Peru. Pete, as we called him, as well as his brother who became a Cambridge economist, were born in Peru, their mother being French. For secondary education they were sent to a spartan school called Rossall in Lancashire, experiencing rain for the first time on board ship between Lima and the UK. Pete was lively and outspoken, so that I found him a breath of fresh air in the broadly dull and conformist atmosphere of the College students. We went to politics tutorials with Norman Hunt, whom we both respected.

After graduation, Pete did a doctorate in economics at a US university, went on to have a career as an investment banker, at various times held cabinet portfolios in Peruvian governments, as well as having business interests in West Africa, and between 2016 and 2018, already in his late 70s, was President of Peru.

In addition, my Italian connections were replenished after meeting some interesting students attending one of the language schools that flourish in Oxford. Their names were Itala, Severina and Maila, who all came from the lovely town of Udine near the Yugoslav border. Itala was my favourite. We went on trips together, including visiting the house of the late orchestral conductor Sir Thomas Beecham in Stratford-on-Avon on one occasion. Many years later, when the invention of the Internet made it possible easily to discover people's career histories, I found that she had pursued a distinguished career as an academic specialising in post-colonial literature, and was married to an architect with interests in East Africa, who designed buildings in Dar-Es-Salaam. I managed to contact her, and send her a card marked 'Una voce dal passato' (a voice from the past). We met in Oxford, and I discovered that her politics had moved decisively to the left (even far left), which I found refreshing after meeting so many youthful radicals who in middle age had joined the Establishment in comfortable middle class complacency.

The most important reason, however, for my second year at Oxford being particularly happy was a created by a purely chance encounter. Most weeks, for my essays I studied in the PPE library, housed in what was then called the New Bodleian. But for one week, early in the year, I had to write an essay on a historical topic that required work in the Radcliffe Camera, repository of much of the Bodleian Library's historical collection. While trying desperately to think how to compose my weekly essay, I was approached by John Field, my former colleague from the JSSL Russian course. He told me that he was organising a skiing party to the French Alps, and asked me if I would like to join. Having never skied before, I readily agreed, and not long afterwards, at the end of February or beginning of March, I was on the night milk train from Birmingham New Street to London Euston (or possibly Birmingham Snow Hill to London Paddington), which was unheated and uncomfortable and took about five hours to reach the capital (but we were brought up tough in those days).

On arrival, I drank a cup of hot coffee at whichever station it was, and took a tube across the city to Victoria. There I met our party, headed by John Field, and also another party, separately organised, from London, which would travel to the same Alpine resort as ourselves, Alpe d'Huez. From the second party I was greeted by an Australian dentist called Brian Turner, practising in Norfolk, who when I told him my name said, 'G'day Arthur, come and meet Audrey, who is on our party.' I shook hands with a young lady of that name. For the first time in my life I set eyes on the person who was to be my wife for fifty-eight years. Audrey and I travelled together on the train to the channel port (probably Dover). We quickly discovered a common interest in modern art movements and exchanged views on obscure painters such as Schmidt-Rottluff. Audrey told me that she was working in the William Morris gallery in Walthamstow, north-east London. On the ferry, like Prince Charles as a teenager on a celebrated voyage to a Scottish island, we drank cherry brandy and continued an animated conversation on the train to Paris. In Paris we had two or three hours to kill before catching the train to the Alps, so we did some sightseeing and Audrey, as I never let her forget, climbed a lamppost in the middle of Paris. We caught a train to the south from the Gare de Lyon, travelled as far as Grenoble, where we were transported by bus to the Alps and then up a long series of hairpin bends to Alpe d'Huez, where we found our respective accommodation and began to learn to ski. Our instructor, a Frenchman with no English called M. Dubois, or M. Dupont, or M. Dutoit, endlessly repeated the following mantra:

Le ski amont en avant, et le poids du corps sur le ski aval.
(The upper ski ahead, and the weight of the body on the lower ski.)

Slowly, we made progress under his supervision, and became passable, though very far from brilliant, skiers. I will say no more about how our relationship developed, except that back in the UK, Audrey continued working at the William Morris Gallery, and I was moving into the busy and challenging final year of my undergraduate course. I had also bought, for about £25.00 in Birmingham, a 1933 blue Austin seven – a vehicle whose engine was so simple that even I could clean out the carburettor when rust entered it from the petrol tank I had bought second-hand from a scrap yard because the existing one was leaking. I even drove it to London and back (top safe speed 30 mph) on at least one occasion. We christened it 'Blue Murder'.

I graduated at the end of my third year, with a good second, but not the first class degree I had thought was at least a possibility. As I waited to be admitted to one of the exams I saw a girl I knew slightly who appeared to be anxious and upset, and I said a few words to cheer her up. When the results were announced, she had come out with a first and I hadn't.

Very shortly after the end of term, Pete Kuczynski and I enrolled as assistants in an international summer school run by the University adult education department. We had to help out with administrative tasks but could also attend lectures. Wanting to do something different from what I had done for my degree, I opted to attend lectures in English literature, including some on James Joyce's Finnegan's Wake, surely the most difficult novel ever written. I met my first Japanese person, a schoolteacher called Mr Watanabe. I did not get to know him well, but he had one or two Japanese magazines with him, and I was intrigued to see that they started 'from the back'.

In 1958, the Soviet Union had somewhat relaxed its policy towards tourism, and it became possible to drive as far as Moscow, picking up an Intourist guide at the frontier. My parents and I decided to take advantage of this, and we booked a tour, with hotel accommodation fixed up in advance, across Europe to Moscow and back. Several of my parents' friends were incredulous that such a journey should be possible, and also that we had actually decided to venture into the 'forbidden territories' of the Soviet Union. We travelled through West Germany, across East Germany into the western sector of Berlin, back into East Germany on the way to Poland. At the East German border post with Poland, we were held up for two or three hours as officials examined the contents of our car, while we watched young soldiers wielding bren guns surveying the river Oder that divides the two countries, through binoculars. On the other side of the river, we found the Polish border post housed in tents, as apparently the East German authorities had moved their border post several miles upstream, and the Poles had to follow suit. With the Polish officials we could converse in French, and the atmosphere in the Polish tents could not have been more relaxed by comparison with the East German border post. When we told them that we going to Moscow, one of the Polish officials laughed and said, 'Make sure they don't send you beyond Moscow!'

At the Soviet border we picked up our guide, Boris Zharkov, a law student studying labour law doing a vacation job working for Intourist. Our discussions (and indeed arguments) with Boris were among the most interesting aspects of the trip. A convinced Marxist, he took umbrage at an RAC brochure we had with us about travel in the USSR, insisting that its (rather mild) criticisms had been written by the British Government. We spent many hours talking with him, grew to like him and as we parted back at the border after returning from Moscow, his farewell greeting was, 'You don't need to take notice of what I say.' He also arranged sightseeing for us in Moscow, and at my parents' request took us to visit medical clinics. To my surprise, my parents were quite impressed by the progress being made in the medical field as they saw it, and more generally, by the rehabilitation of the country since 1945. My father later wrote an (unpublished) short article about our experiences, in which he painted the picture of a society on the move and in some ways admirable – not what one might have expected from an average British conservative. Since I could converse in Russian, Boris left us to our own devices for part of our time in Moscow. One of our problems was that we were unfamiliar with the road rules, and attracted the attention of the police on one occasion. We were able to talk with some individuals in a friendly manner, but attempts to contact them later failed. There was, for instance, no publicly available telephone directory in Moscow, and even armed with a telephone number, as happened on one occasion, I found that the person at the end of the phone kept repeating, 'I don't understand.'

One abiding memory of our journey across Europe to Moscow and back was bomb damage, more or less wherever we went, including bombed out skeletons of buildings still standing in the centre of Warsaw. Some youngish Americans we met in Moscow seemed to have little or no comprehension of what this might mean. I later wondered how unbombed America could really understand what Europe had gone through in a conflict that killed between twenty-five and thirty million individuals – civilian and military – in just the Soviet Union during the Second World War. More than half the population of Leningrad perished in the eighteen-month-long siege of that city.

Let me return to the summer school in Oxford after my university course was finished. I enjoyed the company of a young lady from Strasbourg called Evèlyne, another from Sweden who taught me the days of the week in Swedish, and most particularly a girl from Finland called Silja (Celia). Silja was being pursued by a much older man, an American who worked for the *Reader's Digest*, who, she told me, 'makes me sick'. I suppose it was this situation that threw us together to some extent, as I tried to protect her. There was mutual attraction between us, but we both readily agreed that 'this is not serious'. She in any case had a boyfriend who was a medical student in Finland and told me she wanted to spend her life in Finland. Later, I told Audrey about this temporary relationship, as a result of which we needed to renew our feelings for each other, but this we achieved without too much difficulty in the second half of a journey that I will now describe.

On 15 August 1959, I set out to hitchhike to Yugoslavia. I went through eastern France, into Germany, crossed Austria and entered Yugoslavia at Jesenice, now part of Slovenia. I hitched rides to Ljubljana and then to Zagreb, whence I found a lorry driver willing to take me overnight to Sarajevo in part-Muslim Bosnia. As it became light with the dawn, and we drove through local villages, I seemed to have entered a different world, in which women wore long black dresses, and mosques were frequent. At Sarajevo, I visited the market and bought items in copper. Everything seemed relaxed and peaceful, so unlike the terrible history of the town during the Yugoslav civil war over twenty years later, which split the whole country apart. And then to Dubrovnik, again in an overnight lorry ride over atrocious roads through the mountains, and where on arrival I slept for much of the day on the beach. I found somewhere to stay and attended a music festival.

A few days later, I took a boat up the Dalmatian coast, calling at various islands and also at the town of Split, before disembarking at Rijeka (River) in the north (when it was part of Italy before the war, it was called Fiume, also meaning 'River'). From there I hitchhiked to Udine where I stayed with Maila, from the Oxford language school, and their extraordinarily hospitable family. Maila's father, with her brother, ran a firm making prefabricated window frames. The family was very obviously very well off, and one phrase spoken by Maila's father has stuck in my memory, 'Il Volkswagen, e per I poveretti' (The Volkswagen is for little poor people). Maila and her sister Milla, who was studying architecture, were knowledgeable guides to local sights, including the historic and beautiful towns of Udine and Cividale (My mother later found it hard to believe that Maila and Milla were different names, so let me be precise: Maila is pronounced 'My la', whereas Milla is pronounced 'Mill la').

In the second part of the journey, I met Audrey by prearrangement in the Cathedral square of Milan, whence we travelled by train to Sicily, stopping at Naples and Pompeii on the way. In Sicily, which I had visited two or three years before, I hired a Vespa, of dubious reliability, from a garage in Catania, though it took most of one day to find it. On this machine we visited Piazza Armerina, where only very recently Roman mosaics had been uncovered, showing young women wearing bikinis. We also saw the nearly intact Greek temple at Agrigento. From there we returned to Catania, handed in the Vespa, and went by train to Palermo, where we fell in love with the Palazzo di Monreale, with its exquisitely decorated columns. By the time we were back in England, we had sorted out our problems and had a solid basis for a permanent relationship.

We were married at St Mary's Church, Guildford, Surrey, on 30 January 1960. At the time of our marriage we were both twenty-four, and both virgins, technically at least. After a honeymoon on the wilds of Exmoor, Devon, in the middle of winter, we set out for a new life in a new country, away from family, away from friends, knowing little about what lay ahead of us.

During my last term in Oxford, while preparing for Schools, I had gone out one morning and bought a copy of the *Manchester Guardian*. In it, I noticed an advertisement from the Australian National University (ANU) in Canberra, calling for applicants for doctoral level scholarships. I was applying for a number of different jobs at the time, but the prospects of being awarded a scholarship for a postgraduate course at a British university did not seem promising. My application to the ANU was not undertaken lightly, indeed I took what I considered my best essay in British constitutional history, carefully revised and retyped it, and sent it off with a carefully worded application. I heard nothing for three months, until one morning, back at home, I received a postcard from the ANU administration, sent by sea mail, on which was written simply, 'Thank you for your application, which has been received'. I had by now assumed that my application had gone into the waste paper basket, so the postcard was at least a flicker of light. But within twenty-four hours, my politics tutor Norman Hunt phoned me to tell me that the ANU had informed him they were offering me a scholarship.

Suddenly, Audrey and I had to make a momentous decision, firstly, with our relationship still fairly young, whether we really wanted to embark on a new life together in a country on the other side of the globe. Secondly, we had to think of our parents and how they would react. We soon decided that we would 'go for it', and our parents after some discussion, did not raise any objection. There was, however, a third issue. In my job hunt, which had brought a file of rejections, I had received one offer of a position, which I had accepted, from the Westinform Service, whose offices were based in Piccadilly. This company, owned by a wealthy businessman called Mr Weston, published a weekly bulletin predicting freight rates and other information for the shipping industry. I phoned the company manager to tell him of my offer from the ANU, whereupon he urged me to come and work for the company for at least a few weeks, as they were now short staffed and would need some time to find a replacement for me.

And so, though my mother was none too happy about it, I went to London, found some grotty digs in Highgate, with an elderly, chain-smoking French landlady, near where Audrey was living, and started work with the Westinform Service. The work of the firm had an identical rhythm every week. Since the bulletin had to be published and sent off to clients every Friday, the week would begin in a relatively relaxed way, and then tensions would steadily increase until the Friday deadline. There were, I think, eight of us, seated round a large wooden rectangular table. Facing each other at the end of the table, just under the window, were the manager and his wife. Both were mild-mannered people, but as the tension within the office rose with the Friday deadline approaching, tension would rise to unsustainable levels between the couple at the end of the table, and they would start arguing with, and later shouting at, each other. A chain-smoking woman who was the office secretary clearly thought we were all incompetent, and would occasionally interject some helpfully barbed remark. I took the lesson from this that it was perhaps not a good idea to work with your loved one in the same office.

In early February 1960, we bade farewell to our parents at Tilbury docks and embarked on the SS *Orcades* bound for Australia. We stopped at Gibraltar, Naples (where this time we visited Herculaneum), Port Said (where the local men on the docks spoke English with Glasgow accents), Aden (very poor), Colombo (where we had a day to visit Kandy in the interior of what was still Ceylon, passing through many tea plantations, and encountering elephants and snakes), then across the Indian Ocean to Fremantle (where we had time to visit Perth and were taken in hand by a local lady who seemed to know everybody who was anybody, including the State Governor), and finally disembarked in Melbourne, where we stayed for several days with my cousin Alison and family. I met for the first time my uncle by marriage, a highland Scot who had emigrated to Australia around 1930 to set up a modern TB service in the State of Victoria.

We arrived in Canberra by train early in March and took up residence in University House, the main residential centre of the ANU at that time. At that point it was about ten years old, and had been modelled on an Oxbridge college, though adapted to a warm climate, with curved lines and light colours. The university itself had been founded in the post-war years, with the principal purpose of stemming the Australian brain drain to Europe and North America, and by founding an institution of national, and if possible international, research and teaching excellence, to attract back to Australia internationally known Australian scholars who had discovered pastures new in the northern hemisphere. Among those who were recruited at an early stage by the ANU was the nuclear physicist Sir Marcus Oliphant, who had been at Birmingham University, and before that was part of the team developing the atom bomb. Curiously, I had been at school with his son Michael. Another recruit was the Australian historian Sir Keith Hancock.

At the time the ANU was founded, Canberra already housed an institution called the Canberra University College, founded in the 1930s to teach courses as part of degrees at the University of Melbourne, for public servants transferred to Canberra from Melbourne after Australia's brand new capital was founded in 1913. Several months later the Canberra University College was amalgamated with the ANU, and became its 'School of General Studies', and later still 'the Faculties'.

I became a doctoral student in the Department of International Relations., whose acting head when I arrived was Arthur Lee Burns, an Australian who was working with American specialists on the implications of the nuclear arms race for the stability of the international system.

In my application to the ANU I had stated that, having studied Russian, I would attempt to write a PhD thesis on Soviet relations with Asia, or some aspect thereof. To some extent this was an exercise in grantsmanship on my part, as I had little idea what such a topic might involve. After I arrived in Canberra, it did not take me long to discover that there was nobody at the University with the relevant expertise to supervise a doctoral thesis on Soviet foreign policy, and also there was a serious problem of sources. Arthur Burns, who became my interim supervisor, was very helpful, suggested various topics on which I could focus, but had no specialist knowledge on relations between the USSR and anywhere in Asia. He referred me to a professor of political science, who talked to me rather briefly in generalities, but left me exactly where I had been when I first saw him.

In the course of 'pre-researching' my original topic, I had become aware of Japan. My encounter with Japan will be the subject of my next chapter, but I need to mention at this point that during our first weeks and months in Canberra I was also coming to terms with the university itself and its organisation.

It became evident that in certain respects when I arrived at the ANU, it was a young institution going through teething troubles, and was not entirely well organised. Before I left Oxford I had consulted the Warden of Exeter College, Sir Kenneth Wheare, himself an Australian, about whether I should apply for the scholarship and what he could tell me about the University. He encouraged me to apply, but warned me that the Department of International Relations had been going through a period of difficulties. He also told me that certain individuals in prominent university positions were difficult and I should be careful in any dealings with them. It turned out that the period of difficulties Wheare was referring to related to one Michael Lindsay, a China specialist who had been with Mao Zedong in the caves of Yenan during the war, but after Mao's Communists came to power became disillusioned and openly hostile to them. Sometime in the late 1950s he was convinced that he had been in line for the position of Head of International Relations at the ANU, but had been stabbed in the back by people with their own political agenda. He therefore wrote to Martin Wight, a highly distinguished international relations scholar, persuading him not to apply for the position (or perhaps, to withdraw his application). Martin Wight was part of the celebrated 'English school' of international relations, which also included Hedley Bull, whom I was to know well in Canberra and later in Oxford. Lindsay wrote a book length manuscript which he distributed around the university, denouncing what he saw as the perfidy of certain individuals, or maybe the university more broadly. The Vice-Chancellor shrewdly issued an order to all staff that they were not to respond in any way to this manuscript, thus depriving Lindsay of the publicity that he craved.

In retrospect, one of the problems I had at the beginning was that I had very few fellow postgraduate students in the Department of International Relations with whom to interact or from whom to ask for advice. In fact, I can only remember two: Donald Hindley, who was later to become a good friend, but who when I arrived was in Indonesia conducting field work; and Peter King, working on Cold War arms strategies, who was later to clash rather spectacularly with the new Head of Department, Bruce Miller, after he was appointed a couple of years later. Peter was erudite, but not the most tactful of people. I did of course have friends in other departments, particularly History, whom I could consult.

Arthur Burns asked me to run a public affairs (later international affairs) discussion group. I therefore organised regular seminars to which I invited specialists on various topics and parts of the world. This was a period of raised tension in US-Soviet relations, including the incident when an American U2 spy plane was shot down over Soviet territory, and its pilot, Gary Powers, incarcerated.

When I sought a speaker on Soviet foreign policy, not having found any at the ANU, somebody told me, 'Oh yes, there is a man at the CUC (Canberra University College) who knows about Russia.' This turned out to be Harry Rigby, who was becoming one of the leading world experts on Soviet politics. This must have been before the amalgamation of the two institutions, but it is extraordinary that when I was looking for a supervisor on a Soviet foreign policy topic, nobody thought to mention Harry Rigby. In those days we had none of the electronic aids that today make it so easy to track people down. When I telephoned Harry, who worked in the huts that housed the CUC, his first words to me were, 'Why haven't I met you before?' Why indeed? I went to see him, we found much to talk about, but by that time I was hooked on Japan, so I never became his student. But I did learn from the efficient organisation of his file card index of Soviet politicians, and our families were to become firm friends over many years.

My involvement with the ANU was to last for more than twenty-one years, I became and still remain a great enthusiast for its ethos and achievements, and regard it now as one of the great universities of the world. But at the time I first encountered it, it seemed to be facing serious problems. In particular, it seemed to employ too many individual academics with inflated egos, all cultivating their own spheres of influence and regarding others as rivals. Whether this was a result of the initial recruitment policy of trying to attract the best and the brightest to a 'flagship' Australian university I do not know, but certainly my initial experience was of an institution overly infected by sectionalism. A related issue was that academic staff in the original ANU did not have to teach undergraduates, only to conduct research and supervise postgraduate students. That also, in my opinion, fostered a certain narrowness of focus and insulated academics from the stimulus that undergraduates can bring.

Meanwhile, Audrey and I settled down to life in the federal capital of Australia, flanked by Black Mountain, Mount Ainslie and Mount Majura, with wonderful view of the Brindabellas on the skyline. We made these our weekend playground, walking their eucalyptus-covered slopes in the summer and skiing on higher clear ground in the winter. Canberra was a low-rise city, earlier satirically known as 'seven suburbs in search of a city', but already developing fast. When we arrived the population was barely 50,000, when we left twenty-one years later it was 250,000, and today it is over 400,000.

8

Meeting with Japan

ᴧ

DURING MY FIRST year at the ANU, I had insufficient supervision and was consequently lacking direction. Soviet foreign policy in East Asia was plainly not going to work as a thesis topic, but in the course of pre-researching it I had come increasingly to the view that the most interesting country in East Asia was Japan. In the 1960s most people observing post-colonial Asia from the outside probably agreed that the most important Asian countries were China, India and Japan. Maoist China had many supporters among left wing intellectuals in Western countries, but it was difficult for researchers to access, and as it turned out, its economy would not attain the spectacular heights we are now familiar with for another half century. Post-colonial India had established a complex democratic constitution under the leadership of Pandit Nehru, but the country remained a complex web of languages, religions, castes and ethnicities, while economic development in later years, though it was to be impressive, left millions seeking in vain to escape from poverty.

Of course, I could not have foretold such future developments at the time I was deciding on my path of research, but I was finding positive reasons for choosing Japan as my main focus. In later years I have sometimes told people who ask me 'why Japan?' that when I began to study Japan I knew less about Japan than about Argentina, and all I knew about Argentina was Eva Peron and Fray Bentos beef. But when I think back, I realise that that was not entirely correct. Like most British people of my generation, old enough to remember at least the later stages of the War, I had uncritically accepted an image of Japanese people as extremely tough fighters, even fanatically so. I had heard stories about Emperor worship, refusal to surrender, kamikaze raids, cruelty towards prisoners of war. And yet my comment on an American military film about the Japanese reproduced in Chapter 5 shows that I was also shocked by the extreme anti-Japanese character of that film. The atom bombing of Hiroshima and Nagasaki also affected me as it did so many others, even though I was only nine at the time, and I saw my parents critical of the bombing as well.

When I was a university student I took a fascinating course ('paper' in Oxford jargon) on international relations. One of the books on the reading list was *The Double Patriots* by Richard Storry. This was a detailed study of Japanese army factionalism in the 1930s focussed on the attempted coup d'état by young officers of the Japanese Imperial Army in February 1936. I also bought a copy of *Teach Yourself Japanese*, which, as was common at the time, introduced Japanese entirely through roman script.

I no longer remember how long it took me to decide that I wanted to write a thesis focusing on Japan, but I am fairly sure that it was weeks rather than months from our arrival in Canberra. Whenever it was precisely, as a consequence of my decision I embarked on two tasks that would be essential if I were to prepare myself for this task. One was to study Japanese intensively, and the other was to educate myself in the modern politics and history of Japan. When I look back on that period, and remember that on both of these preparatory enterprises I would be starting practically from scratch, I can hardly believe that I could have embarked on such a course of action with so little concern for the risks involved. It also seems remarkable that nobody at the ANU took me aside and told me that Japanese was a particularly difficult language, and that since I had no experience of Japan I would be hard put to understand the historical, political, social or economic background to whatever thesis topic I eventually chose. Nobody ever said to me, 'but you don't even have a first degree in Japanese'.

And yet, even though in matters of this kind a realistic knowledge of the likely pitfalls is no doubt desirable, broad ignorance (especially on the part of authorities) may also be surprisingly useful. During the first year of my scholarship, I was essentially left to my own devices, so that it was a case of sink or swim. One of the many things for which I have to thank the ANU is that during that first year they let me get on with what I had decided to do, and essentially make my own decisions. When I began writing essays on my reading, Arthur Burns covered them with plenty of red ink, which is precisely what a supervisor is supposed to do. But he did not question my self-imposed trajectory.

I enrolled in first year Japanese at the Canberra University College (which merged with the ANU later in the same year). The head of department was the formidable Professor Joyce Ackroyd, who a few years later, as Professor of Japanese at the University of Queensland, cajoled the Queensland State Government into funding a programme to train substantial numbers of Japanese language teachers to teach the language in state schools in Queensland. This became a model that other states in the Australian federation later emulated. It was only a few years later that Japanese surpassed French as the most popular foreign language taught in Australian schools. Under Joyce Ackroyd were a Japanese war bride called Mrs Clifford, who took most of the elementary language teaching, together with Mr Ito, who had been a schoolteacher in Japan. There was also a rather elderly Japanese academic visitor, Professor Hiramatsu. Mrs Clifford seemed to be a rather vulnerable person, who found it difficult to cope with one or two noisy and impolite Australian students in our group. But she was effective in teaching us the basics of the language. Mr Ito was relatively young and also an effective language teacher. Professor Hiramatsu was a cultured individual who had lived through difficult times in his home country, and expressed anxiety about the future prospects for a stable democratic society. We also received some tuition from a former Australian diplomat with long experience of Japan, Tom Eckersley, whom I had had dealings with as organiser of the International Relations Discussion Group. He had proposed to speak to the topic 'Our Man in Havana: Fact or Fiction?' The title referred to the novel by Graham Greene, and of course Cuba was often in the news in those early years of Fidel Castro. Arthur Burns warned me that such a talk might be problematic, but on the assumption that he would be making an assessment of the political situation in Cuba, I let him have his say. This was my mistake. What he talked about had little to do with Cuba, but revealed an obsessive concern with the activities of Australian and other security services in the early years of the Cold War. That was a tense time in Australian politics (as in the politics of Japan), where banning the Communist Party was on the active agenda of the conservative governments of both countries. I had some sympathy for his views, but sadly the talk was seriously disordered.

The second task I had set myself was to educate myself in the post-war politics of Japan (as well as finding out about Japan more generally). I read a number of Japanese novels in English translation, including that classic of Japanese modern literature, whose title was translated badly into English as 'Some Prefer Nettles'. From these I began to acquire a sense that Japanese society was deeply hierarchical and divided into in-groups and out-groups. This came into focus when I eventually went on to study Japanese political parties, but over the years I came substantially to modify my early impressions of how Japanese social interactions worked in practice.

I also read standard English-language monographs on modern Japan, including such classics as Ruth Benedict's *The Chrysanthemum and the Sword*, written during the war on the basis of interviews with Japanese people long resident in the United States (for obvious reasons, Benedict had not been able to visit Japan to carry out research there). Benedict concluded that Japanese people typically carried an immense burden of obligations to others throughout their lives.

But to understand the nitty-gritty of Japanese politics, I needed a source that would familiarise me with salient political events and issues in the period since the war (and for some aspects before the war as well), and most importantly, would give me some ideas of who were the movers and shakers of the political system over that period. At that time, as I have noted above, there were none of the electronic aids that are the essential tools of researchers today. But I spent many, many hours going through issue after issue of *Keesings Contemporary Archives*, which gave me invaluable information on who was who and what was what, from which I could make deductions about where Japan seemed to be heading.

At this stage my Japanese was far below the standard necessary to read vernacular newspapers. I spent hours, however, in the National Library of Australia (then housed in unattractive temporary buildings), reading the Japanese English language press. Mostly, I chose the *Japan Times*, which still exists having gone through many changes of editorial direction. In those days it was a deeply conservative, United States-centred newspaper, catering principally for expatriate Americans living or staying in Japan. I recall articles by some of its regular columnists. One was a journalist called Paul Aurell. In one of his columns he noted that 'some people' had recently discovered that certain subway stations in Tokyo opened directly into department stores such as Mitsukoshi and Takashimaya. These same 'some people' had therefore taken to getting their drivers to shepherd them into the subway system near to home with precise instructions on how to reach department store-friendly stations, and then collect them there when they had finished their shopping. Expatriates in those days typically lived lives hermetically sealed from the society in which they were living. Few, it seemed, bothered to familiarise themselves with more than a few words and phrases of Japanese – enough to issue the most basic instructions to their maids.

Another *Japan Times* journalist, an economic reporter called Joseph Z. Reday, wrote a column in the late 1950s, when Japan was poised to embark on double-digit economic growth, writing about 'the basic economic poverty of this country'.

Before we left England for Australia, Audrey, who had been working in the William Morris Gallery in Walthamstow, had been studying for her Museums Diploma. She was well advanced, but had not completed it when we moved countries. She therefore arranged a two-week internship at the Art Gallery of New South Wales in Sydney, under its Director, Mr Boustead. So in July 1960, in the middle of the Australian winter, we drove together to Sydney in our ten- year-old Morris Minor. Being impecunious, we stayed at the cheapest hostelry we could find, which was the 'People's Palace', at the lower end of Pitt Street in the seedier end of town. It was not, as its name might suggest, run by the Communist Party, but by the Salvation Army. Sydney has a warm climate, but mid-winter can be surprisingly cold, and so far as I remember there was no central heating. While Audrey was working at the Art Gallery, I went every morning to the Fisher Library at the University of Sydney, where I ransacked the card catalogue for books on post-war Japanese politics, especially the politics of the left, which was already becoming the principal focus of my interest. By the time we returned to Canberra, I had enough material for an essay to satisfy my supervisor.

Incredible as it must seem today, the Art Gallery of New South Wales was insufficiently provided with funds to illuminate its galleries past dusk, which in winter was already well advanced by five o'clock in the afternoon. This meant that Audrey was able to get away early and we could feast on tasty meals in surprisingly cheap restaurants, explore Chinatown and enjoy plays and concerts. We also met some interesting people through Audrey's connection with the gallery.

A source of tension in Australian society was brought home to us late one evening as we returned to the People's Palace. Our venerable Morris was parked outside or just along the road. As we were about to pass the car, two drunks noticed the ACT (i.e. Canberra) plates, muttered 'Canberra!!', and spat at the car. Many 'ordinary Australians' (is there such a thing?) regarded Canberra as a waste of money. My aunt in Melbourne described it in a letter to us before we went there as 'a weird and wonderful place, inhabited mainly by public servants and gardeners'. It was many years before it was able to shake off this kind of reputation and develop dynamism worthy of the federal capital of Australia.

Not long after we returned to Canberra, Audrey was awarded the Museums Diploma.

About a year after we had arrived at the ANU, I finally had a supervisor with expertise on Japan. His name was David Sissons, and since in a real sense I owe my career to David, I must accord him a prominent place in this narrative. During that first year, I had done a great deal of work on the two principal tasks I had set myself, of learning Japanese and finding out about Japan. But I had lacked expert supervision, and still did not have a clear thesis topic to focus on. David, after his arrival, took me in hand in ways that were not always comfortable, but were just what I needed if I was to complete a successful thesis.

First of all, he insisted that I should put more effort into learning Japanese, by arranging exchange lessons with various Japanese graduate students studying at the ANU. This typically meant a two-hour commitment in the evening, where I taught English in exchange for a lesson in Japanese. I was already doing this to some extent, but David told me I should devote every evening to such exchanges (perhaps excluding weekends?). This was hardly conducive to a happy married life (and David still maintained a bachelor's view of such things), so that I fudged the issue to some extent, though I certainly increased the intensity of my Japanese language learning. I was also trying to pick up Japanese language broadcasts with a short-wave radio, but the static made comprehension doubly problematic.

Before his appointment to the ANU, David had spent nearly four years in Japan, researching contemporary issues in the country's politics, and when I first met him he had written well regarded articles on the post-war Constitution, the Governments attempts to reinforce police powers, and – most importantly for me – the main opposition Japan Socialist Party (JSP). I was still struggling with the question of where my focus ought to be placed among the various contemporary issues in what was a fiercely contested political arena. I had been toying with the idea of a general study of Japanese foreign policy, or possibly of Japan-US relations, but I was well aware that these were too vague. David pointed out to me that the JSP was canvassing a foreign policy of neutralism, or non-alignment, in the context of the still simmering and spluttering Cold War. In the late 1950s and early 1960s the JSP was the principal party of opposition, and at times seemed a realistic contester for national power. At the time it still represented large sections of Japanese public opinion concerned to consolidate democratic institutions inherited both from the American Occupation and from indigenous democratic traditions. Pacifism had already taken deep roots in substantial sections of the electorate, and the JSP, despite serious internal divisions, was in tune with that.

David's suggestion was brilliant, and I had no difficulty of accepting it as the focus of my thesis.

As supervisor, David was a hard taskmaster, and at times I became exasperated with the pressure he put me under, as did Audrey even more than I. But it was exactly what I needed if I was to complete my thesis and embark on an academic career. He insisted on economy of language, and clear backing for statements of both fact and opinion. Apart from keeping me up to a high academic standard in what I wrote, he worked to open up avenues for me in Japan, for the time was approaching for a period of research in that country. He arranged for me to have a year's affiliation with the Institute of Social Science of Tokyo University, known in Japanese as *Shaken*. I ended up spending fifteen months at *Shaken*, and it was also my academic home on several later periods of research in Japan.

A complication arose in the planning for my field trip, because in 1961 Audrey became pregnant, and gave birth to a daughter, Kate (Katrina) on 19 November of that year. The circumstances of her birth were not without drama, as Audrey developed an infection and had to be placed in quarantine for several days after the birth. Her doctor asked the advice of another, and presumably more senior, doctor, Dr Harrington, who examined Audrey. But Dr Harrington was killed in an air crash shortly afterwards, when a Fokker Friendship went down on the flight from Sydney to Canberra, killing all on board, including several prominent Canberra citizens.

The birth of Kate meant postponing our journey to Japan for several weeks, but in late January 1962 the three of us left from Sydney on board the *Suez Maru*, of the OSK (Ōsaka Shōsen Kaisha) line, bound for Brisbane and Yokkaichi, a port on the Pacific coast of central Japan. During the voyage France exploded its first nuclear device and the population of Tokyo passed ten million. The ship's purser bore a striking resemblance to His Majesty the Emperor, and to my surprise this caused amusement among the officers. It was a lesson in how much had changed since the times when the Emperor was regarded as a living god. On board this cargo ship were twelve passengers, including a young Japanese man importing race horses from Australia, the horses being housed in a stable that had been constructed on the deck. We met him two or three times later in Tokyo. A middle-aged Australian businessman, travelling to Japan with his wife, asked me why on earth I would choose to study Japan's Socialist Party, when it was the conservatives that were in power. This was a view that I was to meet occasionally in Japan, and it set me thinking about the importance of parties out of power in a democratic system, 'holding the government to account' as the phrase goes. As I was to discover later, however, the problem with the left-wing opposition in Japan was that it appeared frightened of taking power. And if an opposition is not keen on running a government, it is not going to be particularly effective as an opposition. Despite this, however, the Socialists were playing an important role in defending the democratic Constitution with its 'peace clause' – Article 9. All they needed was two thirds of the seats in one or other house of the National Diet (Parliament) and they could block revision. This issue became central to my research in the months that were to follow.

The ship's doctor was an elderly Japanese, whose English was very limited (as was my Japanese, certainly in relation to medicine). But he had a blackboard which he put to good use when we consulted him about a stomach problem Kate was experiencing.

The doctor drew on his blackboard a detailed diagram of a baby's digestive system in order to communicate the nature of the problem. In any case, it was nothing serious.

Our first sight of Japan was the port of Yokkaichi, with its lovely backdrop of mountains. A few women in kimono were on the dockside. The town itself was not beautiful, but it was yet to receive its unenviable reputation as a centre of pollution where children fell sick with asthma.

We disembarked early in the morning, and took a local train to the city of Nagoya, not so far away. At first sight the train appeared to be full of very young postmen in black tunics, until we realised that this was standard school uniform. From Nagoya we took a Tōkaidō line train to Tokyo, in those days before the Shinkansen super-fast lines had been built. In Tokyo we stayed for a couple of weeks at the International House of Japan, a home for academics and graduate students that had been built after the war with strong American encouragement (and money), in the inner suburb of Roppongi. In later years, I stayed many times at IHJ, where at breakfast I would often run into other Japan-specialists from around the world.

I was soon introduced to two other institutions that became central to my research. The first was *Shaken* (pron: Shack-en) – the Institute of Social Science of Tokyo University. After David Sissons' hard work in securing me a place there, I was made welcome and placed under the supervision of Professor Hayashi Shigeru, a political historian of modern Japan rather than a political scientist. He was, however, extremely helpful in giving me introductions to politicians and others knowledgeable in the field I was researching, and in answering my many questions. I was also allotted a desk in his study. Since he was not often there, I had to answer his phone calls, and leave him notes about who had called and why. My Japanese was improving, but I sometimes completely misinterpreted what the caller wanted, or even who the caller was. Professor and Mrs Hayashi became close friends of ours, and visited us for extended periods both in Canberra and later at Oxford.

The other institution that I frequented was the National Diet (Parliamentary) Library), located near the National Diet building. There I spent a great deal of my time in the newspaper clipping section (*Shinbun kirinuki bu*), methodically going through newspaper reports of political developments in the areas that interested me.

During the summer heat and humidity, the only parts of the library that were air conditioned were the book stacks. Those areas occupied by students and others trying to work were not (the term 'sweat shops' comes to mind). I still have notes from that period where my bare arm had been resting on my notes, and the ink was transferred from my arm to another part of the same page.

The man in charge of the press-cutting section was a man called Mr Nakai. His manner was so low-key that he was practically invisible. One day two or three of us foreign students were discussing with some animation a discovery one of us had made in a clipping file. Without realising it, we had evidently raised the decibel count beyond what was tolerable. Mr Nakai came up to us, bowed, and in a low voice began a discourse that was so lengthy and circumlocutory that we were unable to understand its central message. When he realised that we were not understanding he said, 'Please be quiet, *to iu koto desu.*' ('What I mean is: please be quiet'.)

Before we left Australia, David Sissons and I had agreed that the working title of my thesis would be 'The neutralist policy of the Japan Socialist Party'. So once in Tokyo, I needed to find a point of departure for my research. Very soon, I was fortunate enough to discover a book in Japanese outlining the development within the party of this foreign policy orientation, together with a description of internal party disputes that reflected longstanding factional divisions, for it quickly became evident to me that the Socialist Party was seriously divided both ideologically and in personal factional terms. The book was by a party official, Yamaguchi Fusao, who together with his colleague Fujimaki Shinpei, became invaluable sources of information and contacts during the time I was in Tokyo. (Yamaguchi Fusao, *Chūritsu* (Neutralism), Shiseidō, 1959). Both were politically moderate, and fairly pragmatic in their approach to issues of policy. For much of their time working for the party, the Socialists had been a major political force, controlling over a third of the seats in the House of Representatives, so that the idea of an eventual Socialist government was not far from the surface of their thinking. Eventually, however, disillusioned by the power of ideological extremism and the failure of the party in the 1960s to consolidate and improve upon the advances it had made during the 1950s, they both left the party's employ, Yamaguchi-san taking up a university position where his task was to defuse extremist student protest and liaise with student radicals to that end, at the time of the student revolts of the late 1960s. During the period of my interaction with these two intelligent and enlightened men, we became good friends.

Meanwhile, after spending two or three weeks staying at International House, Audrey and I, with our baby daughter, moved into a pre-war wooden house in the suburb of Nishigahara, some twenty to thirty minutes distance by clanking *toden* (trams) from the Hongo campus of the University of Tokyo. Our friends at *Shaken* had helped us find it and negotiate the rent with the estate agent. The landlady, who was living in Hawai'i and whom we never met, was called Mrs Hiroshige, much to the amusement of our friends, though her name was spelled with different characters from the surname of the renowned nineteenth-century artist. This house remained our dwelling for the rest of the time we were in Tokyo. It was a single-storey building with a living area opening onto a tiny garden between the house and the street, separated from the very basic kitchen by a waist-high bench and a child-proof door. The kitchen facilities consisted of two gas rings and a sink. Beyond the kitchen was a Japanese-style bath, in which we could luxuriate, and a toilet. To the side were two bedrooms, ours separated from the outside by a *shoji* paper screen, although when we went out we could secure the house by sliding into place a wooden barrier to the outside of the screen. Behind the house but joined onto it were two tiny rooms inhabited separately by two bachelors, to one of whom Audrey later gave English language lessons (see later).

My supervisor David Sissons had done much to smooth the way for us in securing the arrangements with *Shaken*, and giving me other contacts. His approach to supervision, however, was not to sit back and wait for me to make progress. On the contrary, he required me to send him monthly by airmail a paper outlining the results of that month's research, and later on a draft chapter. He would go through each piece of work I sent him meticulously, criticising in equal measure the structure of my argument, the empirical backing for statements that I made, and the quality of my English. For me, this was a tough regime, but it meant that by the time we returned to Canberra I had written a great part of the thesis in draft form, and it made sense in terms of its structure and argument. This was the most extraordinary learning experience that I have ever known.

David, however, was not only concerned with the academic side of the exercise. He also controlled our finances. Along with my monthly academic report, he required me to send him an accounting of our expenditure for the month, which he would carefully vet, and cull if he thought necessary. I would receive payment from the ANU in accordance with his recommendations. On one occasion he rejected my claim of reimbursement for a punnet of strawberries. Needless to say, Audrey was not best pleased by all this. I am fairly sure that the background to this was his own experience of living in Japan between 1956 and 1960. He had received a scholarship (the Saionji scholarship) from Australia that was supposed to fund him for two years, but managed to eke this out for a much longer period. Being of a parsimonious disposition in any case, he developed a variety of stratagems to avoid spending money, so that my friends (as they became) in the *Shaken* office told me more than once of their amazement at his ability to live on so little. One piece of advice that he gave me before we left Canberra was that I should sign on for the 'rice ration'. When I asked about it at *Shaken*, I found that it no longer existed.

I soon found that the most useful place to work was the National Diet Library. There I met a number of foreign (mainly American) doctoral researchers, like myself, and also one of David's friends, employed as a politics researcher by the library itself. His name was Misawa Shigeo, and I learned a great deal from him about current issues and developments in the politics of his country. He shared the liberal ethos of that era, with its ambition to break entirely with the nationalist politics of the past, and to consolidate a truly democratic regime. At the same time he was a most careful researcher, reliable as a source and analyst of information. He was young, married and hospitable, but I learned that like many at his level in the society of that period, he lived very much from pay packet to pay packet, and was often short of money.

Among the foreign doctoral students I met at the National Diet Library was an American called Donald Hellmann, who was writing a thesis on Japanese relations with the Soviet Union, broadly for the period of the 1950s. Since Soviet foreign policy in Asia had been my first idea for a research topic, I naturally found in him somebody I could relate to in terms of ideas about Japanese foreign policy. He was also open and easy to talk with, so that Audrey and

I became good friends with him and his wife Marge, who was an artist. They had come to Japan earlier than we had, Don knew the ropes better than I did, and he was informative about Japanese studies in the United States, quite apart from his insights into what had been going on in the recent politics and foreign policy of Japan. One thing he taught me that became a central concern of my own research was the importance of factions in Japanese political parties. In researching negotiations for a settlement between Japan and the USSR in the mid-1950s, he had unearthed a good deal of material about the role political factions on the Japanese side played in complicating the negotiations. Even now, more than sixty years later and despite all the changes in the configuration of international relations, an unresolved territorial dispute has prevented the signature of a peace treaty between Japan and its northern neighbour.

Don received his doctorate, went on to publish a book based on his doctoral research (*Japanese Foreign Policy and Domestic Politics: The Peace agreement with the Soviet Union*, University of California Press, 1969), and was hired to teach at the University of Washington in Seattle, where he was to spend almost his whole career. Sometime later he published his second book (*Japan and East Asia: The New International Order*, Pall Mall Press, 1972) arguing that Japan would need to embark on a major programme of rearmament, and that this was most likely to happen. Around the same time, I had been writing articles stressing the strength of opposition to rearmament within Japan itself, and I found myself disputing Don's conclusions. We entered into a long correspondence on these and related issues, but without any real meeting of minds. Although we ran into each other many years later at IHJ, we remained intellectually divided.

While we were living in Nishigahara, Audrey was busy making friends, arranging babysitters, and finding things to do. Among our most memorable friends in Tokyo was a lady whom we knew in the family as 'Sugai-san'. Her full name was Sugai Mieko. She taught aesthetics for a while at *Shaken*, and helped us in all sorts of ways over the years that were to come. She was particularly adept at introducing us to the right people. One day she came to see us and told us that she had fixed up with a local college for Audrey to teach English one day a week, in return for which she would be allowed to use the school pottery. The college, *Bunka Gakuin*

(Cultural Academy), in Surugadai close to the centre of Tokyo, had been founded some time before the Great Kantō earthquake of 1 September 1923, by a man called Nishimura Isaku, who was unhappy with what he saw as the rigid and unimaginative teaching in the state schools of that era, and founded a private school where pupils were given a liberal education concentrating on the arts and culture more generally. Mr Nishimura was himself much occupied with the arts, including painting, pottery and architecture, and saw their function in a school setting as providing a deeply moral and even religious training for schoolchildren. He was also a pioneer of co-education, at a time when virtually all other schools were segregated by gender. (Nishimura Isaku, *Ware ni eki ari* (To my Advantage), Tokyo, Kigensha, 1960, pp. 278-89). By the time Audrey was at the school, he was old and ill, and died of cancer during her period teaching there. But his assistant, a young woman called Miwa-san, was kind to Audrey and helped her understand the workings of the pottery studio within the school.

Audrey had taken pottery lessons in Canberra, and was anxious to develop her skills in ceramics. On one occasion we invited some Japanese friends to dinner — not easy to make with such primitive cooking facilities. One of our guests commented that this was the first time he had been invited to a dinner where the hostess had bought in the food but made the plates.

So far as babysitting was concerned, on the days she was at the school she employed the young daughter, Reiko, of one of the *Shaken* professors, to look after Kate. Over fifty years later, we are still in touch.

During the hot mid-summer of 1962, Audrey took the baby to England to show her to her grandparents. While she was there I went by train to the Shinano valley in Nagano prefecture, north-west of the capital, to spend a week or so in the mountains of that beautiful region. It was a relief to leave Tokyo and its stifling heat. I stayed at an inn, and climbed the slopes of Mount Shirouma (White Horse). I travelled by chair lift for the first part of the climb, but on the way back I found that the chair lift had closed for repairs, so that I had to walk down the rest of the way in the gathering dusk, and as a result was late back at the inn, to the concern of the staff.

I returned to Tokyo and re-installed myself in the Nishigahara house. I turned on the electricity, which I had turned off as I left for Nagano, anxious about an ancient wiring system in a wooden house. An hour or so after I returned, there was a gentle knock at my front door, revealing one of the two bachelors from the rooms at the back. He asked me about my travels, and my experiences of climbing Mount Shirouma. After the conversation had gone on for a while, he said to me, 'I am sorry to have to tell you this, but when you left the house you turned off the electricity, so that we have not had any electricity since you left.' Horrified by what I had done, I expressed my deepest apology; to which he replied, '*Sore dewa, tsugi no kikai ni wa, yoroshiku o-negai itashimasu.*' (So, on the next occasion, please think of us.) In fact, '*yoroshiku o-negai itashimasu*' is almost impossible to translate into English, but a more literal version might be, 'I humbly request that you do well by us.' Whatever the niceties of translation, after he left I fell right through the tatami matting into a pit of shame below.

This unfortunate episode led me to reflect on the nature and function of politeness in Japanese society. I wondered what would have been the response had the same thing happened in Australia, 'Ya turned me bloody electrics off, ya silly galah!' – or worse. Japanese people are not always polite. Towards the end of our stay in Tokyo I was in a shipping office in Tokyo trying to book a sea passage back to Australia. There was a dispute between the offices of the company I was visiting and the offices of the OSK which had rescheduled its passage and therefore cancelled the ticket I had already bought. I asked that this company recover the fare from the company that had cancelled my original passage. The company was prepared to do this but met with a refusal from the other company. I listened in to a telephone conversation in which a woman official of the company whose offices I was in expostulated to her counterpart in the delinquent company (my translation), 'Why does your company operate such totally idiotic and irrational procedures?' Point taken: the problem could now be easily sorted out.

Japanese discourse is nevertheless infused with considerably more polite expression than that in most Western countries. Learning the correct *keigo* (politeness) usage is a bane for all students of Japanese. There are several levels of speech, and selecting the most appropriate one for a given situation is not always easy. This is not just a language learning problem but is also a problem in socio-linguistics. No doubt most societies have mechanisms to smooth over relations between different groups. But in the Japanese case the use of polite expressions based on hierarchy ('I humble myself before your respected self') seem designed to minimise socially disruptive friction. Language within groups (e.g. families) is generally much less flowery than between them.

One implication of politeness language is that relations between groups are in themselves intrinsically disruptive, and need a mechanism such as *keigo* to prevent them getting out of hand.

And this takes me on to the subject of factions within political parties, which became such a central issue in my doctoral thesis.

9

Trying to Write a Thesis

ᴊ

MY EXPERIENCE OF trying to write a thesis taught me practically from the outset that writing twelve chapters was materially different from writing twelve unconnected essays. The maximum length permitted by the ANU for a PhD thesis was 100,000 words, and most theses ended up between 80,000 and the maximum. This meant that you must have a coherent argument that transcended the concerns of individual chapters. At the same time, I instinctively believed, and still believe, that the best research should be embedded in empirical exploration of reality. This is not to say that the generation of theory is unimportant, but that unless it is underpinned by empirical understanding of the actual world, it is likely to end up as largely irrelevant to practical concerns. A few times in my career I have read reviews of my work that took me to task for underplaying the theoretical implications of what I have written. Such criticisms were mostly fair, but I hold fast to my view that without a deep understanding of the real world, based on hard empirical investigation, any theoretical insights that emerge may well be flawed or of limited interest.

David Sissons, my supervisor during most of my serious thesis writing, was much more extreme than I was in giving priority to empirical concerns. Indeed, I have never met anybody who pursued every path that his research opened up with such dedication to detail and to covering every last inch of ground as was David. In his research, for instance, on Japanese pearl divers in Northern Australia, I believe that he felt it necessary to investigate in meticulous detail the background to information given by every headstone in the Japanese cemetery at Broome before he could venture to write anything about the subject. Somebody once said to me, 'David does

not understand the concept of a sample.' More seriously Arthur
Burns, who preceded David as my thesis supervisor, once expressed
to me the opinion that 'David is an absolute non-generaliser'. With
that opinion, however, I do not entirely concur. Having helped edit
a posthumous edition of David's writings (Arthur Stockwin and
Keiko Tanaka, *Bridging Australia and Japan: The Writings of David
Sissons, Historian and Political Scientist*, 2 vols., Canberra, Australian National University Press, 2016-2020). I have discovered that
the end product of his research in many cases was a statement of
firmly grounded generalisations that were powerful enough to challenge widely accepted assumptions about the course of history. This
was what was to make him, in later years, a major – even great –
interpreter of Australian interactions with its turbulent and ambitious Asian neighbour to the north.

My own early attempts to penetrate the arcane world of Japanese
left wing politics once I had landed in Japan were handicapped by
my inadequate knowledge of the Japanese language. I did not know
enough of the language to conduct interviews until I had lived
in Tokyo for at least three months, assimilating as much relevant
vocabulary as I possibly could. And in some of the early interviews
I would take somebody with me to help out, not as an interpreter,
because I was determined not to use interpreters, but as a backstop
to make sure I did not wholly misunderstand at least the most crucial pieces of wisdom that I was being fed.

Very early in this process, I learned some practical lessons about
interviewing in difficult linguistic conditions. The first was to avoid
if possible scheduling an interview over a meal. Interviewing is difficult enough, requiring close prior preparation and intense concentration during the interview itself, so that the distraction of having
to manipulate chopsticks to eat your tempura can seriously harm
comprehension. The second was to have some kind of shorthand
– however primitive – to facilitate note-taking. Some of my fellow
graduate students used tape recorders in interviews, but I decided
early on not to do this, since what might be gained in terms of
accuracy was likely to be offset by a reluctance to divulge information that might be politically sensitive. Today, some people take
notes on a laptop or similar electronic device, but those did not exist
at the time I was conducting research for my thesis. I have never
learned Pitman's, or any other, shorthand, but it made sense for me

to work out in advance a number of basic abbreviations relevant to the topics I was discussing. Also I often found that I was writing some things down in Romanised Japanese because the actual Japanese expression used could give fruitful clues to the mind-set of the person being interviewed. Thirdly, I was careful never to schedule more than one interview in immediate succession. It is hard enough to capture the essence and as much detail as possible of a single interview, whereas two or more in succession will mean you lose detail and even essence. The fourth point – and this is particularly important – was that I tried to make sure that there was a convenient coffee-shop round the corner from the place of interview, so that immediately the interview was finished I could race round there, order a coffee, and write out as accurate an account as possible of the interview. Being Tokyo, coffee shops were easy to find. It was not so easy, however, if I was with a group of people, or if – as sometimes happened – the interviewee proposed some kind of hospitality or entertainment as an adjunct to the interview.

A much broader, and final, aspect of interviewing was a less mechanical consideration that I learned the hard way as the result of successive interviews. In retrospect this seems clear, but it was something that I rather neglected in the earlier stages of my research: in advance of an interview, be as well briefed as possible about the background of the person to be interviewed. This became obvious to me as a result of my experience of interviewing a political activist called Satō Noboru. He was not an elected politician, but rather an official in the Japan Socialist Party (JSP) and a key intellectual force behind the 'Structural Reform' movement led by Eda Saburō in the early 1960s.

When I first interviewed Satō, I found him rather stiff and formal. I put to him the question, 'Are you from the left wing or the right wing of the party?' He replied, 'Left', without much further explanation. I came away from the interview feeling frustrated that I had not got as much out of it as I had expected. But over the following few days I found out more about him, and discovered that he had been an activist in the Japan Communist Party (JCP), but as a result of complex faction fighting in that party, had defected to the Socialists in 1958. So when he said 'Left', he neglected to mention that he had actually changed his party allegiance. I therefore contacted him again, and with due apologies requested a second interview.

The atmosphere during the second interview could not have been more different from that in the first. He was relaxed, told me a great deal of useful information and even gossip, and explained carefully why he had changed parties and the hopes he and his colleagues were investing in Eda's 'structural reform' initiative.

My acquaintance with Satō brought me face to face with one of the most fundamental issues exercising Japanese left wing parties in the 1950s and 1960s: that of Marxism. The ideology of the JCP was founded in Marxist thought, influenced and even directed by the Soviet Union (and to a lesser extent by China) so that its internal disputes were couched in Marxist language and concepts. This was also true, however, with the JSP, although its interpretation of Marxism was very different from that of its Communist rival. It is dis-spiriting to find that, as I write this, the British Labour Party leadership operates under significant Marxist influence. From the second interview with Satō I remember a particular phrase, 'since we are Marxists', but when one of my own students, Stephen Johnson, interviewed him for his own research on opposition parties several years later, Satō was no long arguing in Marxist terms. My own interpretation of Satō's transition is that as a man of intelligence and essentially liberal instincts he was coming to terms with the fact that although Marxism in the immediate post-war period was a radical blueprint for renovation after the disasters of a fascist regime and catastrophic military defeat, Japan was already in a phase of economic recovery that required more moderate and sophisticated solutions. Like many on the left, he was never going to accept that the political corruption, inadequate welfare policies and pro-American foreign policies of the ruling Liberal Democratic Party (LDP) were simply the price to be paid for rapid economic growth, but he recognised that the Left must adapt to a situation in which standards of living were rapidly improving. It was this way of thinking that led him to change parties and promote a movement of radical reform in what was still the principal party of opposition, the JSP. Perhaps the best way of characterising this is to see it as a movement to modernise the Left and make it relevant to changed economic circumstances.

On a day in November 1962, I was attending the annual congress of the JSP in the Kudan Kaikan in central Tokyo, a widely used conference centre that was showing its age. Eda Saburō, the party

Secretary-General, made an important speech explaining his notion of 'structural reform', and this was followed by fairly desultory discussion. The main excitement was provided by verbal sparring between party activists and sections of the press. Around this time also, Eda had outlined what had become known as the 'Eda Vision', describing in vague but inspiring terms his vision for a future Socialist government. In August 1962 Eda had outlined to a provincial audience his 'vision' of a future socialist society, based on four pillars: the high living standards of the United States, Soviet levels of social security, British parliamentary democracy and the Japanese 'peace' constitution. Leaving aside how far the Soviet Union in the early 1960s should have been seen as a model exemplar of social security, Eda's 'vision', had it prevailed and been consolidated as JSP policy, might well have given the party the modernising impetus that it needed in order to become a genuine contender for political power at the national level.

It was getting late in the evening and I was anxious not to miss the last train home, so I left. Next morning, I learned on the news that I had missed one of the most important events in JSP history: at a late night vote of the Congress, the Structural Reform programme had been defeated. This was to lead to years of hard left leadership and erosion of the Socialist vote by newly emerging parties. However vague and insubstantial Eda's programme had been, at least it connected with popular aspirations. What replaced it appealed largely to ideologues.

I must now return to my remarks at the outset of this chapter, affirming that discrete chapters do not add up to a thesis. I had a thesis title, 'The Neutralist Policy of the Japan Socialist Party', suggested to me by my supervisor. I knew that the concept of 'neutralism' had emerged in the late 1940s in Pandit Nehru's India and elsewhere in Asia, as a way of escaping from the polarities of the emerging Cold War. As it seemed to observers at the time, States and their governments were finding their choices of orientation to world affairs increasingly constrained by a rigid choice: you were either pro-American, or pro-Soviet; you had to position yourself firmly in one camp or the other. Neutralism (later often referred to as 'non-alignment'), was a method of escaping from such bipolar thinking, which carried with it the unwelcome connotation of being subordinate, either to the Americans, or to the Soviets.

In this respect it differed from traditional neutrality, on the model of Switzerland or of Sweden, which simply meant staying out of wars between powerful neighbours.

Within the JSP, neutralist ideas were often expressed using the term 'positive neutrality' (*sekkyoku chūritsu*), implying that the aim was not simply to stay out of war, but rather to promote world peace. The aim of non-alignment was to change the international system away from bipolar nuclear confrontation towards something more flexible and less dangerous. As such it appealed to ex-colonies such as India, Burma and Indonesia, which were feeling their way towards affirmation of their independence and establishment of a type of power status separate from that of their former colonisers. Since most former colonisers (Britain, France etc.) were now to be found in the American-led camp, a neutralist strategy tended to be relatively more critical of the United States than of the Soviet Union. In the case of Japan from the late 1940s onwards, peace movements grew rapidly in support following the catastrophe of Japan's Asia-Pacific War. 'Japan the only country to have been sub-jected to nuclear attack' became a powerful slogan, while being linked with the United States in a security treaty from 1951 gave the peace movement a strongly anti-American flavour.

In the Japan Socialist Party, neutralist ideas supplied a useful pol-icy focus. They fitted well with rising pacifist sentiment, appealed to the anti-American resentment that was becoming dominant in the party, and seemed not especially at odds with elements of Marx-ist thinking that prevailed on the left of the party. Those uncon-vinced by the neutralist message, within the party or outside it, often attacked it for being skewed: not equidistant between the two international camps, but anti-American and pro-Soviet.

As I grew more familiar with the detail of debate within the JSP concerning neutralism, I gradually became aware of a phenomenon that in some ways transcended the ideological content of the issues being discussed. This was to take on the character of a set of struc-tural problems relating to party politics in general during my later research. A classic definition of a 'faction' in Western political sci-ence literature was that of the pre-war American political scientist Harold Lasswell, who regarded political factions as essentially tem-porary and opportunist groupings of politicians coming together for pragmatic advantage, but without any real sense of loyalty towards that grouping. It followed that factions and parties were fundamentally different political phenomena: whereas factions, broadly speaking, had the characteristics of a 'flash in the pan', parties were much more substantial. Parties were expected to present a carefully worked out set of policies, to be able to rely on relatively stable support from defined sections of the electorate, and to enjoy an 'image' that was easily recognisable. One way of looking at British political history from the nineteenth century onward is to regard the political system as being in gradual evolution from one based on poorly articulated factions to one based on well organised parties.

To a considerable extent these distinctions were normative: factions were seen as remnants of an underdeveloped political system, whereas the prevalence of political parties was held as key evidence of sophisticated and modernised politics. The development of British politics throughout the nineteenth century and into the twentieth was widely seen as bound up with the advance of political stability based on the consolidation of parties.

The problem for my research on Japan was that parties and factions did not clearly follow the distinction between them that was fundamental to Western political science. Factions were often less ephemeral and more solidary that the Lasswell model maintained. There were factions that could boast a longer history than the parties of which they were currently a part. Within parties also, factions were often embedded centrally in the decision-making process of the party itself. Now while it is true that not all factions in *Western* political systems were ephemeral, opportunistic and unprincipled in Japan, the centrality of factions to the political parties of which they were a part contrasted sharply with the situation in many political systems in Western Europe, for instance.

Of course, it is possible to argue that this apparent contrast may be primarily a question of language. The Japanese word for 'faction' is 'habatsu', which embodies certain implications about leader-follower relations and about hierarchy. In my research I found that relationships between individuals within a 'habatsu' were frequently long-term and highly structured. Generally speaking, they were also hierarchical and involved in fund raising.

For the periods I was researching, all major political parties (and some smaller ones) were divided into competing factions. A widespread assumption in the secondary literature was that factions in the ruling LDP were essentially groupings of individual politicians, linked together according to traditional principles of hierarchy and mutual support, for purposes of fund raising and power maximisation. By contrast, it was asserted that factions in the JSP were ideological in inspiration, ranging from overtly Marxist on the left to social-democratic on the moderate right. In the course of my research, however, it became evident that reality was much more complicated than this, both in the LDP and in the JSP. So far as the conservative LDP was concerned, there were indeed traditional features of factional organisation, but to a significant extent they also represented different ideological positions on major policy issues. Even in the 1970s, when the 'classic' structure of LDP factions still for the most part prevailed, a bitter struggle for power between the Fukuda and Ōhira factions was indeed a contest between two ambitious leaders. But it was not only that. Fukuda maintained hard line right wing views on sensitive issues such as the 'peace' constitution, whereas Ōhira held fast to moderate policy positions on most issues. A later successor of Ōhira as head of the same faction (the *Kōchikai*) Miyazawa Kiichi, strongly opposed revising the constitution, even though revision (especially of the 'peace clause', Article 9), had been official party policy since the party was founded in 1955. This flies in the face of a general assumption that LDP factions have little to do with policy.

Conversely, one of the things that became evident in my earlier research on the JSP was that although ideology was often a powerful driving force in that party's factions, those factions, much like the factions within the LDP, were structured as power maximising and fund raising organisations aiming to control the party apparatus. Several of those I interviewed emphasised how crucial factions were to the way Japanese politics worked, and on more than one occasion when I turned up at an interview I had arranged with a single individual, I found other members of the same faction present as well.

Every month during our stay in Tokyo, I spent most of my time in the National Diet Library and other libraries, as well as a good deal of time interviewing. Some of the experiences that came my way during this intensive period of research gave me insights into Japanese behaviour and social norms, as well as into politics. On one occasion I asked permission to consult the archive of the Socialist politician Asanuma Inejirō (who was assassinated by a member of the far right during the 1960 general election campaign) held in the library of Waseda University. This had no doubt been negotiated through friends at *Shaken*, which was an institute of Tokyo University (Tōdai), where I was based. Now Tōdai is widely regarded as the leading state university, while Waseda is one of the most highly rated universities in the private sector. I was greeted by the Waseda librarian with rather less of the celebrated Japanese politeness than I had become accustomed to. He put the archive at my disposal, but indicated to me later that the library was about to close, some time before what I knew was the official closing time. I can only assume (from other experiences also) that institutional sectionalism was at least part of the explanation.

In the English language literature on Japan at the time, the idea that Japanese institutions, political and other, worked on the principle of consensus, was widespread to the point of approximating holy writ. My experience of conflict in a shipping office, recounted in Chapter 8, shows a counter example from ordinary life. In political affairs, my research suggested that conflict was at least as common as consensus. It slowly dawned on me that Japan was as conflict-ridden as anywhere else. I gradually formed the hypothesis that, far from consensus being a naturally occurring aspect of Japanese society, it was a social mechanism designed to mitigate the ill effects of a society in which conflict (especially group conflict) played a conspicuous role. This was borne out by my research on the Japan Socialist Party in the mid-1950s. The San Francisco Peace Treaty in 1951 ended the Allied Occupation and returned independent sovereignty to Japan, with the exception of Okinawa, which remained under American military control. At that juncture the JSP split into two more or less equal parts, known informally as the Left Socialist Party and the Right Socialist Party, though formally each retained 'Japan Socialist Party' as their title. By 1955 the Cold War, which in 1951 had come dangerously close to degenerating into real military conflict, seemed to be on a path towards détente between the US and USSR, following the death of Stalin in 1953. In 1951, the Left Socialist Party opposed the Peace Treaty, opposed the Japan-US Security Treaty that came into effect at the same time, and also refused to accept the early measures of rearmament that had been ordered by the Occupation after the Korean War broke out in 1950. By contrast, the Right Socialist Party accepted the San

Francisco Peace Treaty, but was divided over the Security Treaty and also over rearmament. So far as neutralism was concerned, the Left Socialists were prepared to accept it, with an anti-American spin, whereas the Right Socialists were much more sceptical.

Following the ending of the Allied Occupation and the restoration of Japan's formal sovereignty, the two rival socialist parties gradually began to explore how they might come together again as a single party. This was facilitated by a lessening of international tension following the death of Stalin in 1953. In October 1955, after some two years of negotiation between the two sides, the two parties merged into a single 'Japan Socialist Party'. Negotiations had been conducted for the most part along factional lines, but for them to succeed, two conditions had to be met. The first was that both sides understood that it would be to their own advantage for unification to succeed, even if that meant abandoning or modifying parts of their policies. The second condition was that language had to be used in the final agreement that somewhat blurred the divisions of opinion that still existed. These two conditions are no doubt essential for success in most processes of negotiation, the world over. But there is – and was in this instance – a problem with the second condition: if divisions are simply papered over in a way that makes it difficult to determine in what precise policy has been agreed, that is a recipe for storing up trouble for the future. And that is exactly what happened over the succeeding years.

A surprising example of 'papering over' exhibits the flexibility of the Japanese language. During the 1955 negotiations the Right Socialist Party, because of its interest in collective security, insisted that the Japan-US Security Treaty should be retained, pending the establishment of collective security under the auspices of the United Nations, or a four power treaty, inspired by the Locarno Treaty of 1925, which had been advocated as a possible way forward in Europe in a speech by Winston Churchill on 11 May 1953. The Locarno Treaty had involved a mutual guarantee of the frontiers of France and Belgium by Germany, Belgium, France, Great Britain and Italy.

The Left Socialist Party, on the other hand, argued that the Japan-US Security Treaty should simply be abolished. This rather fundamental difference of view was bridged by a linguistic sleight of hand. The first syllable of the word for 'revise' (*kaitei*) was combined with the first syllable of the word for 'abolish' (*haishi*) to make *kaihai*, whose translation into English would seem to be 'revise-abolish'. My electronic dictionary translates *kaihai* as 'revise and [or] abolish'. The widely used Kenkyusha dictionary translates it as 'alteration and abolition, reorganisation, or a change, as in reorganising a ministry'. Kōjien, the Prince of all Japanese-Japanese dictionaries, explains it as *aratameru koto to yameru koto to* (to revise and to put an end to). I think we may conclude that *kaihai* was just the right word, in its strategic imprecision, for the purposes of reconciling the otherwise unreconcilable. I do not suggest that this represents some specifically Japanese capability, since the English term 'strategic ambiguity' has come into our language and is quite widely used in the political and corporate worlds, often to good effect.

When we arrived in Japan early in 1962, the ANU had allowed me a year's fieldwork, but as the year approached its end it was clear both to me and to my supervisor that one year was not going to be enough to complete all that I needed to do in Japan. I applied for a three months' extension, which was granted, meaning that we did not return from Japan until May of 1963. David had himself arrived in Japan on sabbatical from the ANU late in 1962, so that we were able to discuss my work face to face. The extra three months enabled me to conduct many extra interviews, and arrive at a much more rounded understanding of my subject matter than if I had only been able to spend a year in Japan.

I remember a gathering during this final period of research in Tokyo, no doubt somewhere in its parliamentary district. I was talking with a small number of journalists and perhaps others about the current politics of the Socialist Party. I had recently interviewed a number of JSP politicians and was reasonably up to speed with very recent developments. And so I held forth on what I had learned. Much of the conversation up to that point had been between the journalists themselves. But after my intervention, one of the journalists looked at me and said, 'Ah, yoku wakaru na' (Ah, you really know what's happening, don't you"), and from then on I was fully part of the conversation. This no doubt gave me a nice warm feeling of being appreciated, but more importantly it confirmed the lesson I had much earlier learned in my discussions with Satō Noboru, that a researcher in Japan needs to earn respect and thus allowed to share information through competence and knowledge. Some

social anthropologists would no doubt argue that what I have just
described represented my move from 'out-group' to 'in-group' status in that particular group, but I think that it was much more than
that: it suggests you have to *earn* your entry into the 'in-group';
laggards are not easily tolerated.

Although I had had to work extremely hard during our fifteen
months in Tokyo, Audrey and I with our baby daughter Kate were
able to enjoy family life in a new and fascinating environment, living in a teeming and vibrant city, and making many new friends.
It seems that we were something of a phenomenon in the Japan
of those days, where foreigners were less often seen than they are
today. One Sunday we decided to follow the railway line that passed
fairly near our house, and travel by train as far as the city of Ōmiya,
a little over 100 km. to the north of Tokyo. From Ōmiya station
we proceeded to walk, with Kate in a sling on our backs, as far as
a Shinto shrine that we had identified in advance. I should note
here that Kate was (and is) a redhead, and attracted the attention of
local people as we left the station. As we walked towards the shrine,
we soon gathered a crowd of people following us along the street.
Women would come up to us and ask Audrey personal questions,
including whether she was breast feeding the baby, questions that
were direct, but expressed with Japanese politeness, and all entirely
in Japanese. On that day we experienced what Andy Warhol once
described as 'everybody's fifteen minutes of fame'.

In the 1960s, there were enough foreigners in Tokyo for their
presence to make little impact on passers-by, but that was hardly
the case in small towns outside the capital. Once, several years
later, I was walking along a shopping street in a provincial town (I
forget where). I was walking fast, and at an intersection I turned
sharp right and came suddenly into the sight of two teenage girls
approaching me in the opposite direction. On seeing me, instanta-
neously, and in unison, they screamed - AAAAARRRRGH – at this
hairy barbarian bearing down upon them.

While we were living in Tokyo, we made many friends, including young ladies who came as babysitters for Kate. Many of these
friends were from networks connected with the Institute of Social
Sciences (*Shaken*) at Tokyo University, where I had my base. Among
these was Reiko, daughter of a *Shaken* law professor, who later came
to stay with a family in Yorkshire, which found to their surprise that

she called their city 'Reeds'. Our families are still in touch, more than half a century later. And then there were three sisters who came to baby-sit, from a Roman Catholic family, unusual in Japan. Occasionally, I would prevail on one or other of them to translate short pieces I had written into Japanese. They had a brother who later ran a well-regarded institute in Tokyo for Japan-US understanding.

This takes me back to the time I was spending in the National Diet Library ('Diet' meaning 'Parliament'). While at the library, I had come to know a number of librarians who worked there, and I was asked to teach a class on English conversation, which I did on Saturday mornings. Since Audrey was also teaching English to various groups and individuals, we swopped notes on teaching technique, as neither of us was formally trained to be a language teacher. With the library class I came up against the difficulty many Japanese people have with distinguishing between 'R' and 'L'. In Japanese there is no letter 'L' since 'L' is assimilated to 'R'. Reiko pronounced 'Leeds' as 'Reeds'. So one day at the library I devised a way of teaching the class to distinguish between these two sounds, which to us appear quite different, but to Japanese appear to be the same. I told the class that I would say the words 'grass' and 'glass' in random order repeatedly for several minutes. 'When I say "grass" raise your left hand, and when I say "glass", raise your right hand'. I proceeded with my recitation of these two words, and at first their responses were essentially random. But after a few minutes the pattern began to change, and I saw mainly left hands going up in response to 'grass', and right hands being raised when I said 'glass'. I congratulated the class on successfully identifying the difference between the two, and inwardly congratulated myself on a successful language teaching outcome. And then one female member of the class said, 'yes, we were lip-reading'. I felt deflated.

I should add that the Japanese language also lacks the letter 'V', which is assimilated to 'B', and there are several other English sounds that do not exist in Japanese, including a number of consonant-vowel combinations. English 'si', for instance, becomes Japanese 'shi'. We pronounce 'love' as 'luv', but none of the sounds represented by those three letters exists in Japanese pronunciation. So if you want to write 'love' in katakana (the Japanese syllabic alphabet used mainly to transliterate foreign words) it comes out as 'ra-bu'. Just to conclude this brief diversion into Japanese linguistics, let me add that you cannot end a Japanese word with a consonant, except for 'n'. On this point, Japanese somewhat resembles Italian: 'Buon giorno, Signorina.' Nor does Japanese go in for consonant clusters in the middle of words.

As the year 1963 progressed, we knew that we would soon have to leave Japan and return to Australia. Our return was set for May of that year, and we would be bound for Sydney, this time from the port of Kōbe, in the Kansai region that includes Ōsaka and Kyōto. We would have spent fifteen months of intense activity for both of us, in a country whose culture was still not widely known in non-Asian countries, communicating so far as possible in a non-European language, as inexperienced parents of a small baby, as (in my case) a graduate student trying to research and write a doctoral thesis about a turbulent political party of opposition to the established government, in a country that was still recovering from a disastrous war and trying, with partial success, to transform its political system along democratic lines. Audrey, meanwhile, apart from coping with the tasks of a new mother, was making new friends, mainly Japanese, teaching English and making pottery at Bunka Gakuin, and exploring that overcrowded and fascinating city called Tokyo.

Tokyo in 1962-3 was already home to some ten million people, a majority of whom had flocked into the city from other parts of the country since 1945. Allied bombing during the war had left huge areas of the capital city devastated, and even though enormous numbers of new dwellings, office blocks and factories were being constructed or reconstructed, many of these were of poor architectural quality, vulnerable to earthquake damage and, as for dwellings, providing minimal living space. Many railway stations – particularly Ueno station north of the centre – were temporary home to migrants mainly from northern Japan, or elsewhere, seeking to make a living in Tokyo.

At the time there only two underground lines in Tokyo, the pre-war Ginza Line linking northern suburbs, through the up-market Ginza district, with suburbs to the south; and the post-war Marunouchi line, which wound round from the Ikebukuro hub in the north-west, clockwise through the Ginza area as far as Shinjuku in the west, the biggest of the regional hubs, and out further into the western suburbs. The extension beyond Shinjuku had only just been completed when we arrived in early 1962. By contrast, there are now twelve underground lines in Tokyo, with super-modern equipment, including gates on platforms that slide open in exact unison with the opening of the train doors. But the above ground Yamate (now Yamanote) line took, and still takes, millions of passengers every day in a circle round the city and through the various regional hubs (Ikebukuro, Ueno, Akihabara, Tokyo central station, Shimbashi, Shinagawa, Meguro, Shibuya and Shinjuku). In addition, you could travel on many other lines radiating out from the various hubs. There was also a network of elderly two storey electric trams (toden) running along major roads, but they have now been mostly superseded. While we were in Tokyo in the early 1960s, there was an army of mostly young men ready to clip your ticket as you entered a rail platform. When they were not clipping tickets they would invariably wave their clippers around to make monotonous and mono-tonal music. These bored young men have long since retreated before electronic devices.

When we were first there Tokyo was a low-rise city, with no high-rise buildings because of earthquake restrictions. Several years later these were relaxed as the result of new technology, so that many areas of the city have been converted to high rise – Shinjuku being the most spectacular of these. Tokyo is still a crowded city, but it cannot be compared with the extent of overcrowding, particularly on public transport, that we experienced when we were first there. I remember travelling on a bus in Tokyo, which was filled to perhaps three times its capacity, the many standing passengers so closely packed that it was difficult to breathe. But even in such conditions nearly everybody remained studiously polite. In my experience public transport is generally safe, though I have experienced problems with drunks late at night. Women, however, are much more likely to encounter problems than men, and this has become a big issue in the media.

I don't think that we knew much about Japanese food before we went to Japan for the first time, and I doubt if we had even heard of sushi, tempura, sukiyaki, shabu-shabu, yakitori, tōfu or soba before we started being interested in Japan. The world then was a far narrower culinary environment than it is today. Interestingly enough, Chinese and Indian cuisine was widely known outside Asia but not Japanese to anything like the same extent.

In May 1963, we made our final departure from Tokyo. We had a good deal of luggage to transport (including the manuscript collection of a Socialist politician I had bought on behalf of the National Library in Canberra from a second hand bookshop, so that we needed assistance in getting ourselves and our cases from Nishigahara to Tokyo Central Station. My supervisor David Sissons, who was by then on sabbatical leave in Tokyo, offered to assist us. We became worried, however, when at three quarters of an hour after our agreed time of departure, he still had not arrived. He did eventually turn up, but since frugality was sewn into his soul, he had travelled the journey from his place to ours on the 'toden' (tram), which stopped every few hundred metres. We did in the end manage to get to Tokyo Central Station with his help, presumably in a taxi (I forget).

We had left ourselves several days to explore Kyoto and Nara before our ship – the *Tenos*, of the Australia-West Pacific Line – set sail for Sydney. We were allowed to board the ship, secure a cabin, and then explore the hinterland of the Kansai, for the days before the ship sailed. We fell in love with the Shisendō (Immortal Poets' House) on the eastern side of Kyōto, with its maples and *shishiodoshi* – a kind of bamboo tube what slowly fills with water from a stream, and then when the tube is full, its balance changes and it moves on its pivot, discharging the water, creating a loud noise as it falls against a rock, designed to scare off deer and other animals. The Shisendo, as its name implies, is conducive to quiet contemplation, in poetic mode, of such a beautiful place.

The port of Kōbe in those days was busier than any port we had ever seen. When a serious earthquake hit the town thirty-one years later, the port was badly damaged, and it lost much of its trade, perhaps permanently. Once again, the *Tenos* was a cargo ship carrying a small number of passengers, who seemed to have emerged from the pages of a novel by Somerset Maugham. One was an imperious lady who was the wife of the director of the Japan branch of a major oil company. She was travelling to Australia to wind up an estate. She took pains to denounce the satirical TV programme 'That was the Week that was', running in the UK and elsewhere at the time, which established the name of David Frost and others. We had not seen it but my parents had written saying they had enjoyed it, and I did not hesitate to convey that opinion to her. There was another woman on the ship, an Australian who looked down at heel and manifestly belonged to a class inferior to that of the oil company director's wife. The latter did not hesitate to inform the other woman that she knew her son, 'who is involved in various rackets in Japan as I am sure you know'. A journalist called Bob Blazey, after I told him about my research in Japan, attempted to recruit me into the Australian security services. I declined.

On this voyage, Kate was now sixteen months old, and understood at least one word of Japanese: *abunai* (dangerous, i.e. don't!). Since she was now a toddler, she was restrained by a tether that we either held or tied to some immovable object when we were on deck.

Soon, we were back in Canberra, and the ANU.

10

Back to Australia

ㅅ

A STRANGE ASPECT aspect of life back in Canberra was that for a while at least, we found ourselves looking at Australia almost through Japanese eyes. It seems that his is not an isolated phenomenon. A journalist (later Japanese university president) Gregory Clark, who had spent several years reporting from Tokyo, returned to Australia and wrote a piece in *The Australian* describing entering a bank in Sydney on his return. There he witnessed a customer who was carrying a cat chatting about the cat with the bank clerk who was cashing her cheque for him. He reacted to this with astonishment, realising that such a scene could never take place in Japan, where formality in a client-customer relationship would almost always prevail.

Curiously, I had a not dissimilar experience many years later, after flying from Japan to the UK. I had been in Japan for several months, and this was a two-day visit to Oxford, then quickly back to Tokyo. I had written several letters, and had them in Japanese envelopes, which in those days lacked the means to close them securely. I went to the main Oxford Post Office, and asked whether they had any gum with which to secure the envelopes. The clerk behind the counter replied in a plummy but deadpan voice, 'Unfortunately not.' It may seem strange to a British reader, but that reply seemed to me extraordinarily rude, and was unimaginable to me in a Japanese context.

Our reactions on returning to Canberra after fifteen months in Japan probably involved several components: we were going from late spring straight into late autumn. We were moving from a teeming, exciting Japanese city into Australia's 'bush capital'. We were exchanging a traditional Japanese house in a back street for an unattractive university flat facing onto a main road. But over the period we had stayed in Japan, and being young and adventurous perhaps, something of the ethos of Japan had seeped into us, and we missed it.

But the phase passed fairly quickly, as we both had a great deal to do right from the start of our return. In my case, I was indebted to my supervisor for coercing me into drafting a substantial monthly paper or (in later months) a draft chapter. Yes, I hated it at the time, but it meant that by the time I was back in Canberra I had drafts of what was probably a majority of the twelve chapters I needed to write. I had brought a great deal of material back with me and had at my disposal the Japanese language resources of the National Library. But I was expected to submit the thesis during the next year, 1964, I think by a date in October.

Meanwhile, Audrey was re-connecting with her Canberra friends, getting back to her pottery as much as was feasible at the time, and looking after Kate. And also we were expecting our second child. Jane was born on 26 January 1964, Australia Day.

I was becoming concerned about finding a university position once I had finished my thesis. I applied for a lectureship in the just established Centre of Japanese Studies at the University of Sheffield, and also for a position in international relations at the London School of Economics. In neither of these applications was I successful. But in the later months of 1963 the ANU advertised a lectureship in the Department of Political Science within what was then called the 'School of General Studies' (later 'The Faculties'). I applied and was interviewed by the Head of Department, Professor Leslie Finlay Crisp (known to all as 'Fin Crisp'). I had met him before, and indeed Audrey had been among his assistants when he was organising an international conference back in 1960. But it was immediately evident to me from the interview that Fin was a pretty tough character, ready to fight his corner with exemplary vigour. He knew that at about the same time I had applied to the LSE, but by the time of the interview I had not heard the result. He told me that he was not happy with the fact that I had applied to the LSE while also applying for the position in his department. I replied that I had done so because I needed a fall-back position should I be unsuccessful in my ANU application. The upshot was that I was offered the position and accepted it. I believe that my main competition was Colin Tatz, a South African anti-apartheid campaigner who was now directing his attention to Australian government policy towards the Aborigines. We knew each other quite well as we were now living in a university flat nearer to the university than before, where Colin and his family were our neighbours. He graciously congratulated me on the result.

Landing my first academic job, and landing it at a university that I knew well, was a matter for rejoicing. Our financial situation would now be secure, though we would hardly be affluent, and I would not have to worry about job hunting while finishing my thesis. We had one lively daughter and another soon to be born. We now had a degree of stability for our family, and could plan for the future on the basis of settled variables.

There was, however, one problem that seriously exercised us. This was the reaction of our parents back in England, whom we had led to believe that we were going to be away for about three years and then return to the UK. My mother in particular was shocked to learn that I would be on the academic staff of the ANU and potentially might not be coming back at all. I was an only child and my parents would be retiring before many years were out. Audrey's parents were younger, and if they were upset they did not put it in writing. My parents, however, were planning their 'trip of a life-time' and would arrive for a few weeks with us in October. In those days international travel was more exotic, less convenient and less 'normal' than it has now become, so that many people of the older generation found themselves bereft if their children went off to the ends of the earth. So in retrospect it was fortunate that my parents could come and experience the environment in which we lived, and make the acquaintance of their first granddaughter. At any rate their visit went off reasonably well. While in Canberra they went on a tour of the Snowy Mountains hydroelectric scheme, and on their way home through the United States they were entertained by friends in San Francisco and New York. Writing now from the perspective of mature years, I think that we did not fully appreciate the problems that confront people approaching old age, but even had we been more understanding, I could hardly have turned down at that juncture the offer of a job that would launch me into an academic career.

My first serious job began early in 1964, but I still had my thesis to finish, at the same time preparing lectures, some of which would be on subjects with which I was not wholly familiar and would require a fair amount of reading and thinking. Happily, I was given a reprieve from teaching for the first term of the new academic year. But when that period was up, I had a double load, and since I was still writing my thesis and had a great deal to learn about teaching, I was under a good deal of stress. At the end of one lecture I gave, a student came up to me, and in that refreshingly unadorned and egalitarian Australian style he said to me simply, 'You look done!' But at least the thesis was going fairly smoothly, and I just managed to finish by the deadline.

In those days there were no laptops, and it was normal for a graduate student to pay a typist to type a fair copy of the thesis. Since multiple copies would be required, it was necessary then to use a Gestetner machine, on which you had to fix waxed sheets, one per page of the thesis, which you put through the machine one by one to create copies. This was a long and tedious process, made even more difficult in my case because I found that the waxed sheets I had bought had the wrong pattern of holes at the top of each sheet with which to fasten them securely to the roller. I therefore had to procure a special tool to reconfigure the holes. On the night before I had to take the thesis to be bound, Audrey and I spent the evening and well into the night at the Politics Department producing the required number of copies. Audrey returned home in the car at about one o'clock in the morning (we must have made babysitting arrangements), I stayed to finish the job until about four in the morning, and then rang for a taxi. Since there was practically no traffic at that time of night, the taxi driver drove through the town as though on a motor racing circuit, and once home I had two or three hours sleep. After breakfast I told Kate I had finished my thesis and danced with her all around the living room.

The ANU at that time had many undergraduates who were taking part-time degrees. Nearly all of these belonged to the public service, as Canberra was the centre of national government. Being part of government, they were naturally interested in politics, and a fair number of them chose to take courses in the Department of Political Science, in which I was now a lecturer. As many as half our students were part-timers. Some of them were not only part-timers but also time-servers. Since a university degree would help with promotion in the public service and they were given an amount of time off to attend the courses, they would enrol, do just enough work to pass, but contribute little to tutorial discussion. But there was another category of part-timers, who were both ambitious and intellectually aware, so that they put a great deal of effort into their courses and enlivened the atmosphere in tutorials. Such students, generally older and more mature than students straight out of school, were able to draw on their own experience of working within government, and were a useful resource for lecturers to have in tutorials.

The structure of an undergraduate degree in the Arts Faculty was a combination of 'majors' and 'sub-majors'. A major consisted of three 'units' (roughly equivalent to a 'module' in British academic-speak), and a minor, consisting of two. A unit was a specific course leading to an examination at the end of it (though much later, and controversially, coursework became part of the overall assessment). A student in the Faculty of Arts was also allowed to take a certain number of units in other faculties, for instance the Faculty of Economics. An extraordinarily complex set of regulations existed concerning what combination of units constituted a major, what a sub-major, and what combination of majors and sub-majors were permissible. I remember one mature age student, determined to create the broadest set of intellectual experiences he could engineer for himself, who spent hours and hours of his time and that of the faculty administrators arguing for greater flexibility in the administration of the rules about what courses could be taken together. He would have been better advised to do more work on the courses themselves.

A further level of complexity was added by the distinction made between a pass degree and an honours degree. A pass degree, which was what most students opted for, was taken over three years, whereas an honours degree required four years. In order to qualify for entry to the fourth year, a student in his or her earlier years (second and third, I think), had to take a number of units 'at honours level'. This required extra reading, and a higher pass level was required to pass the unit.

Teaching was conducted through lectures and tutorials. Lectures were supposed to last between fifty and fifty-five minutes, and typically a lecturer gave two lectures per week for students taking the same unit. The academic year (early March to late November) was divided into three terms of unequal length (the third was much shorter than the other two), and a major would last over the whole academic year. (Many years later, semesters replaced terms, after a chaotic period in which the university attempted to allow some faculties, principally in the natural sciences, to teach in semesters, and others, mainly arts and social sciences, to teach in terms.)

A 'tutorial' needs to be defined. In the Oxford system an undergraduate tutorial is a discussion between a lecturer and no more than two students. It is supposed to encourage intense exchange of information and ideas between academic staff and students, and is a selling point for the university, but of course it is very labour-intensive. At ANU (and other Australian universities), the average number of students in a tutorial was between ten and fifteen (occasionally more). At the beginning of each term (later semester) each lecturer would receive a computer print-out listing the names of students who had enrolled in the relevant unit. Unfortunately, students were allowed a period of grace (two weeks?) in which they could change courses. This meant that one's course was well under way before it was clear which students were actually taking it. Moreover, unlike Oxford, attendance at tutorials was not compulsory. Often, students would appear at the first couple of tutorials and then disappear, although they would have to turn up to hand in written work. Tutorials, therefore, were a curiously fluid environment in which to teach, although a perversely useful spin-off from all this was that the students who remained were generally well motivated and did some work.

In my early years of teaching I provided the Japan section of a major on 'Asian politics'. Within the same course my colleagues David Corbett and Ian Wilson taught the politics of India and China respectively. A few years later, after David left to take a post elsewhere, India was taught by Thelma Hunter. In order to give the course theoretical coherence, we used the then fashionable and influential work of the American scholars Gabriel Almond and James S. Coleman, *The Politics of the Developing Areas* (Princeton University Press, 1960). We had to learn, and teach to our students, a whole new vocabulary for understanding politics (particularly politics in non-Western political systems), that substituted 'political articulation' for interest group activity, 'political aggregation' for bringing together different political views together in political parties, 'rule making' for legislation, 'rule implementation' for the activities of the executive, and 'rule adjudication' for the activities of the judiciary. This vocabulary shift went back to the (seriously indigestible) sociologist Talcott Parsons, and ultimately to the great Max Weber. It was linked with systems theory, also fashionable at the time, which sought to bring order to the understanding of political (and other) social phenomena by analysing such phenomena in terms of self-regulating systems. Systems theory later came under widespread criticism for its alleged conservatism, in playing down the possibility of system-change, or even system-destruction. Critics argued that politics in many 'developing areas' exhibited radically different, and more fluid, characteristics than systems theory allowed for.

However that may be, the work of Almond and others dominated studies of non-Western political systems until the late 1960s, when it began to be challenged by elements in what came to be called the 'New Left'. In relation to Japan, Princeton University Press published a whole series of books on the development (including political development) of Japan from the opening of the country that began in the 1850s.

One nagging problem with this course, was that politics in the three countries could hardly have been more different, and that made comparison problematic. China from 1949 was ruled by the Chinese Communist Party, and became a Marxist (or Marxist-Leninist-Maoist) state. India was a post-colonial state, created in an act of decolonisation from Great Britain that in a bloodbath split the sub-continent into grudgingly co-existing parts. India under Nehru developed a political system on a democratic model, with the lengthiest constitution in the world, with the Indian population divided along extremely complex religious, linguistic, class and caste lines. By contrast, Japan harboured a relatively homogeneous population (though the extent of homogeneity has sometimes been exaggerated), and under American guidance, or some would say coercion, introduced a brief and rather general democratic constitution, essentially on the British model, which also included a clause (Article 9) that formally outlawed military potential.

A few years later we decided to change the course format, allowing students to choose two out of the three countries to study. This had a dramatic and to us unexpected effect: Numbers choosing to study Indian politics fell precipitately, whereas the numbers wanting to study China and those wanting to study Japan were about the same. We asked students why they had abandoned India, and one student answered as follows, 'We feel that the politics of India has very little to teach us.' The student who gave this answer became famous in Australia late in 1975 as the Governor-General's official secretary announcing Sir John Kerr's dismissal of the Whitlam Labor (sic.) Government on 11 November. His name was David Smith (by 1975 Sir David Smith) and a photograph of him announcing the dismissal with Gough Whitlam looking over his shoulder 'went viral', as we would now say, throughout Australia.

I look back with some nostalgia to teaching 'Asian politics', from which I learned much, not only about Asia outside Japan, but also about the challenges of applying political science analysis to countries outside a fairly narrow range, largely in Europe, the legatees of European empire, Australasia and the United States of America. In later years I occasionally met older generation political scientists who were uncomfortable about studying the politics of countries such as Malaysia, because their politics 'is not sophisticated', or variants on that theme, reflecting a residual colonial outlook. But there is politics almost everywhere, even in small groups, reflecting human behaviour where there are competing opinions on policy or divisions over power. None of this should be exempt from reasoned scrutiny, linked to the discipline of political science.

Returning to my early introduction to teaching, nearly all our interactions with students were conducted in what were known as the Childers Street Buildings. These were single storey wooden buildings, built during the war, with classrooms and offices off long corridors, inadequately heated by electric bar heaters in winter and stiflingly hot in the height of summer. There was one largish lecture theatre, much in demand for teaching. How these buildings had never caught fire and burned down was a mystery. Our Head of Department, Professor Fin Crisp, was curiously attached to these buildings, where he had founded the Department of Political Science around 1950, and reluctant to leave them when more permanent accommodation became available. He was also fiercely opposed to the amalgamation of the former Canberra University College with the ANU in 1960, not long after we arrived in Canberra. I think this was because he feared teaching, which he revered, would play second fiddle to research.

I soon found that members of a discipline department cannot expect to teach exclusively about the politics of a country with which they are most familiar. And so it was with me. Some of my earliest teaching was on British politics. Because there were so many part time students working throughout the day, my Department put on classes in the evenings, with classes starting at 7.00 p.m. and 8.00 p.m. It was to those groups that I taught British politics to first year students, some five years after I had graduated in Philosophy, Politics and Economics from Oxford. Australian students of that era had little familiarity with even the names of most British politicians, so I had to start the course from a rather elementary level. They were much more familiar with their own politics, although almost entirely from media sources and discussions with family and friends. I remember setting an essay on the role of the monarch in British politics of the time, and found that some of them attributed to Queen Elizabeth II a great deal more power than she could exercise, either constitutionally or in practice.

The ANU was, in the 1960s, a fairly small university by Australian standards. But it differed from the rest in two respects. The first was that it enjoyed special government funding, to finance the research arm of the university, known as the Institute of Advanced Studies. The other was that it was in the city that also housed the federal government, and was physically close to the politicians and public servants, many of whom were doing part-time degrees in its classrooms.

As the 1960s drew on, a new factor entered into Australian and world politics, namely the Vietnam War. This was felt acutely in Australian universities, and most especially, among their student populations. When, in 1964, Sir Paul Hasluck as External Affairs Minister announced that Australia would contribute troops to support the American anti-Communist campaign in Vietnam, the question arose how these troops should be recruited. This was resolved by the re-introduction of conscription for twenty-year olds. This did not mean that all those men aged twenty would be conscripted. The required number of men were to be conscripted by lot. Some 365 marbles were placed in a container, each with a birth date inscribed upon it, and those whose birth dates were removed from the container were conscripted into the armed forces, earmarked for service in Vietnam.

Later in the decade, university protest erupted in a number of countries, including France and the United States. Opposition to national involvement in the Vietnam War was the key trigger for these student campaigns, though domestic politics as well as university politics also played their part. In Australian universities what was widely perceived as the unfairness of a randomly selected system of conscription sharpened the determination of the protesters. I myself witnessed the importance of this issue in stimulating often highly disruptive activities on campus. How to deal with student protest seriously divided the university, with some academic staff and members of the administration taking a conciliatory line and other favouring confrontation. Fin Crisp, an old Labor man, strongly favoured the latter approach, and protested vehemently against attitudes in parts of the university that dialogue with radical students should be pursued. This came to a head when the composition of faculty meetings was changed to allow student representation on faculty. Fin strongly opposed this, maintaining that informal communication with students was sufficient. As it turned out, at least in the arts faculty meetings, some student representatives were positive and helpful additions to our discussions.

The situation, which by 1969 had become very tense, also had serious repercussions within the Department of Political Science. A number of us regarded Fin, who had been seen as a left of centre radical some fifteen years earlier, as increasingly authoritarian and difficult to communicate with. He had appointed to the department a journalist friend of his of strongly right wing views, and it appeared to us that he was communicating with him and not with us. We were unhappy that Fin seemed to be introducing the politics of the Australian Labor Party branch in Canberra into the politics of the department. These events occurred a long time ago, but I now regret – to some considerable extent – my own part in what happened subsequently. A few of my colleagues and I formed a group that came to be known as 'The Six'. We were a motley crew, ranging from the right to the far left in our political beliefs. On the right was Kathy West, who was conducting research on the ruling Liberal Party. I was there, a centrist with left of centre leanings perhaps, working on the politics of Japan, so was Frank Castles, a specialist on welfare systems, Ian Wilson, writing on Chinese politics, Robert Cooksey on aspects of foreign policy and international relations, and Bruce MacFarlane who wrote largely on Australian politics from a Marxist perspective. Of these Kathy was on the right, Frank and I were broadly centrist, Ian, Robert and Bruce could be identified as more or less left wing, while Bruce was the most extreme left winger.

At a departmental meeting we confronted Fin, and proposed a fairly radical reform to the first year politics major, so that it would no longer start with British politics, go on to the politics of Australia as a kind of British outpost, and rely heavily on the textbooks of Jennings, which we regarded as outdated. By pre-arrangement, I took the leading role in this meeting. Fin was clearly shocked at being challenged in this manner, especially by me, whom I think he had regarded as his protégé, and countered it as best he could.

Some days later, he summoned the department to a meeting, to our complete surprise bringing him with us the Vice-Chancellor, Sir John Crawford, a distinguished economist and former public servant having strong links with Japan. We had not been informed in advance of this meeting's nature and purpose, nor that the Vice-Chancellor would be present, but Jack Grainger, an Englishman who was by far the most conservative member of the department and not previously a confidant of Fin, had been briefed in advance and used the meeting to make a well prepared and blistering attack on student radicals and those in the university who in any way supported them. We, for our part, did our best to advocate once again our proposals for curriculum reform. No doubt a number of other issues were aired as well. By this time these issues were being reported and discussed in the local newspaper, the *Canberra Times*.

And then came the bombshell. Fin rejected our proposals with the following words, 'I cannot commit my successor.' We were nonplussed, as we had never imagined that he was planning to step down from the headship of the department he had founded years back, or to retire. We later learned that the reason was medical: he was suffering from a heart condition that we had not known about. He duly stepped down though he retained an office in the department, an arrangement that I protected when I was acting head for a period several years later. We surmised that perhaps his recent behaviour might have something to do with his heart condition. Sometime afterwards, his successor was appointed, namely Professor Gordon Reid, a specialist on parliaments, especially the Australian federal parliament.

Gordon was a very different personality from Fin, essentially low key, lacking evident political preferences and easy to get on with. Curriculum reform took place under his guidance. Several years later he was appointed Governor of the State of Western Australia.

My regret at this episode is compounded by the fact that Fin had been very kind to me after appointing me to my first academic job, and I used to ask him for advice on things I had not previously done, like lecturing techniques and writing references for students. He was also, as I knew, a pioneer in the serious study of Australian politics from the 1950s. But he had become seriously authoritarian as the unannounced meeting with the Vice-Chancellor indicated.

Fin and I never did make up our differences, even after I came back off leave in the 1970s, when I rather hoped that an opportunity to do so might present itself. But I never took the initiative myself, and nor did he. In the early 1980s, after we had left the ANU for Oxford, Fin died suddenly of a heart attack. When I wrote a condolence note to his widow, Helen, I included the statement, 'Both of us were too proud to apologise'. And I am sad that that was the case.

Meanwhile, our family had increased in number. Rupert was born on 1 October 1966 and Timothy on 23 December 1968. Before we were married we had decided that we would aim to have four children, and now we had fulfilled that promise. We had had no need to argue about it, since we were both at one in wanting a family that would add variety to our lives. I had been an only child, while Audrey was one of two, having a younger sister, Julia. By good fortune, we had two daughters followed by two sons. The 'swinging sixties' were our child-producing sixties. And then, in August 1968, we moved into a house that we had bought with the help of a university mortgage with fixed interest rates. It was a very basic single storey house in a brand new suburb that was part of the newly developing Canberra region of Belconnen. But it gave us the prospect of extending it in the future.

A little before that, in the second half of 1967 and into 1968, I was able to go on sabbatical with the family to the University of Sussex, but living in the nearby town of Lewes. In Brighton I interacted with Indian and African specialists, and was able to develop my interest in political factions by making comparisons particularly with factions in India. This was our first time back in Britain for over seven years, and the first time for our children. Our country of birth had changed in various ways, and so had we. Our parents had aged. Not long after we returned to Canberra, my first book was published, based on my doctoral thesis (*The Japanese Socialist Party and Neutralism*, Melbourne University Press, 1968).

In 1970, Audrey bought her first gas-fired pottery kiln, and now had a workshop as well. She had been developing her pottery skills and with these new facilities she was able to make much faster progress. And the children were growing up as well. Sometime later she built her own kiln, which worked magnificently, out of fire bricks. In the run-up to Christmas every year, she held a pottery exhibition and sale in our garden, recruiting the older children and their school friends as sales assistants. The weather was warm and nearly always dry. It provided a useful addition to our income. Audrey also organised musical education for our children. She recognised early that Kate had exceptional musical potential, and encouraged her to learn the clarinet, making sure she practised. Kate went on to have a career as a professional clarinettist. Jane learned to play the violin to a more than respectable level, while later on Rupert played the trumpet and Tim the drums. In 1970, Kate and Jane went on a tour with the Canberra Youth Orchestra to a Youth Orchestra festival in Aberdeen, Scotland, performing also at various places elsewhere in the UK and in continental Europe. This was preceded by a major fund-raising campaign in Canberra, in which the parents of most of the musicians participated actively.

Before we were married, we speculated about our future as a married couple, not being too serious about it, but trying in very general terms to imagine how it might be. By that time we knew we were going to Australia, which created many unknown variables for us. We gave ourselves a notional fifty years, meaning that since we were marrying in our mid-twenties, after fifty years we would be in our mid-seventies. I suppose that that was a statistically likely assessment given life expectancy in 1960. Perhaps it may seem strange that we should have thought in such terms, but we also lightly touched on the point that over a period of half a century the law of averages made it seem not unlikely that we might face unexpected crises or even disasters. We were right.

The problem with disasters is that you can prepare yourself mentally for a possible disaster, but you will have no idea what shape such a disaster might take. In any case, it was not something that greatly bothered us, since over ten years of marriage life had been kind to us.

In November 1970, Audrey's sister Julia was visiting us from the UK during a period of leave from the civil service, where she was rising in her profession. We took her for a few days to Broulee on the south coast of New South Wales, where we rented a beautiful holiday home belonging to one of my colleagues at ANU. On the last day of our stay, Julia and I went for a final swim off the beach. We walked out along a spit of sand where water came up barely to our knees. The spit then extended along to the south, continuing parallel to the beach. The distance between the spit and the beach was from memory not much more than 100 yards. Unwisely, I suggested we should take a short cut and swim through deeper water to the shore. Unfortunately, we were caught in a ferocious rip, which was pushing us backwards and under water. It was something I had never previously experienced. I can remember going onto autopilot, swimming free style as hard as my arms could flail the water, while hardly understanding what I was doing. Julia was a breast stroke swimmer, but that was insufficient for the conditions. I survived but she did not. There was no way I could have saved her and there was nobody else on the beach.

This was a huge family tragedy, we had to call the police, telephone Audrey's parents and deal with all the aftermath of a death. Audrey returned to England to be with her parents for a while. I was left with a huge legacy of guilt. For a while it put our marriage under strain, but with some hard work we came through that.

The Australian political scene was livening up in the early 1970s. A conservative coalition between the Liberal Party and the Country (later National) Party had been continuously in power for 23 years, since 1949. For much of that time the government was led by the formidable Robert (later Sir Robert) Menzies, a devoted Anglophile and traditionalist, who stepped down as Prime Minister in 1966. His immediate successors, Harold Holt (who disappeared while swimming in Port Philip Bay near Melbourne), John Gorton and William McMahon, presided over a fractious and unimpressive government, so that when the time came for general elections in December 1972, the prospects for a change of government seemed good.

The ALP (Australian Labor Party), with its strong trade union base, had found it difficult to break through into government over the same period, especially after a split in its ranks in the late 1950s over allegations that the then ALP leaders were 'soft on Communism'. A breakaway group, with strong backing from the Roman Catholic Church, formed the DLP (Democratic Labor Party), and were able to make use of the preferential system of voting (in the UK called 'the alternative vote') to ensure in many constituencies that ALP candidates were not elected. This was done by instructing its supporters to place ALP candidates last on the ballot paper, where the voter had to rank candidates in numerical order of preference. This hurt the chances of the ALP, even though the DLP was never able to elect a single candidate to the House of Representatives (In the Senate, elected by proportional representation, the DLP was able to win seats).

The ALP, meanwhile, was going through a period of radical renewal, under the able leadership of Gough Whitlam, who had trained as a lawyer. Much of the traditional baggage of the party was cast aside, and it was able to fight the December 1972 elections for the lower house on the basis of a widely attractive set of policies. The party campaigned under the slogan: 'IT'S TIME'. For the first time in twenty-three years conservatives were no longer in power, and Whitlam became Prime Minister in a single-party ALP government.

Among the policies of the new government was a phasing out of the notorious 'White Australia policy', which had excluded almost all non-white immigration since Australian federation in 1901. Policies based on White Australia had been slightly loosened already by the conservative governments of the 1960s, but Whitlam was far more radical. In the years that have followed, Australia has changed from a country made up almost exclusively of people originating from the United Kingdom, Ireland, continental European and other predominantly white nations, to the vibrantly multicultural and multi-ethnic nation it is today.

The Whitlam Government faced a number of difficult problems along the way. One was inexperience. No minister in his cabinet had ever occupied a government position before, and some of them were not up to the job. There were ideological differences within the government. Whitlam was probably trying to do too much too quickly, and did not pay enough attention to the economic consequences of overspending, thus fuelling inflation. It seems likely that he was deliberately moving with speed because he feared electoral defeat and was concerned to put into legislation as much of his programme as possible. If so, he was a realist, because his government lacked a majority in the Senate. He was forced into another general election a mere eighteen months after having been elected in 1972, but he won that with a slightly reduced majority.

This, however, was not the end of his problems. In 1975 the Senate, where he lacked a majority, denied supply to his government. That meant, in effect, that he was going to run out of money to pay the public service and to conduct other government activities. He resorted to unorthodox methods to raise alternative funds. But that ultimately compounded the problem, and in a situation which by November had developed into a major crisis, the Governor-General, Sir John Kerr, who as a fellow lawyer had been appointed by Whitlam himself, acted unilaterally to dismiss the Whitlam Government on 11 November 1975. A general election was called, and the Liberal/National coalition returned to power under Malcolm Fraser as Prime Minister. A controversy still remains about how far the Governor General had been able to discuss the dismissal with the Queen, and what advice he was given. Relevant documents still remain to be released.

11

The 1970s: A Surprising Decade

⋏

BY THE 1970s we were well settled in Canberra. The children were at school and enjoying multifarious activities, including sport and music. The schools they went to were within walking distance of where we lived. I often cycled to the university, using a recently constructed network of cycle paths, many of which went through bushland. Occasionally, I would walk to work across the native bushland of the shoulder of Black Mountain. It took me about an hour, and I would encounter kangaroos, wallabies and the occasional echidna – a kind of inflated hedgehog.

Since our family was growing up, we needed more space, and decided that we should build an extra room at the back. Like most Canberra homes, ours was single storey, but we had enough land to extend horizontally. Audrey, with my encouragement, proposed to direct the project herself. Kate can describe what happened next much better than I can, so I will reproduce her account:

> In the mid-1970s Audrey became the first woman in Canberra to be granted the coveted Permit to Build. She delighted in entertaining us all with the response to her interview for the application, which was 'Well... you'd better send ya husband in to see us love'. Her response to that was: 'My husband is an academic and wouldn't know one end of a hammer from the other'. She then successfully subcontracted all the workmen for our first house extension – a rumpus room at the back, with trademark 1970s burnt orange ceiling interlaced with dark timber beams.

I can add the following to Kate's account. The building official who interviewed her was a Mr Huckstep. Audrey believed that what

160

clinched the agreement was her answer to Mr Huckstep's question, 'What can you tell me about soffitting?'

Between July 1973 and June 1974 I was granted a year's sabbatical from the ANU. We spent the first half at the University of Oxford and the second half attached once again to *Shaken*, the Institute of Social Science at Tokyo University. In Oxford I had a visiting position at St Antony's College, more specifically at its Far East Centre under Richard Storry, a historian of Japan, whose *History of Modern Japan* (Penguin, 1960, and later revised editions) was a widely used textbook. From 1937, Dick Storry had taught at the Otaru Commercial School (which after the war became Otaru University) in Hokkaidō, where he was able to observe at first hand Japan's slide towards a catastrophic war. During the war itself, he fought in various theatres of the Asia-Pacific War, and in one or two instances discovered that some of his former pupils from Otaru were on the other side of the line. And then during the American occupation of Japan after the war was over, Dick became one of the very first graduate students at the ANU in Canberra, though he spent the bulk of his period of attachment to the ANU conducting research in Japan. There he studied factionalism in the Japanese armed forces during the 1930s. This was to culminate in his book *The Double Patriots* (Chatto and Windus, 1957), about factional conflict in the Japanese armed forces during the 1930s. This was a book that I myself read as part of an International Relations paper at Oxford as an undergraduate in the late 1950s. It was a pioneering work in the field.

While I was in Oxford in the second half of 1973 I began work on a project to write a textbook of Japanese politics. This had been commissioned as part of a series describing the political systems of various countries, under the direction of Professor Max Beloff, Gladstone Professor of Government and Public Administration at Oxford. He was a prominent Conservative, who not long after I met him in Oxford became Vice-Chancellor of the University of Buckingham, an initiative designed to introduce private enterprise into the management of universities. An important part of my brief was that I should give as much information as possible about how Japanese politics actually worked in practice, rather than bring in too much political science theory. I was not a Conservative, but the brief suited me well, because I was of an empirical rather than theoretical bent (though recognising the value of theory in certain areas of investigation). Moreover, I had been further influenced towards such attitudes by my super-empiricist thesis supervisor, David Sissons.

At this stage in my career I was an inexperienced author, and writing what was to be a textbook was a new challenge. I had examined the existing range of textbooks, by that time mostly rather dated, and devised a structure that was not particularly original, combining political history and background with chapters on specific parts of the system, and towards the end of the book on key political issues. But I was also attempting to write from a different standpoint from that of previous textbooks that were mostly written by American authors.

I agonised for a long time in trying to find a suitable title. In the end I came up with *Japan: Divided Politics in a Growth Economy*. The title puzzled some reviewers, as well as a few of my students. At the time a curious orthodoxy had developed, to the effect that Japan was a 'consensus society', and that its politics reflected social norms in the sense that the approximated a well-oiled machine. A widely used phrase – much loved by non-Japanese journalists, but also used by some academics at the time, was 'Japan Incorporated', or more snappily 'Japan Inc.' My research on the Japan Socialist Party had shown me a very different reality, one of endemic conflict. When I broadened my interests to focus on the ruling Liberal Democratic Party, I also found a highly factionalised party, closely linked with a bureaucracy suffering from severe sectional tendencies, and this did not seem to fit easily into patterns of naturally occurring consensus. Rather, as I have argued elsewhere, consensus was a combination of devices needed to put order and stability into a system that was often riven by personal and institutional conflict. The atmosphere of the time (so different from today) was also one of widespread political activism and confrontation with authority. I realised, however, that this created a complex mixture. As I wrote in the book's Introduction:

> The juxtaposition of conflict and consensus, tension and stability, is probably the aspect of Japanese politics and government that is least easy to understand from the outside (p. 4).

In the book's brief final chapter, titled 'Conclusions and Dilemmas', I wrote:

...on some basic issues of politics there has been so little agreement or meeting of minds between the main political participants of right and left as to negate what are usually taken as the requirements for pluralist democracy.

I went on to elaborate on the dilemmas that the society and political system was facing in the mid-1970s, but followed this by a surprisingly up-beat assessment of Japan's prospects. I stressed the modernity of contemporary Japan, its

...sophisticated range of social, economic and political institutions, a highly developed structure of authority, a competent and experienced economic bureaucracy, near total literacy and the habit of attaching enormous importance to education, a meritocratic selection process for positions of responsibility in government and elsewhere, and an urban population that was increasingly articulate on political matters.

Finally, I introduced a theme that would also run in later editions, namely the need for a realistic possibility of alternative government. I was becoming increasingly uneasy with single party dominance. As I put it rather tentatively in the final sentence of the book:

Future governments will have to be particularly responsive to the demands and sensitivities of a broad-based and predominantly urban electorate if the health of Japanese politics is to be maintained.

The book went into four editions, each one involving quite radical revision and updating. The first edition was published in 1975, the second in 1982, the third in 1999 and the fourth in 2008. The first edition was translated into Bahasa Indonesia and the second into Japanese. Between the second and third editions the publisher changed from Weidenfeld to Blackwell. The title remained the same between the first and second editions, but with the third and fourth editions the main title became *Governing Japan*, though in both editions a subtitle remained, in the third *Divided Politics in a Major Economy*, and in the fourth *Divided Politics in a Resurgent Economy*. Whether 'resurgent' was appropriate in 2008 is a matter for debate.

Over the life of my textbook (and it might just possibly have still more life ahead of it), enormous changes had taken place in Japan, most notably demographic decline, periods of economic stagnation and the rise of political nationalism under the intelligent but authoritarian government of Abe Shinzō. Japan though has still the third largest economy in the world. The world also has enormously changed.

But I need to return to the 1970s. We spent the second half of my sabbatical in Japan, from January to June 1974. Our friend Sugai-san had found a house for us at Hayama, on the coast of the Miura Peninsula south of Tokyo. It was a traditional Japanese house, with Shōji paper screens and a sizable garden, walking distance from the Emperor's summer holiday residence, known as the Goyōtei. The owner was an elderly lady called Asano-san, who spoke no English, and lived in Tokyo while we were in her house. Our three older children went to a school in the beautiful town of Kamakura, further up the coast, called *Seisen shōgakkō* (Sacred Spring Primary School), run by a Catholic order of nuns. They travelled there together, without supervision, first on a bus, then on a train for one stop, and finally on a train that took them to the school. The language of instruction was Japanese, so they had a hard time at first, but they picked up some of the language, and made good friends. Since the girls had red hair, they found it difficult to blend in, but later remembered the experience of Japanese school with some nostalgia. Tim went to a kindergarten in Hayama, where his white hair made him the 'white sheep of the family'. Audrey pursued her pottery interest, taking lessons with a potter in Kamakura. She taught effectively even though she started on the whisky at eleven o'clock in the morning. Audrey also took the older children on a pottery tour to various parts of the country, absorbing much of the spirit of Japanese pottery. Kate went to clarinet lessons and Jane to lessons on the violin. Somehow, Audrey managed to arrange all this, with some help from friends.

Very near to the end of our stay, I spent nearly a week at a conference in Fukuoka, a long way to the south-west of Tokyo. During that time Asano-san had returned to her house to prepare it for the staff of a company – twenty or more individuals – who would stay there on holiday. When I returned, I found Audrey, who had never bothered much with learning the language, chatting quite confidently in Japanese with the landlady, having picked up much vocabulary in only a few days.

We returned to Canberra half way through 1974. The Whitlam Labor Government was still in power, but was in difficulties because it lacked a majority in the Senate. The countdown was beginning towards the eventual dismissal by the Governor-General of the Whitlam Government on 11 November 1975 – probably the most controversial act and certainly the most serious crisis in Australian government since the war. In a famous speech immediately after the dismissal, Gough Whitlam called upon the Australian people to 'maintain your rage'. The subsequent general elections resulted in a conservative government, but it was many years before the mutual ill-feeling generated by the 1975 crisis eventually died down.

In 1975, I was invited to spend nearly a year as 'academic in residence' in the government's Department of Foreign Affairs. This was a completely new departure for me and I was not given much idea what I was supposed to do. In the event I was assigned certain tasks and fulfilled them as best I could. Meanwhile, I observed with interest the workings of an Australian government department. At first, I was put into a room on my own in a room with no external light, which I hated, but eventually I was able to move into an open plan area, and interact more easily with other people at their desks. Every morning a batch of telegrams would land on my desk, most of them on issues that were no concern of mine. I remember, for instance, a lengthy issue about camels. King Saud of Saudi Arabia was seeking to improve the blood stock of his camel population. Australia offered to help by sending him a number of camels wandering free in central Australia, the descendants of those used in camel trains during the nineteenth century. During the time I was in the Department, the 'Law of the Sea' negotiations were proceeding, and I saw a humorously subversive 'report' parodying some of the absurdities that appeared over exclusive fishing zones. This of course was an issue that vitally concerned Japan, given the crucial importance of fish for the diet of ordinary Japanese. There were huge issues concerning Vietnam and Cambodia (then under the murderous Pol Pot regime), and Australia was generous in allowing large numbers of mainly Vietnamese refugees to settle in Australia. Over a few months the number of Vietnamese restaurants in Canberra rose from zero to fourteen. I also became used to the special vocabulary used in the department. Leaving work early was known as 'flexing off', and I had to 'flex off' often because I was still giving lectures at the ANU. I also became used to the word 'presentational', as in 'This is a thoroughly lousy idea, but it is presentationally attractive, so let's propose it to the Minister' (I parody a little).

But after a while I was able to follow the negotiations for a Treaty of Friendship and Co-operation between Australia and Japan. I was not taking part in the negotiations, but I saw all the documentation as it was produced, and soon realised that this was a fascinating example of an international negotiation. The principal purpose of the treaty was for each nation to accord to the other equality of treatment in a wide range of areas, and this included most-favoured nation (MFN) treatment. This meant that Japan should grant Australia, and Australia should grant Japan, treatment on commercial and other matters that was at least as favourable as each state granted to other states. This is a standard procedure in international law. The problem was, however, that Japan argued for ' retrospectivity and prospectivity' in MFN treatment. That is to say that, for instance, since Australia had granted to the United States in the late 1940s permission for General Motors to establish a wholly-owned subsidiary on its territory to manufacture Holden cars, Australia should now, several decades later, accord the same treatment to at least one Japanese automotive company. And the same was supposed to apply to future changes.

This was an extremely complex matter to disentangle, but two Australian diplomats in particular, Garry Woodard and Ashton Calvert, worked with their Japanese counterparts with remarkable ingenuity to reach a satisfactory solution. (For a much later assessment, see my article: 'Negotiating the Basic Treaty between Australia and Japan, 1973-1976', *Japanese Studies* [Sydney], vol. 24, no. 2, September 2004.)

By the time the treaty was formalised, the Whitlam Labor Government had been dismissed by the Governor General, and a conservative government under Malcolm Fraser had taken its place. But the Treaty (often known on the Australian side as the 'Nara Treaty') survived the change of government. A rather extraordinary, but surely welcome, long-term sequel to the battle royal between those two titans of Australian politics in the 1970s, Gough Whitlam and Malcolm Fraser (whom Whitlam in one of his inflammatory speeches after the dismissal referred to as 'Kerr's cur'), was that the two men in old age became close friends, and on various issues political soulmates.

The second half of the 1970s was a hard-working time for me, with a range of activities, on top of the usual routine of teaching and writing. Funding had become available to set up an intensive Japanese language course, and I was centrally involved in its administration, along with Sydney Crawcour, and Antonio Alfonso, who succeeded Syd as head of the ANU Japanese Department. We hired a Japanese national, Miyaji-sensei, to be in charge of the course. An early task was to select a set number of applicants to join the course, out of the many who had applied. No upper age limit was applied, but a striking lesson that we learned from experience with overseeing the course was that there was a sharp inverse correlation between age and progress in learning Japanese. One partial exception was a lovely lady called Janet Barriskill, a potter like Audrey, who was to go on and spend long periods making pots in pottery areas near Nagoya, where many potters shared the surname Katō. We became close friends with her and her family, who lived at Avalon Beach north of Sydney. So far as the language was concerned, though she was no longer young, by sheer persistence and hard work (and later as a result of long periods living and working in Japan) she became a fluent Japanese speaker.

During the late 1970s three equally (though differently) colourful characters taught Japanese in Canberra. Since I was teaching political science, not language, we were in different departments of the university, but I saw a great deal of them, working together in a range of tasks. The first two I have mentioned above: Syd Crawcour and Tony (Antonio) Alfonso. Syd (whom I visited in Melbourne around Christmas 2018, when he was already ninety-four), had learned Japanese to a superb level of fluency, in part, he once told me, by sitting in on school lessons in Tokyo on '*kokugo*' (national language). Like David Sissons, he had first been in Japan during the American occupation after the war, where he had formed pessimistic and often cynical views, both about the ways in which the Americans were administering Japan, and also about the character and intentions of many Japanese politicians and officials following the war. He was a man with a truly extraordinary memory for detail. One evening in the 1960s, I casually asked his advice about

Japanese cameras, as I would shortly be visiting Japan and wanted to buy a decent camera. Some three hours later he had told me the technical details of every single camera then on sale in Japan, all from memory. Professionally, he was an economic historian specialising in the Japanese economy from the mid-nineteenth century into the early twentieth century – a time when the Japanese language was very different from Japanese today. Apart from writing on economics, he had also written a textbook on 'kanbun', widely used among the elite in early modern Japan as a means of writing Japanese with something close to Chinese grammar. Syd was an Australian of strong opinions, which he had no compunction about expressing in whatever company. These included withering assessments of particular individuals, in Japan and elsewhere.

Tony Alfonso was a Spaniard who had written a series of textbooks on learning Japanese according to modern linguistic principles. At the time, these were regarded as the best textbooks on the market. Some of his colleagues in the Asian Studies Faculty seemed to regard him as a reincarnation of Don Quixote. But on the selection committee for the Chair of Japanese, a referee for another candidate wrote to the effect that 'you have just about the best candidate in the world in Dr Alfonso, so why are you bothering with other candidates'. I happened to be a member of the committee. Some of the committee members were inclined to laugh this off, but together with the Professor of Linguistics I helped swing the verdict in his favour. This is the only time that I have seen a reference that supported a different candidate from the candidate that the referee was supposed to be supporting.

The third colourful member of the Japanese Department was Roger Pulvers, again a man with a truly remarkable linguistic gift. He was American, of Jewish parentage, who in his university training had studied Polish and Russian, and had published significant translations of literary works in those languages. He was politicised by the Vietnam War in the mid-to-late 1960s, and left his native country for Japan, where he assimilated the language in a very few years. It was from Japan that Syd Crawcour recruited him to join his team at the ANU in 1972. Before the end of the decade he had renounced his American citizenship and become a citizen of Australia. He has since made an amazing reputation for himself writing novels and plays, in English and Japanese, directing theatrical performances and for journalistic writing. (Roger Pulvers, *The Unmaking of an American*, Balestier Press, 2019).

One visiting fellow at the ANU in the mid-to-late 1970s was the political scientist Fukui Haruhiro, who was teaching at the University of California, Santa Barbara, where I also visited him on one occasion. He had come to Canberra in the aftermath of the Nara Treaty negotiations, and we were planning a book analysing these fascinating, essentially bureaucracy to bureaucracy interactions, beginning under the Whitlam Government, and concluded under the administration of Malcolm Fraser. I was familiar with the documentation and had interviewed many of the participants on the Australian side. Haru, as he was generally known, went ahead and interviewed some of the negotiators on the Japanese side. Gradually, we were putting together the material for what should have been the definitive book on the subject, providing we were able to obtain permission to write a book on what was still in some aspects a sensitive subject.

Sometime after Haru returned to Santa Barbara, there was an unexpected turn of events. Haru wrote to me to say that he had been approached by Greenwood Press to be editor-in-chief of an encyclopaedia of political parties of Asia and the Pacific. He asked me if would agree to write the section on the political parties of Japan. This would mean writing substantive entries on Japanese parties going back to the Meiji period when the first parties were organised. With considerable reluctance I agreed. I knew that this would have serious repercussions for our Nara Treaty project. On the other hand, from my earliest research on Japanese politics I had been concerned with political parties, and the opportunity to write on parties in Japan from the earliest emergence in the Meiji period to the present was tempting.

In the end I agreed. I assembled all the reference materials that I was likely to need, and began work. My brief was to write entries on all Japanese political parties except for local parties on Okinawa. Even though I already had a good deal of knowledge concerning political parties since 1945, my understanding of pre-war parties was superficial. Moreover, how should one define a party? For instance the First Lobby Association (*Dai-ichi hikaeshitsukai*) was formed in July 1928 out of several pre-existing groups. It suffered several defections only two months later, and I commented as follows:

The association's membership seems to have been very fluid, and it was finally disbanded in January 1930, although a few months later a similar group of small parties was formed under the name of *Dai-ichi hikaeshitsu* (First Lobby).

Were these groups genuine parties, were they factions, or were they floating groups within the Diet that divided much like cells in a human body? I gathered a number of them under the title of political parties, but I had (and retain) serious doubts about whether I was right to do so. At the other end of the spectrum of size and importance I devoted twelve and a half pages to the Liberal Democratic Party that had ruled Japan for most of the period since the war.

This project did indeed impact adversely on our Nara Treaty book plan. The book was never written. All that came out of the research was my article in *Japanese Studies,* cited above. In retrospect that is a shame, but I learned a great deal about the historical antecedents of the political parties I had been researching, and that should be placed on the positive side of the ledger. One lesson that it had taught me was the sheer richness of party culture in Japan, even under the pre-war regime that was only democratic in part, and where democracy was hampered by inbuilt authoritarian institutions and practices.

During the 1970s, I was supervising my first doctoral students. These included Alan Rix, who wrote his thesis on Japan's overseas aid policy. Alan published widely on Japan and later became a central figure at the University of Queensland in Brisbane. Aurelia George (later Aurelia George Mulgan), wrote her thesis on the politics of agriculture in Japan, and went on to have a distinguished career writing about Japanese politics and foreign policy, especially its economic aspects, including trade and defence. My friend the economist Peter Drysdale and I co-supervised James Horne, with whom I had many fascinating discussions. Subsequently he was a public servant in Canberra, had postings in Tokyo, and became a leading expert on water policy in Australia, that driest of continents. I also interacted closely with Hayden Lesbirel, who did a pioneering study on the geographic placing of nuclear power stations in Japan, based in Brisbane. I was an examiner of his doctoral thesis.

In addition, I supervised a number of theses on areas of the world outside Japan. Most memorably, one of my doctoral students was Amin Saikal, who had left his native Afghanistan at a time when that country was facing invasion and revolution. He wrote a thesis on the politics of Iran under the Shah. His timing was perfect, because very on his thesis was published by Princeton University Press, under the title: *The Rise and Fall of the Shah*. The book became a best-seller. He was later a most active Director of the Centre for Central Asian and Islamic Studies at the ANU, where he became a leading voice within Australia on the understanding of the Middle East.

The 1970s were also a decade during which I first ventured into translation. This was prompted by the presence at the ANU of Professor Banno Junji, who was to become one of the leading political historians of modern Japan. He spent two periods as visiting fellow in Canberra once early in the decade and once towards its end. At the time of his first visit, he had recently published a seminal book in Japanese, titled *Meiji kenpō taisei no kakuritsu* (The Establishment of the Meiji Constitutional Regime) Tokyo University Press, 1971. He had been one of the principal leaders of student revolts against revision of the Japan-United States Security Treaty in 1960, and had gone on to translate political activism into a fascination with the history of his country's politics from the opening up of Japan in the 1850s until the descent into war between 1937 to 1945. Professor Hayashi regarded him as probably his most brilliant student.

During his first stay at ANU we became good friends and I offered to translate his major book into English. In making this offer I was seriously underestimating the scale of the task that this would entail. I was trained in contemporary Japanese, but written Japanese in the mid-to-late nineteenth century was a far cry from the contemporary language. In his book were many quotations from documents of that period, so that when I came to grapple with those passages, I had great difficulty in making sense of them. Japanese as written in the Bakumatsu period (1853-1868) bore about as much relationship with Japanese of the 1970s as English written somewhere between the times of Chaucer and Shakespeare did with 1970s English. During the Meiji period (1868-1912) the language was being modernised and therefore becoming easier to understand, but even in the 1930s there were many conventions of writing that contrasted with those of the post-war period.

During his second stay in Canberra, Junji helped me with the translation, and we spent weekly sessions thrashing out how best to translate difficult passages. Events that were to come, however, seriously delayed this translation project, I had many more demands on my time, and in the end it took around twenty years. Even so, during this process, Junji and his wife Kazuko became our closest friends in Japan.

Let me now explain what I mean by 'events that were to come'. In June-July 1979 I paid one of what had become fairly regular visits back to the United Kingdom, principally to see my parents in Birmingham, and also my parents-in-law in Guildford. I was particularly worried about my own parents, whose health was plainly precarious. While I was in the UK, I also visited Oxford, where I met Dick Storry and his wife Dorothie, as well as Brian Powell, a specialist in Japanese drama, whom I had first met in the late 1960s. I had just read that the Nissan Motor Co. Ltd. was providing funding to set up an institute of Japanese studies in Oxford. Brian explained to me something of the background to the Nissan 'benefaction' (Oxford term) and urged me to apply for the post of Professor and Director of the institute-to-be. My diary entry for 9 July 1979 includes the comment, 'This will require a lot of heart-searching.' Yes indeed.

On Sunday 30 March in the late Canberra summer of 1980, when the heat of summer is slowly merging into autumn but the eucalyptus fails to indicate the season since it sheds leaves the year round – we held a party at home to celebrate three things: 1. Twenty years of marriage; 2. Twenty years in Australia; and 3. The new house extension.

No. 3 was the product of Audrey's success in procuring a 'Permit to Build', described above, allowing her to direct the building project herself. No. 2 celebrated our substantial commitment to Australia, indicated by the fact that a few years before that we had taken Australian citizenship. And No. 1 signalled that our marriage had prospered, and we now had the family of four brilliant children that we had planned. The diary informs me that the party lasted 'from 12.00 p.m. to 4.00 p.m', and that 'perhaps 120 people came through the evening' (this suggests that '4.00 p.m.' was a fictitious end point). As presents, most people brought us pot plants. In the end we had so many that we had to give some of them away.

The party suggests success, happiness, stability, a settled existence, opportunities ahead in Australia. But since I had returned from the UK half way through the previous year we had been discussing whether or not I should apply for the new Oxford chair. I had the bit between my teeth, though with some reservations; the family was less keen. Our children considered themselves thoroughly Australian, and there was no question which national team they supported in test matches (especially the sports-mad Tim). Audrey wondered how she would re-establish herself as a potter in Oxford. The children worried about schools in Oxford. From my point of view the possibility of an Oxford Chair, the challenge of setting up a new institute of Japanese studies, and being closer to my elderly parents, were strong positive factors. If I stayed, I was due for a three-year stint as head of the Department of Political Science, and having spent six months as acting head I knew all too well just how fractious that department was. But leaving ANU would mean leaving many close friends, and in a broader sense, leaving the beautiful country that we had made our own.

In the end, I applied, and was summoned to an interview in Oxford in early December of 1980. I was asked how I would propose to develop the institute. I replied among other things that I would want to introduce a course on Japanese politics for students of Philosophy, Politics and Economics, and was told that I would have to fight for it, but would have a good chance of success. There were discussions about the secrets of Japanese modernisation from the Meiji period, why I thought Japan so important, could I teach through Japanese language texts, did I have experience in fundraising?

After the interview, I shopped in central Oxford for an hour or so, and then returned to the Eastgate Hotel, where a message awaited me to ring the Vice-Chancellor. When I did so, he told me the job was mine if I wanted it. I put through a telephone call to Audrey from a wall phone in a tiny cubicle in the bowels of the building, timing it to take account of the time difference with Australia. Not feeling well and awaiting a gall bladder operation, Audrey was muted in her appreciation of the news, but after I returned to Canberra, she apologised for her lack of enthusiasm.

The question remained whether I should accept the position or not. We discussed it as a family, and agreed that I should accept.

But although Oxford wanted me to take up the post at the beginning of the academic year the following October, I held out for the start of 1982, because I had six months' sabbatical due to me from January 1981, on condition that I then remained to teach in the second semester from August to December of the same year.

Reactions from friends and colleagues were a mixture of surprise, regret that we were leaving and enthusiasm at hearing that I had secured a position at Oxford. Only two people directly criticised me for my decision to leave. One was an ANU natural scientist called Jim Bowler, who had been a committed and useful participant in the discussion groups we had held in the early seventies about the Vietnam War. Clearly, he had a great love for his country and didn't like to see me abandoning it. The other was our old friend Harry Rigby, prominent and enlightened specialist in the politics of the USSR. In a conversation where the two of us were calmly discussing my impending departure, he slipped in the remark, 'It doesn't make much sense in terms of the future development of Japanese studies in this country.' That really hurt, and made me question our decision in my own mind, though I was now almost irrevocably committed.

We would still have a year before we were to leave for Oxford, but for me, the first half of it would be spent in Tokyo. For much of that period I would be on my own, but Audrey, now still recovering from her operation in late December, would join me for a few weeks in the northern spring. And so, I left for Tokyo in early January of 1981.

After I had spent a week or two in Tokyo, my doctoral student James Horne invited me to spend the rest of the six months staying with him and his partner Tomoko at a house belonging to Tomoko's mother in the western suburb of Ogikubo. I was delighted to accept. Tomoko was one of the Japanese language tutors at Oxford, and was a source of professional advice about the Japanese language both to James and to me. When she heard me speak Japanese she commented that while I was evidently experienced in speaking the language, my speech was far too formal and used *keigo* (polite forms of speech) much more than was natural in a household (which was how she described our living arrangements). Perhaps my Japanese was influenced by my supervisor at *Shaken*, Professor Hayashi, a delightful person but brought up in the pre-war period. So during the months I spent in Ogikubo I had to rethink some aspects of the way I spoke the language, and of course I learned a great deal of new vocabulary. Tomoko was a strict teacher, and would not let me (or James) get away with errors of grammar or vocabulary.

When Audrey came, in early spring, the two of us arranged a pottery-viewing trip down the country as far as the south-western island of Kyūshū, staying at various *minshuku* (similar to youth hostels) throughout the trip. The highlight was our stay at the pottery town of Hagi, in Yamaguchi prefecture at the westernmost tip of Japan's main island. Hagi was at the centre of what had been up to 1873 the leading feudal domain known as Chōshū. We had booked at the local minshuku for two nights but ended up staying for five. While there we visited one of the most famous potteries in Japan, which had been founded in 1663 by the Miwa family, and had been run by the same family ever since. Like most other potters in that most traditional of pottery towns, the current potter at the time we visited was Miwa Kyūwa, known as Miwa X (tenth generation), and was recognised by the government as a 'living national treasure'. Hagi pottery was exceptionally traditional because the town's potteries supplied highly prized tea ceremony bowls, which fetched elevated prices among tea ceremony specialists throughout the country. The bowls were generally of earthy colour overlaid with a translucent beige glaze.

Several years later, in Kyūshū, we visited the tiny pottery village of Onta (Little Deer Field), up a winding road in the mountains of Oita Prefecture, where we stayed overnight at an inn. The village echoed day and night with the sound of heavy blocks of wood on axles, powered by stream water, constantly pounding clay. Some seventeen families lived in the village, of which around twelve were families of a potter. Here again we encountered a place where ancient tradition was prized.

My studies of Japanese politics made good progress during this period, and I was able to study the beginnings of a long-drawn-out change in the nature of the political system. I shall say more about this in later chapters. One Sunday, late in June, I wrote a letter of resignation from the ANU. It was one of the hardest letters I have ever had to write.

At the end of June, we returned to Canberra, where I completed my teaching requirements. And we made preparations for our departure from Australia for pastures new in our original home country.

12

Old Country, New Country

ᴧ

LEAVING AUSTRALIA AFTER twenty-one years was not simply a matter of going home, even for us, and certainly not for the children. Great Britain had changed, we had changed. Our children spoke with Aussie accents. People couldn't quite place us. One evening, I was invited to dinner at Templeton College, and found myself sitting next to the Bursar. Knowing that I had spent several years in Australia, he said, 'I'm glad you haven't picked up an Australian accent; that would have been *so* embarrassing.' Though I was sorely tempted to put on an Aussie accent just for his benefit, I refrained from doing so.

We arrived in Oxford in the middle of the most severe winter for many years. Our children, used to snow only on ski slopes, found it hard to imagine that snow could blanket a city, burying cars.

When we arrived at Heathrow Airport, we were met by our old Australian friends Hedley and Mary Bull. We had known them at ANU, where Hedley was Professor of International Nations, but in 1977 he had been appointed Montague Burton Professor of International Relations in Oxford. He was author of one of the most influential books in the study of international relations in modern times, *The Anarchical Society*, arguing that even in the absence of a central international government (meaning that an international system is 'anarchical'), under certain conditions relations between states are such that together they may be regarded as a 'society'. Hedley was to be an important supporter of mine in my early years in Oxford, while my colleagues and I were attempting to develop a new institute. Sadly, he died of cancer in 1985, and so missed the collapse of the Soviet Union, depriving us of what would have been his wise analysis of its implications.

The Nissan Institute of Japanese Studies had been formally inaugurated the previous September in a ceremony that I attended, having flown in from Canberra. The Nissan President, Mr Ishihara Takashi, made a speech in which he commended the study of modern Japan in the United Kingdom, where his company was planning major investment, strongly encouraged by Margaret Thatcher, which was to result in the building of a brand new automotive plant in Sunderland, Tyne and Wear.

The previous July, I had flown from Japan to the UK on Aeroflot to participate in the selection of a candidate to fill the modern history position at the Nissan Institute. And over the months following my arrival in Oxford, we were searching for a candidate to teach about the economic system of Japan.

Our choice as historian of modern Japan was Ann Waswo, an American who had taught at Stanford, the University of Virginia and Princeton, was inspired to study Japan from reading about the 1960 protests against revision (meaning perpetuation) of the Japan-US Security Treaty and by controversies in the US about whether Japan was on the verge of becoming Communist, by boredom with Gibbon's *Decline and Fall of the Roman Empire*, and by a Stanford Professor, Thomas, C. Smith, who encouraged her to visit Japan and study its history and language. She became principally a social historian, writing on agricultural tenancy in pre-war Japan, housing and housing policy in post-war Japan, and Japanese society in general. She arrived in Oxford just two weeks after I arrived myself.

Our international search for an economist resulted in the appointment of Jenny Corbett, an Australian who had studied extensively in the United States, principally at the University of Michigan, Ann Arbor, where she obtained a doctorate. She joined us the following year. She was conducting research into macro-economic issues in Japan, Japanese banking and finance, and also branching out into studying broader financial and economic issues in the Asia-Pacific region. I had known her for a long time, including in Japan, and her father David had been a senior colleague of mine in the Department of Political Science at the ANU for a couple of years from my teaching debut in 1964.

I should add that at St Antony's, in addition to the three of us who were Nissan Fellows, and language tutors, there were two long-standing St Antony's Fellows in Japanese Studies. These were Brian

Powell, a literature and in particular theatre (Kabuki) specialist, and James McMullen, who researched Japanese pre-modern history and religion, especially Confucianism, in the context of Japan. Both of them were generous and useful allies for us in the Nissan Institute project. Later in the decade they both moved to undergraduate colleges, which they made receptive to the recruitment of undergraduates wishing to engage in Japanese studies.

Apart from the three of us in tenured positions at the Institute, we appointed annually a 'Nissan Visiting Fellow', as part of our agreement with the Nissan Company. These Fellows did not have any formal teaching commitments, but conducted research in their own areas of specialisation. One of our early visitors in this category was Professor Hayashi Shigeru, who had been my supervisor in Japan when I was researching my doctoral thesis in 1962-63.

An issue of some complexity for us in the early years of the Institute was how to fit in a new country-specific institute into the Oxford system based principally on colleges. It had been decided before I arrived that the Nissan Institute would be physically located at St Antony's College, one of five or six colleges that admitted exclusively graduate students, and was known as the most internationally-minded college in the whole university. In a sense the Nissan Institute was the successor of the former Far East Centre of St Antony's, which in its later years had been headed by Dick Storry. Sadly, Dick died of a heart attack only a few weeks after my arrival, having retired the previous autumn. But his widow Dorothie came to be a great support for us at the Nissan Institute in later years, giving hospitality to many of our Japanese visitors.

The first three appointments at the Nissan Institute brought with them fellowships at St Antony's. This could not be guaranteed, however, for future appointments. This was a problem for us with some later appointments because if a fellowship was offered at a college whose principal teaching activity was teaching undergraduates, it was likely that the person appointed would be expected to spend a great deal of time tutoring undergraduates in that college in a general discipline (say, economics), at the expense of teaching in that discipline as applied to Japan. Happily, from our point of view, the precedent was eventually established that, in practice, new appointments would be accompanied by a fellowship at St Antony's. To those unfamiliar with the detail of the Oxford system, this may well seem an arcane and unnecessary problem, but we had some difficult political fights over it in later years.

An important phrase in the agreement between the University of Oxford and the Nissan Company promoted the introduction of the study of modern Japan 'into mainstream curricula of the University'. This was, in essence, a reflection on the pre-existing situation where the study of Japan, as well as other Asian countries, was confined to faculties that specialised in the study of the languages and cultures of non-Western countries. Traditionally, they would be called faculties of oriental studies, though by the 1980s 'Asian Studies' was becoming more common. 'The Orient', after all, is a word that views Asia from the perspective of 'the Occident', in other words the West, and is not indigenous to the region. For the same reason, I have never much liked 'Far East', nor indeed 'Near North', used by Australian governments during the Second World War.

A key policy issue was involved here. What could be called the 'ghettoisation' of Asian, as well as other non-Western, university studies, was seen to reflect a legacy from the colonial period that needed to be rectified. This was particularly acute in the case of Australia, where Japan had become by far its largest trading partner, and where foreign policy was shifting in emphasis towards its northern neighbours, seeing them as trading partners, not 'dangerous other'. An editorial in the *Australian Financial Review* in the early 1970s was given the mildly corny title, 'Making mates out of partners'. Despite this atonality, however, the editorialist accurately foresaw the long-term development of close working relations between the governments of Australia and Japan, as well as professional and social interaction between their peoples in many fields of endeavour.

In the United Kingdom as well, though perhaps with less urgency, things were moving in a direction that made it possible to propose placing Japan within the mainstream curricula of the University as a practicable proposition. For those, however, who thought this was a good idea, there was a practical problem. One possible implication of placing the study of Japan into 'mainstream curricula of the University' was that Japan-specialists should be appointed in discipline-based departments. This, indeed, had been my situation during the whole time that I had been teaching at ANU. In a world where academics were generally mobile, if a Japan-specialist in, say, a department of political science, moved elsewhere, then that position might well go to a political theorist, or a specialist on American politics. My departure from the ANU left the study of Japanese politics in a precarious position in the political science department, though it did survive for a while. So 'deghettoisation' bore with it the danger of 'deJapanisation'.

Much later on, the University of Oxford devised an ingenious solution to get round this problem, but that was not until after the new millennium had begun. This was to combine area studies with studies based on different disciplines in the same 'school'.

In our case, we were an institute specifically designed to promote the study of Japan within the University, but Fellows whose primary academic home was at the Institute also did teaching for departments. As for me, I was able to argue my case at a meeting of the Faculty of Social Studies, against sharp opposition, and eventually succeeded in persuading the Faculty to introduce a 'paper' on 'The Politics of Japan' into the later year options of the degree in Philosophy, Politics and Economics. One faculty member expressed the view that, 'We might perhaps be able to introduce the study of Japanese politics into a masters course in a few years' time.' But I won my case.

Ann Waswo was similarly successful in persuading the Modern History Faculty to introduce a paper on 'Modern Japanese History' into the optional courses available in that faculty. Jenny Corbett faced greater difficulty in persuading the economists to accept an option on the Japanese economy, but was nevertheless able to do a great deal of lecturing within that faculty. It seems that many economists see their discipline as necessarily abstracted from the economies of specific countries, even though much of the material for their theories comes from experience of the economies of Europe and North America.

Another important element in our teaching schedules was of course lecturing. We all advertised courses of lectures each term in the University *Gazette*. In the Oxford system of those days academic staff could put on lectures on subjects that were not necessarily an integral part of a specific 'paper', and there was no obligation on students to attend specific lectures. This system had a certain libertarian feel to it, and seemed reminiscent of a time when great philosophy professors would deliver a series of lectures from on high that would change the course of human thinking for ever. I was brought up, however, in a more mundane tradition from my teaching at the ANU, where there are defined courses in which lectures and tutorials are an integral part of the whole, and students are at the centre of the exercise.

In my early days back at Oxford, I occasionally met academics who seemed surprised that I was doing any lecturing at all, since according to them as a Professor I was not obliged to do so. This I regarded as a nineteenth-, rather than a twentieth-, century attitude. To be fair, Oxford has now moved a long way on from attitudes that I encountered in the early 1980s, but they were already changing at that time.

My colleagues and I were also keen to develop graduate studies of Japan, and we readily took on the supervision of graduate students writing doctoral theses, as well as occasional masters theses. To mention just my own experience of supervising theses on Japanese politics, those I supervised on Japan at doctoral level included several on aspects of political opposition, which was my own particular area of expertise. But I also supervised a thesis on education policy reform, one on a particular Liberal Democratic Party internal faction, one on fisheries policy, one on Japan's great political thinker Maruyama Masao, one on political corruption, several on foreign policy, and one – for which I was joint supervisor – on the organisation of the *manga* industry. I supervised theses on the Republic of Korea, including one by a former radical student (Korean), who years later was to come close to being chosen as the President of his country.

One highly successful initiative that we pioneered was a book series on topics relating to Japan. It originated from a visit I received, around 1985, in the early days of the Institute, from Peter Sowden, at that time working for the publisher Croom Helm in London. The launch of a series of books that introduced aspects of Japan to the reading public had been one of our ambitions almost from the start, and Peter Sowden, with the backing of Croom Helm, proposed a sensible and attractive way of organising such a series.

It seems worthwhile reproducing the first paragraph of my preface to the first book published in the series. The tone of it suggests the pioneering excitement of promoting a series of books on Japan in the heady atmosphere of the 1980s:

> Few countries in the world today can be unaware of the increasing international impact of Japan. From the ashes of defeat in 1945, Japan has risen to become one of the most dynamic and successful economic powers in the world today. The broad outlines of how this has been achieved are reasonably well known. There are, however, many little-documented aspects of contemporary Japan, and many thinly-understood facets to the Japanese experience of modern development. Japan is neither unique (as sometimes asserted), nor merely a copy of the outside world, but rather a fascinating source of human experience which deserves to be tapped and disseminated far more widely than it now is.

What I think I was trying to suggest here was that Japan was worth studying, not just for its own sake – just as Sir Edmond Hilary had climbed Mount Everest 'because it is there' – but because it was rapidly becoming an example worth emulating in the outside world.

Not everybody in the outside world saw Japan at the time through such rose-coloured spectacles, nor was my enthusiasm particularly original. The Harvard scholar Ezra Vogel published in 1979 a book entitled *Japan as Number One: Lessons for America* (Harvard University Press, 1979). In some ways the book was as much about the United States and its ills as about Japan and its successes. In a few places the approach of the book is too binary. Vogel at one point argued that his country might do well to emulate the Japanese example of having a single emergency phone number for the whole country. From this I learned for the first time the bizarre fact that the US *does not* have a single emergency number. The United Kingdom would have been as good an example as Japan – or France, or Germany, or Australia, two of which are federal systems.

But during the 1980s increasingly negative attitudes towards Japan were appearing in the media, especially in the United States. The so-called 'Gang of Four', including the celebrated scholar of Japan the late Professor Chalmers Johnson, became vocal in castigating the Japanese system as predatory in relations with the outside world, and especially the United States. Japanese firms at the time were active in taking over such venerable American institutions as Columbia Pictures. In 1989 the Dutch journalist Karel van Wolferen, also a member of the 'gang of four', published a book entitled *The Enigma of Japanese Power*, in which he argued that the Japanese politico-economic system was deeply irresponsible, with nobody prepared to take responsibility. He cited President Truman's adage concerning the presidency of the United States that 'the buck stops here'. In van Wolferen's view, however, in Japan 'the buck just keeps circulating'.

A year or two after the launch of our book series with Croom Helm, that company was taken over by Routledge, so that all later books in the series were published in what was now called the 'Nissan Institute – Routledge Japanese Studies series'. Only two books were published under the Croom Helm label, and after the takeover they were given the Routledge imprimatur.

The first of these had a remarkable *succès de scandale*, and launched the series therefore with an unexpected flourish. It was titled *The Myth of Japanese Uniqueness*, and the author was Peter Dale, a polyglot Australian scholar (originally a classicist but familiar with many different cultures, including Chinese and Japanese) permanently resident in Italy. Peter argued that much academic as well as journalistic, writing in Japan was pervaded by assumptions about the unique character of the Japanese people, different therefore from that of any other people on earth. This body of writing was widely referred to as *Nihonjinron*, roughly translated as 'what it means to be Japanese'. It proved to be highly controversial, attracting both enthusiastic supporters and defiant detractors. Sometime in the 1980s the European Association of Japanese Studies (EAJS) held one of its triennial conferences, at which a session was organised specifically to discuss (or perhaps more accurately demolish) the arguments of Peter Dale's book. I was not able to attend, perhaps because I was in Japan at the time. But if I had attended, I would have defended the book, on the grounds that it was a provocative and controversial piece of work, also brilliant and original in its conception and detail, even though in places the author went too far and placed Japanese writers unjustly in the category of nationalist believers in the uniqueness of the Japanese people. As a matter of fact, I had spent a great deal of time editing Peter's original manuscript, making it more readable and cutting down its length by about fifty per cent.

Before we left the ANU, I had known two Melbourne academics, Ross Mouer and Yoshio Sugimoto, who with several co-authors were also writing about *Nihonjinron* from a critical standpoint. Whereas their methodology was essentially sociological and statistical, that of Peter Dale could not have been more different. Peter was writing from a literary and cultural standpoint, using his deep knowledge of comparative culture to demonstrate the shallowness and bias of much *Nihonjinron* literature. A further reason why I believe that both Peter Dale's book, and the writings of Sugimoto and Mouer, have had a useful effect, is that they were noticed in Japan itself, and induced a more critical approach (in some circles at least) to the dubious nostrums of many *Nihonjinron* writers. And indeed, the discourse has now moved on.

Some of the books published in the Nissan-Routledge series were specialist monographs with limited appeal but representing good research on a particular topic. Some books, in contrast, had much broader appeal. The most spectacularly successful of these was *Understanding Japanese Society*, by Joy Hendry, who has now retired from teaching at Oxford Brookes University. Her title has been a standard textbook in many courses at universities in the United States and elsewhere, and has recently been re-published in its fifth edition. I believe that her book, over its five editions, has sold more copies than almost all the other books in the series put together.

At this time of writing, more than 100 books have been published in the series, making it almost certainly the most prolific series devoted to things Japanese in English.

One initiative that was taken during the 1980s was to increase the undergraduate Japanese studies course from three years to four years. This was something I strongly supported, because Japanese is a complex language (especially its writing system), and it was unrealistic to expect even a linguistically gifted undergraduate to reach a high working level of fluency in the language in as little as three years. The problem was, however, that we did not have the resources of personnel to extend the course to a full four years. It was also highly desirable for students to spend a considerable period of study in Japan as part of their course, and that was difficult to arrange if the course was confined to three years. An arrangement was therefore worked out whereby Oxford first-year students in Japanese would take a course in the Department of Japanese at the University of Sheffield, one of the best Japanese departments in the country.

This caused some controversy in the University of Oxford, particularly from some colleges that found it difficult to fit such an arrangement in with their normal procedures. I myself, however, was strongly in favour of the scheme, in part because it made sense in terms of extending our students' exposure to Japanese, and also because I believed that it was a bonus, in terms of life experience, for students to be exposed to two very different universities. I remember, however, talking with one young lady who had applied to take Japanese studies at Oxford, and who was appalled at the prospect of having to spend time at a northern university. I reflected that the notorious British class system was still alive and well in the 1980s.

The British Ambassador to Japan in the early 1980s was Sir Hugh Cortazzi, whom I had known, on and off, for some years. After he retired from the diplomatic service he began a second successful career as a writer on Japan. He was also concerned with the health of Japanese studies in the UK, and was instrumental in raising funds for Japanese studies in Cambridge. Not long after he had returned from Tokyo he wrote to me asking me to meet him in London, which I did. At the meeting he expressed his displeasure that Oxford was sending its first-year students in Japanese to the University of Sheffield. I explained our practical reasons for doing so, and included my own strong feeling that students would benefit from an experience of two contrasting universities. He argued quite forcefully against me, but I held my ground. In later years, we found common cause in our similar critical views on authoritarian trends in Japanese politics following the election of the Abe Government in 2012. Sadly, Hugh died in August 2018. Our first-year students went to Sheffield for several years, and for the most part they were appreciative of the experiences it had given them. There were some dissenters from this view. Eventually, the arrangement ended because Sheffield had changed its first-year course in ways that did not suit us.

Only a few weeks after we arrived in Oxford, the United Kingdom was at war with Argentina over the Falklands/Malvinas. For me the idea that the country of my birth, to which I had just returned after some twenty years at the other side of the globe, should find itself at war with Argentina, of all places, required a major effort of adjustment. I felt no joy at the fleet setting sail from Portsmouth, nor at the crowds patriotically waving them on their way. Later, I grasped the fact that Argentina was under the sway of a nasty dictatorship led by the opportunistic General Galtieri. But when Margaret Thatcher lauded Senator Pinochet in nearby Chile, a dictator also, whose preferred method of getting rid of his opponents was to drop them out of aircraft into the sea, I found myself disillusioned with the political leadership of the country I had returned to.

There was of course a great deal more to the Thatcher regime in the 1980s than policy towards Latin America, although I still find it galling that it was the sheer chance of finding a war and thumping the 'Argies' that saved her government, which was deeply unpopular in its early stages. But there are many examples in history of leaders who have used external war to boost their popularity and even save their regimes. I was attracted to the Democratic Labour Party, which had broken away from the main Labour Party in 1981, until it eventually imploded later in the decade. In retrospect I have to admit that the 1980s were a time of national renewal under the Thatcher regime, but even with the advantage of hindsight I find it difficult to regard the politics of that period with unqualified enthusiasm. When Margaret Thatcher made a speech arguing that there were individuals, and families, but there was no such thing as 'society', I found such an ideology deeply unattractive. Society – indeed also community – are surely essential parts of how human beings find peace, security and a decent life. The alternatives involve unbridled competition and lack of regulation where the richest and strongest prevail while the poorest and weakest lead miserable lives.

In this period also I continued researching the politics of Japan. The most significant Japanese political leader during the 1980s was the Prime Minister (1982-1987), Nakasone Yasuhiro. Like Margaret Thatcher in the UK and Ronald Reagan in the United States, Nakasone was a right wing conservative, seeking to reform national institutions so as to promote choice and competition in areas such as education, and most significantly, to turn Japan into a 'normal state' in foreign and defence policy. This meant that he was serious about wishing to revise the 'Peace Constitution' of 1947 and to place the Self-Defence Forces on a similar footing to the armed forces of NATO member states. Previous LDP leaders had paid lip service to this aim, which was embedded in the party platform, but did not do much about it in practice. Nakasone also stood out among a succession of prime ministers many of whom were easy to forget, as a powerful personality who could interact easily with world leaders.

Towards the end of the decade, the Japan Socialist Party, which had been the subject of my doctoral thesis, began to take a new and (to me) interesting turn. It was still the leading opposition party in numbers of parliamentarians, but was generally seen as in decline and running out of relevant ideas. Towards the end of the decade, however, the party elected as its leader the first woman to lead any Japanese political party, Doi Takako. In terms of personality she was an attractive leader, charismatic, appealing far beyond traditional socialist voters, and her positive messages to women brought many female voters onto her side. I had the good fortune to interview her and found her wide ranging in her understanding of international affairs, open-minded, a reformer and obviously attractive on the personal level. The JSP won over many new voters, made major electoral gains and seemed set to challenge the Liberal Democrats, though few expected that the JSP would actually be able to replace the LDP in government.

Sadly, for the future of Japanese politics, her success was short-lived. It became evident that her most important concern was to preserve the integrity of the Constitution, and that her understanding of economics was hardly exceptional. She rode on a popular platform of opposition to 'consumption tax' (a kind of value-added tax), without fully realising that added taxation was necessary if improved welfare policies were to be implemented. Within her party itself, moreover, she found herself cold-shouldered by a traditional male-chauvinist party elite.

Nevertheless, I think it is reasonable to single out Nakasone Yasuhiro and Doi Takako, as two politicians who began to upset the long stability of the political system and nudge it into new directions during the 1990s and beyond.

Meanwhile, our lively family had not stayed still. Audrey was rapidly establishing herself as a well-known Oxfordshire potter, she had organised the conversion of a garage in the garden of our house into a working pottery, had bought a new gas kiln, and was holding, or participating in, regular exhibitions of her work. She joined the Oxfordshire Craft Guild and was later elected as its president. Just like when she was making pottery in Australia, she was primarily concerned with form and less with decoration. She had a sharp eye for what constituted a perfect pot, and came close to realising such an ideal in her own work.

Our children were developing rapidly towards adulthood, an exciting, but often difficult, stage to traverse. When we left Australia, Kate was half way through her Honours BA in music course at the Canberra School of Music, and although she came with us to Oxford during her summer break, she returned to Canberra to resume her studies. Before the course was even finished, she was recruited as Principal Clarinet by the Elizabethan Melbourne Orchestra (now known as Orchestra Victoria). As well as a variety of concerts, interstate and Victorian regional touring and education initiatives, this orchestra plays with Opera Australia, Victorian Opera and the Australian Ballet. Kate worked full time with OV for many years, before leaving to pursue clarinet teaching, examining with the Australian Music Exam Board as well as freelance gigs and chamber music performing.

Jane had graduated from secondary school just before the family moved to Oxford, and after some time in Oxford embarked upon a Professional Chef's Diploma at Westminster College in London. Later in the decade she went with her geologist fiancé (later husband), Russell, and worked in South Africa, later in the United States, the UK and back to Australia. After working as a pastry chef and later running two successive hospital kitchens, she changed course, and as well as bringing up her family, became an interior decorator with a brilliant sense of design.

Rupert had the later part of his schooling in Oxford, and then, always the mildly counter-cultural countryman, took a tree-surgeon course at Merrist Wood College in Surrey, made a good living looking after trees and gardens, and became a talented photographer. Timothy, our youngest, had most of his secondary education in Oxfordshire, was accepted into Oxford University to read geography, prior to which he took a gap year for travel.

Towards the end of the decade, I became aware that the Nissan Company, and specifically its President, Mr Ishihara Takashi, was interested in promoting further development of the Nissan Institute, and seemed prepared to make a substantial second donation of funding for the purpose. I did not learn this directly from Nissan, but I found out that Mr Ishihara had summoned a meeting of all the Japanese visiting fellows that we had harboured annually since the inauguration of the Institute, and asked their opinions on what further developments might be worth pursuing. I believe that all nine of these attended the meeting. By pure coincidence, I happened to be in Tokyo on the day that the meeting took place. Several of those present contacted me directly to brief me on what had been said at the meeting, and those who did not I managed to contact myself. But from Nissan I heard nothing, not even that the meeting had taken place, either then, or at any later time.

Based on the intelligence I had collected about the intentions of Nissan, and based on our own priorities, I sent a carefully worded request for further funding to Nissan, after consulting with the University and with St Antony's College. We put together a package, consisting of three principal items: funding for a new building to house the Institute, for two new academic positions, and for a conference on the Japanese standard of living. We also, at the suggestion of one of our former Japanese visiting fellows, asked for a small amount of money to help a particular African student in Japanese studies at Oxford, who was facing financial difficulties.

Putting together this package was not entirely easy. We came up against the interests of the College contrasting with the interests of the University. Nissan from the time of the first 'benefaction' in 1979 had insisted that their largesse should go to the University, not to one of its colleges. Up to the point of our new funding request, we had inhabited a refurbished Victorian building, owned by St Antony's College, in Church Walk, a short distance outside what was referred to in Oxford-speak as the 'curtilage' of the College. But now we were proposing to construct a new building *within* the curtilage. Moreover, we wanted to unify, so far as possible, the library collections relating to Japan, in a bespoke library space within the new building. These included the existing Japanese collection of the Bodleian Library (the central university library), and the Japan-related part of what had been collected by St Antony's as its Far Eastern collection. The teaching collection within the Oriental Institute would be excluded because it was needed for teaching purposes within that Institute (It has been amalgamated with the rest of the collection only very recently, as part of a general centralising of Japanese studies within the Nissan Institute.) Things have moved on.

This met resistance on various fronts. Some College Fellows argued that it was unprecedented, and if not unprecedented then undesirable, for a university institute to be located within a college, as it might dilute the autonomy of the College. I felt that the College had already sold the pass on this question by agreeing to house the Nissan Institute (admittedly not within the 'curtilage') after the first funding had been given in 1979. This objection was compounded by the proposal to incorporate a portion of the Bodleian Library within the new building. St Antony's was exclusively a college for graduates, whereas the new library would be used by undergraduates as well as postgraduates. This seemed to me a weak objection, since undergraduates using the Nissan Institute Library would not have access to other facilities of the College. In any case, teaching of undergraduates already took place within the College. Another problem, seen as less important but still raised by objectors, was that a substantial part of a book collection amassed by the College ought not to be simply handed over to a library that was part of the University library system. The name of the late Richard Storry, a passionate college man who had collected much of the St Antony's Japanese book collection, was cited in defence of this position. We had to explain that since Dick's day circumstances had changed. Another objection, though I only became aware of it much later, came from scholars working on pre-modern Japan. This was that separating off the Bodleian's Japanese collection from its Chinese collection would sever the intimate links that existed between pre-modern Japan and China of the same period, including linguistic overlap between the two cultures. I took the point but suggested that a social scientist studying modern or contemporary Japan would need to consult discipline-specific as well as Japan-specific collections of written sources, and these were in different libraries.

The idea of funding for two new Japan-related positions did not meet serious resistance from the College, but the problem was that the funding Nissan seemed willing to grant was inadequate to endow these posts in perpetuity. And we duly held the conference on Japanese standard of living, as well as receiving funding for the African student.

As the decade of the 1980s was approaching its end, my colleagues and I felt a certain satisfaction at what we had achieved in a few years. We were assisted by the fact that the Japanese economy was booming, commentators were using the term 'economic miracle' to describe what was happening, and the 'Japanese model' was being widely discussed. In many circles, what Japan was doing was also controversial, as shown by the writings of Chalmers Johnson, Karel van Wolferen and others. I attended conferences in continental Europe where speakers gave vent to splenetic outpourings of alarm about the dangers coming to be posed by Japan.

There had been difficult negotiations on economic matters between Japan and the United States throughout much of the 1980s about trade, investment and other economic matters. The atmosphere in the UK was not so extreme, but it was not forgotten that the Japanese motorcycle industry had 'wiped out' British motorcycle manufacture during the 1970s. When I wrote to my parents telling them I was returning to Britain to head up an Oxford University institute of Japanese studies my father wrote back ironically saying, 'When you drive your Nissan Primera through Cowley, be careful that they don't stone the car.'

But economic booms do not last for ever, and by the late 1980s asset prices, meaning principally land prices, had reached astronomical levels. For instance, the value of land in central Tokyo – specifically Chiyoda-ku, which includes the Imperial Palace – was calculated to be approximately the same as the value of all the land in Canada. Companies were using land as collateral for loans, the repayment of which became dependent on such assets retaining their extraordinarily high values. The Ministry of Finance has been widely blamed for failing to control an economic 'bubble' that had gone out of hand. Stock prices had also reached unsustainable levels. When the inevitable happened and the bubble burst early in 1990, the economy went into a long period of stagnation. The shine went off the 'economic miracle', and this caused serious problems for Japanese studies outside Japan as well. Those who had been advocating 'Japanese solutions' for problems in their own countries began to rethink their positions, so that American economic models came back into fashion.

As a family, we were not particularly affected by these issues in Japan, but just before Christmas of 1987, in the matter of a few seconds, the bottom dropped out of our world.

13

Affliction and Accomplishment

ᴧ

THE YOUNGEST OF our four children, Timothy, graduated from Magdalen College School in Oxford, where he had spent the last two years of his schooling after attending state schools, in July 1987. He had been admitted to St Hugh's College, Oxford to read geography, but was allowed to take a gap year, in which he planned to travel. In August, he participated in a cricketing tour of Zimbabwe, and in the later months of the same year, went inter-railing, together with two Australian friends, in several countries of Western Europe. In December, he secured a job at a *Gasthof* in the ski resort of St Anton, in Austria. Tim was a talented cricketer, sports mad, but he was also a culturally aware, ambitious and personable nineteen-year-old. He was the sort of young person who easily lifted the spirits of those around him.

On 23 December 1987, in clear weather and easy skiing conditions, this experienced young skier inexplicably skied off the snow onto rocks and was killed.

I will not attempt here to describe the long period of grief and radical disorientation that this wrought on his family, his girlfriend and his friends more generally. In the years that followed I was determined that his already remarkable life should not be forgotten, and wrote *The Story of Tim*, Paul Norbury Publications, 1993 (copies available free from the author: arthur.stockwin@sant.ox.ac.uk).

We learned several lessons from this devastating experience. You do not 'get over' such a loss in a mere six months, as a few of our acquaintances seemed to believe. Many people were most kind to us, but in general the average person is not well schooled in dealing with the grief of others. The death of a young person today is far more exceptional than it used to be, and for most people experience of it is lacking. I felt anger, to the point where I was frightened of my own reactions. I found that grief and anger overlap. Such an experience may also – and I am speaking mainly for myself here – radically upend your assumptions of what life is about and how the world is supposed to be ordered. In this sense it can lead to severe disillusionment, and with that also depression. You have to rethink the world, and that is hard. And finally, there is no end point: you cannot simply go on as before, because your expectations cannot return to what they were before. That is not to say that there is no way through (and this depends to some extent on one's beliefs) but that the path ahead cannot simply replicate the path behind. I personally found no satisfactory answer to the question: 'Why do bad things happen to good people?'

We all dealt as best we could with what had happened, and we were all involved in the world of work and the world of school, which requires concentration of effort, and thus distraction. I watched in love and admiration at Audrey's ability to organise the family in such awful circumstances.

For me, the period after Tim's death coincided with our negotiations with the Nissan Company for extra funding, with the key purpose of erecting a new building for the Institute. Crown Prince Naruhito participated in the ground-breaking ceremony for the new building, by 'turning the first sod'. The new building opened its doors early in 1993. This transformed our operations, and among other things made it possible to amalgamate the Japanese collections in the Bodleian Library (except for those required for teaching the language and culture of Japan at the Oriental Institute) with books and other materials we already had in the original Nissan Institute building.

The other principal use to which we put the new funding was for two new academic positions. Although it took some while before we were able to make appointments to these positions, once the appointments were made we had reached critical mass, and were able to paint on a broader canvas. The first position was filled in social anthropology, by Roger Goodman, who had written his doctoral thesis at St Antony's College on Japanese 'returnee children', meaning children of Japanese parents posted abroad who, after returning to Japan and to Japanese schools, had missed out on substantial portions of indigenous schooling. A major issue he grappled with in the thesis was how far the 'returnee children' came back home into a situation where they suffered discrimination as 'not properly Japanese', and how far, to the contrary, they came in adulthood to be treated as a privileged elite with special insight into how the world works outside Japan.

The second position was in economics, but the selection process raised in sharp form the question of college affiliation. One of the undergraduate colleges made a bid for the position, which from our point of view was problematic because we feared that the college would require the successful candidate to devote an inordinate part of his or her time to teaching general economics, rather than furthering the understanding of the Japanese economy, which did not necessarily follow all the rules of 'general economics'. As it turned out, the first attempt to make a selection failed to come up with a satisfactory candidate, the undergraduate college lost interest in the position and withdrew its bid, so that the position was transferred to St Antony's. On the second attempt at selection we appointed a Canadian economist, Marcus (Mark) Rebick, a specialist in Japanese labour economics, who wrote extensively on how far traditional patterns of labour relations (enterprise unions, permanent employment contracts in large firms, and so on) were giving way to free-market practices under the influence of globalisation.

One thing that this second position established was that in principle future appointments to the Nissan Institute would be fellows of St Antony's College. Some argued that this was not how the college-based Oxford system was supposed to work, but from our point of view it created a welcome boost to efficiency and commitment to the study of Japan.

Meanwhile, the sense during the 1980s that we had a following wind behind us because of the spectacular achievements of the Japanese economy excited a mixture of excitement and apprehension in many parts of the world. When this came to an end with the downfall of Japan's 'bubble economy', leading to a long period of economic stagnation, this had an adverse effect on Japanese studies around the world. In the United Kingdom there were cutbacks, and some departments and centres of Japanese studies were axed, most notably at the universities of Stirling and Essex, which were vulnerable as relatively recent foundations with insecure funding. Much later, in the 2000s, the much older and well established Centre of

East Asian Studies at the University of Durham came under attack from the university Vice-Chancellor, and even though a massive campaign was organised to save it, it nevertheless bit the dust.

In the longer term, the study of Japan in all its aspects in British universities not only survived but prospered, and continued to attract good students, but the 1990s were a lean time. Much the same was true for other countries, such as the United States and Australia, where there had been substantial investment at university level in the study of Japan. So far as the Nissan Institute in Oxford was concerned, we were in the position of having a single financial benefactor, the Nissan Company, but during the late 1990s it was going through a difficult period. It was only after the company, now led by the remarkable if controversial M. Carlos Ghosn, recovered in the 2000s, that further funding became a realistic prospect.

The years 1989 to 1991 marked a crucial turning point in the history of the world. The Soviet system imploded, fourteen of the fifteen former Soviet federal republics became independent of the Russian heartland, and the Cold War in its existing form came to an end. The prospects looked good for a united Europe, even though some ancient disputes in Eastern Europe were revived, most disastrously with civil war in what was still Yugoslavia.

In Japan, not only did the renowned economic success story of the 1980s come to an end from the beginning of the 1990s, but the Shōwa Emperor, in the sixty-fourth year of his reign, died after a long illness on 7 January 1989. This was sensational news locally, where none but the elderly remembered any emperor but him. Even the least nationalist of the newspapers were scrupulously careful to refer to the deceased Emperor using reverential language, some of it of antique origin.

The Shōwa Emperor was widely known outside Japan as 'Hirohito', though few in Japan referred to him by that name. He was normally referred to as 'Tennō heika', which may be translated as 'His Majesty the Emperor'. In part because, even after 1945, discussion of the Emperor's role in pre-war and wartime politics was treated widely as a taboo subject, controversy about his war responsibility was not extensively aired, except among specialist historians, some of whom were circumspect about what they wrote. Much government material was deliberately destroyed in the weeks following the surrender. All this left the way open for various conspiracy theories about his role to circulate, especially but not exclusively among non-Japanese writers. In 1971, the journalist David Bergamini published a book of more than a thousand pages, titled *Japan's Imperial Conspiracy,* claiming that the Shōwa Emperor 'led Japan into war against the West', as phrased in the subtitle. Despite the appearance of thorough and extensive scholarship that the book creates, the question arises whether an order that went out under the name of the Emperor was necessarily an order **by** the Emperor. Indeed, the same question could be asked about government orders under the name of King George VI during the Second World War. In other words, titular power and real power are not necessarily the same thing. The book was widely criticised and discredited by serious historians in the years that followed, and is now rarely referred to. Moreover, in recent years memoirs by imperial chamberlains have provided much new documentary material, which fails to back up Bergamini's arguments.

It seems implausible that all the backstage manoeuvrings that occurred within Japanese government during the 1930s have yet been uncovered, and successive post-war governments have shown touchy sensitivity to any material that might show the Shōwa Emperor in a bad light. Even so, the idea that the Shōwa Emperor personally directed his country's path to war runs in the face of what we know about how the political system worked in the pre-war period. The Emperor was not entirely a puppet and the Emperor *institution* had substantial power, but neither was he a personal dictator, despite what had been widely believed in Western countries during the war.

In February 1991, shortly after the death of the Shōwa Emperor, a journalist named Edward Behr produced in the United States a docu-drama entitled *Hirohito: Behind the Myth.* In it, he claimed among other things that the Emperor *personally* ordered the attack on Pearl Harbor. He also asked rhetorically why, given that the Emperor made a broadcast in August 1945 ending the war, could he not have prevented the outbreak of war by vetoing the Pearl Harbor attack in December 1941. It would seem that the answer to that question is fairly straightforward, but not in the sense that Behr intended. In 1941 his cabinet was united in its determination to go to war. In 1945 he faced a power vacuum in circumstances of national military defeat. He lacked the power to act in 1941, but not in 1945. Another consideration, raised by the historian

Stephen Large, was that given the feverish atmosphere of politics in the 1930s, he was under a real threat of assassination by ultra-nationalists if he stepped too far out of line (*Emperor Hirohito and Shōwa Japan*, Routledge, 1992).

The Behr film made an impact in the United Kingdom as well as in the United States. The feisty former British Ambassador to Japan Sir Hugh Cortazzi engaged vigorously in the controversy the film had unleashed. I was involved in the dispute as well to some extent, and we cooperated as best we could.

During 1990 and 1991 Audrey and I spent a period of sabbatical in Japan and then in Australia and the UK. The most interesting period of the whole sabbatical was the period when we stayed at the University of Hokkaidō in Sapporo, the principal city in Japan's northernmost island. It became evident to us early in our stay that Hokkaidō was in some ways different from the rest of Japan. It had only been seriously settled by Japanese during the late nineteenth century, so that it had not much more than a hundred years of history as home to Japanese people. The indigenous people of Hokkaidō, the Ainu, were a quite different ethnic group, with their own language, unrelated to Japanese, their own culture and religion. The Japanese incursion had devastated the Ainu, whose life had been based on hunting and fishing, and their numbers had drastically declined. But Ainu activists were now working to revive the language and culture, and assert their identity, separate from that of Japanese people. The Japanese authorities, local and national, were working to keep the lid on such activities, in an assimilationist drive that gave the Ainu some opportunities for cultural development, but clamped down on any signs of separatism.

We soon realised that Japanese people in Hokkaidō were rather less wedded to traditional attitudes and culture than those in most other parts of Japan. This made it perhaps less interesting from the standpoint of traditional culture, but people in general seemed less inhibited by attitudes entrenched in historical assumptions about the uniqueness of Japan and similar nostrums. Politically, this meant that the island as a whole was at that time (not today) somewhat further to the left than the rest of the country. As a very rough analogy, (which may not work in relation to politics) I am tempted to compare this with the differences in general attitude between the United Kingdom and Canada.

Nevertheless, some time-honoured practices were alive and well even in Hokkaidō. Audrey and I were invited to witness a session of debate in the prefectural assembly housed in the *Dōchō*, or provincial equivalent of the parliament building. On arrival, we had a lively discussion with officials servicing the prefectural assembly, and received a dossier to introduce us to what we might expect in the debate we were about to experience. When we took our places in the visitors' section of the chamber, we soon found that the dossier we had been given was almost entirely a verbatim transcript of the debate we were in the course of hearing. The only departures from the script that we detected came from the two or three Communist Party members. We felt we had been given, not the minutes of the **last** meeting, but the minutes of the **present** meeting.

This indeed was an admittedly extreme example of a widespread practice in Japanese politics, particularly at local level, where decision-making takes place, not necessarily in formal assemblies, but behind the scenes in meetings where issues are thrashed out beforehand between the participants. The function of the subsequent formal assembly is to ratify what has been decided, rather than to decide. It brings to mind a meeting I was once involved in in Tokyo between an eminent Oxford law professor and two or three of his Japanese counterparts. The latter explained that an essential purpose of legal institutions is to inhibit, rather than to facilitate, disputes coming to court. The Oxford law professor expressed his utter astonishment at such a strange system, which seemed to fly in the face of his expectations honed over a long career. Another comparable example is the notorious one of police preparations for prosecution. It is very rare in Japanese criminal cases for a case prepared by the police to be overturned by a court. Here again, the real decision-making takes place behind the scenes rather than in an open forum.

I need, however, to enter a caveat here. Now that we are well into the twenty-first century, we see some resistance to such lack of transparency, however entrenched it may seem. Even though contemporary institutions for the most part follow time-honoured practices of this kind, they are not universally accepted. I come back to what I wrote earlier, that the celebrated notion of consensus as a characteristic of Japanese society and institutions is not a naturally existing consensus but one that is imposed, or engineered, because of the fear that otherwise conflict will spill over into disruptive strife and social unrest. But there are those who challenge it.

Our stay in Hokkaidō coincided with fascinating developments between Japan and Russia. We were in Sapporo between June and September 1990, and in August Audrey and I, together with our Oxford friend Jacky (who had also lost a child in an accident), flew to the eastern part of Hokkaidō, hired a car and toured the Nemuro peninsula and the coastal areas to its north. This was a truly beautiful area, reminding us of parts of southern Germany, and very different from most parts of Japan that we already knew. We stayed at inns, all pre-booked from Sapporo, and were greeted with wonderful hospitality. This was an area of natural beauty largely undiscovered by foreigners like ourselves. At one *ryokan* (Japanese-style inn), we were served with a delicious salad, and ordered cold Japanese beer. After a minute or two, I noticed that exactly at the meniscus of the beer in the tall beer glass, there was a crack that extended right round the glass. Clearly, the beer had been refrigerated at too low a temperature. I summoned our waitress and with a dramatic gesture, lifted the top section of the glass into the air. The expression on that young lady's face was unforgetable.

Visible from various spots along that coastline were the islands of Shikotan, Habomai and Kunashiri (Russian Kunashir) that had been taken from Japan in September 1945 by Stalin's troops. These islands, together with the much larger island of Etorofu (Russian Iturup) further north, had been claimed by Japan ever since. There have been many negotiations between the two sides over the years, and at times a compromise solution seemed possible, but under the hard-line Putin the chances of a settlement have faded. We caught sight of the nearest islands once or twice, though mostly they were shrouded in mist. At one location we visited, a museum on the coast, was giving the Japanese case for their return. I also photographed a propaganda poster on the roadside showing an evil-looking Soviet soldier threatening a map of Japan. This had undoubtedly been put in place by some ultra-rightist organisation. I showed my photograph at a conference sometime later in Sapporo, where one of the participants – no doubt with access to government – promised to have it taken down. Whether this was done I never learned.

During our stay in Sapporo, however, with the Soviet Union close to collapse and barriers to personal contact between Russia and Japan breaking down, the local media ran a story for some weeks that suggested happier outcomes might be possible if local peoples were freed of political constraints. A young boy living with his family in Yuzhno-Sakhalinsk (the principal city in the Russian island of Sakhalin directly to the north of Hokkaidō and parallel with the Russian coastline going north) had fallen into a container of boiling water and been badly scalded. Officials of the two sides got together and arranged for the boy to be flown to Sapporo for emergency treatment. This was successful and he survived. His mother appeared on Japanese television and thanked Japan 'for saving my son's life'. This episode symbolised a possible cooperative future for the region that was later largely nullified by hard-nosed political considerations.

There is one other experience worth recording during our stay in Sapporo. I gave a series of lectures in comparative politics to undergraduates at the University. In so doing I received a similar reluctance on the part of Japanese students to engage in discussion that several of my colleagues have also experienced. I would finish my lecture a few minutes ahead of time and ask for questions or comments. None, or few, came; except, that is, from one student whose name was Sakurada Jun. He was seriously handicapped, suffering from what was probably cerebral palsy. He could walk, but had very little use of his hands, so that he needed assistance from his friends to feed himself. Sometimes, when he was sitting down, his head and back would fall forward out of his control. But at the end of every lecture he would come up to me and discuss the arguments I had put forward. One time he suggested to me what he calculated to be an ideal cabinet line-up of the Japanese politicians he most admired. To my surprise, He asked if we could speak in English, which he spoke passably well, despite never having been outside his home country. Most of the other students were reluctant to attempt any conversation in English. We got to know each other well, and would take lunches together, sometimes with other students. After I left Hokkaidō, I lost touch with him, but several years later I discovered that he had published several books on the politics of Japan, and had made a career for himself in that field.

In reflecting on this case, I came to the conclusion that the reluctance to engage on the part of most of the students I was teaching probably resulted from two broad factors. One was the strongly conformist atmosphere that inhibited the expression of controversial ideas unless they had been taken up by the majority; and secondly because the standard of living was high by international standards, and most students probably led a fairly comfortable life. Sakurada-san, by contrast, had needed, since childhood, to battle with a severe disability, and could not afford not to plough his own furrow, irrespective of how many conformist norms he was transgressing, if he was to make a mark in the world. He was also, of course, intelligent, but the key factor was motivation, and the motivation that principally stimulated him was his determination to succeed despite his disability.

During the period we were in Hokkaidō, the domestic politics of Japan was in a particularly interesting phase. The Japan Socialist Party, which had been the subject of my doctoral dissertation at the ANU in the 1960s, was going through a transformation. In 1986 the first woman to lead a Japanese political party was elected to the presidency of the JSP. Her name was Doi Takako, whom I had interviewed in Tokyo not long after she became President. She had been a member of the National Diet for several years, but once she took on the reins of office she inspired a remarkable revival of the party. The JSP won an overall majority in the second chamber, the House of Councillors, in July 1989, which was a national sensation at the time, with some commentators predicting an imminent change of government. In the subsequent House of Representatives elections held in February 1990 the party did not come near to winning a majority, but it added fifty seats to its existing seat total, so that a good deal of the initial momentum was maintained.

Ms Doi had charisma, and proceeded to recruit a large number of new candidates for election, among whom were many women. She campaigned against corruption, at a time when there was a spike in corruption cases involving LDP politicians, some of them breathtaking in their chutzpah. She proposed economic reforms designed to benefit ordinary people rather than entrenched elites, and she campaigned on welfare issues and human rights. She opposed the government's unpopular 'consumption tax' legislation (similar to value added tax), though in doing so she was potentially depriving a future Socialist government of the financial means with which to improve social welfare and other services that needed improving. In foreign affairs she put forward an internationalist vision and as a long term defender of the 1947 'peace' constitution, she proposed to strengthen constitutional barriers to substantial rearmament.

About half of the fifty JSP members newly elected in the lower house elections of February 1990 formed themselves into a proto-faction called the 'New Wave Society', consisting of the most progressive elements of those newly elected. While we were living in Hokkaidō, I met some members of this group in Sapporo, and later travelled with them by train in various parts of northern Honshū, the main island of Japan. I also attended a weekend school at a private conference centre in a cabbage growing region among the mountains of Gunma Prefecture north of Tokyo, presided over by the JSP politician Eda Satsuki, son of Eda Saburō who had pioneered 'structural reform' of the JSP in the early 1960s. When I returned to Sapporo, I found a box of perhaps twenty cabbages sent to us through the post as a present. I hate cabbages.

The unexpected boom in electoral support for the JSP was short-lived. I commented in an article published later as follows:

> Thus in the nearly 5 years of Doi Takako's chairmanship the party appeared to have come full circle, from political irrelevance to political irrelevance, by way of a period in which the Socialists were briefly and intoxicatingly discussed as the future party of power.
>
> ('On Trying to Move Mountains: The Political Career of Doi Takako', *Japan Forum*, vol. 6, no. 1, April 1994.)

Even so, the political legacy of Doi Takako was far from negligible. The JSP victory in the upper house elections of July 1989 created for the first time a precedent for a 'twisted Diet', in other words a parliamentary situation in which the two houses had differing majorities. It also presaged a period that lasted most of the 1990s in which party politics was unstable and difficult to predict. In June 1993, the LDP split, with two separate groups breaking away and forming new parties, while the previous year a new group titled the Japan New Party was formed with the intention of reforming the political system. The leader of this party was a young-looking and charismatic prefectural governor called Hosokawa Morihiro. In July, the LDP was defeated in general elections, and Hosokawa became Prime Minister in a multi-party coalition government with reformist ambitions but a marginal electoral majority. The power behind the throne, however, in this first non-LDP government since 1955, was Ozawa Ichirō, a controversial ex-LDP man and former acolyte of Tanaka Kakuei. Ozawa had recently set up as a new party the larger of the two breakaway groups from the LDP. For good or for ill, Ozawa was a major figure as a political maverick for the next two decades.

The Hosokawa Government was a shaky coalition that lasted a mere nine months. After a brief interim period in 1994 the Liberal Democrats managed to claw back power through a deal with the JSP and another small party, whereby the post of prime minister went to the Socialist leader, Murayama Tomiichi, but in terms of numbers the government was dominated by the LDP. Nevertheless, the previous Hosokawa Government had inaugurated a radical reform of the lower house electoral system, from a multi-member district system to a system combining single member districts with electoral blocs based on proportional representation. The new system, which was to have profound effects on future political developments, was finalised by the successor government (with its large LDP component), but it was the Hosokawa non-LDP coalition that had done the 'heavy lifting'.

To summarise briefly what happened over the rest of the decade, Ozawa founded a new party that took from the Kennedy period in the United States the English title 'New Frontier Party'. The NFP became the principal party of opposition, but after just over three years it disintegrated, and out of the chaos that ensued another, more durable, party emerged, the Democratic Party. One of my graduate students discovered a member of the National Diet who had changed party affiliation a total of seven times, and a joke was circulating that some Diet members didn't bother to update their business cards because they realised that these were likely to be superseded by changes of affiliation even before they were printed.

Towards the end of the decade the political situation gradually stabilised, and the Democratic Party, which later also incorporated Ozawa and his followers, managed to consolidate itself as the principal party of opposition. Eventually, from 2001, a new government emerged, whose principal element was the LDP, under a remarkable leader, the apostle of neo-liberalism Koizumi Junichirō. But that is a story for the next chapter.

The 1990s were not only politically unpredictable but also economically difficult. The collapse of the so-called 'bubble economy' in 1990 led to economic stagnation summed up in the phrase 'The lost decade'. Commentators were already warning of the consequences of a low birth rate and an aging society. The amazing economic dynamism of the 1980s was replaced by a generalised uncertainty and malaise in the 1990s. Two events in mid-decade added to an atmosphere of anxiety and aimlessness. One was a major earthquake centred on the eastern port city of Kōbe, costing the lives of over 6,000 people. The other was the release of toxic sarin gas on Tokyo Metro lines by a bizarre sect known as *Aum Shinrikyō* killing about a dozen people and injuring hundreds. One of the effects of this latter event was to discredit many unrelated forms of religious expression in Japan's spiritual marketplace, not only that of the perpetrators. The government also brought in legislation targeting religious extremism.

One exercise in which I had been regularly involved over a number of years was that of selection committees for scholarships to enable students in Japan and the Republic of Korea to study at postgraduate level at the University of Oxford. The scholarships were funded by the Swire shipping company (formerly Butterfield and Swire) and were therefore known as the Swire scholarships. The company was large, but essentially a family firm, run by the Swire brothers. Selection normally took place in Japan a week or two before the selection in Korea, so that in successive years I would spend two or three weeks in Tokyo, followed by a few days in Seoul.

My participation in Korea began in1984 and that in Japan rather later, I think in 1988. Thus every year, normally in September or October, I would fly from Tokyo to Seoul. The time it takes for a flight between the two cities is about two and a half hours, so that when I arrived in Seoul I was seeing it half through Japanese eyes, since I had been in Tokyo a very few hours earlier. Some differences were immediately apparent. The Japanese drive on the left, the Koreans on the right. The languages are quite different, using different writing scripts. But the people look much the same, and even now I find it difficult to recognise whether somebody is Korean or Japanese (or Chinese, though there the differences are more marked, particularly in relation to clothing). But once I was engaged in conversations with Koreans I came to realise the extent of the psychological gulf that separated the two peoples. Crude though the characterisation might be, I came to explain the difference by identifying two points, some way apart, on the surface of a table. I would then describe the path a Japanese person would take to move from one point to the other, by making a line with my finger, replete with curves and detours. And then I would show the way a Korean would make the same journey. My finger would race in a straight line from one point to the other. Now any such generalisation will throw up many exceptions and variations. But in a broad sense Koreans tend to be direct, the Japanese rather more indirect.

Of course, historical factors come into play as well. When Korea was a Japanese colony between 1910 and 1945, the Japanese authorities imposed a harsh regime upon the Korean people. Koreans were required to assume Japanese names, young men were conscripted into the Japanese imperial forces and any dissent was harshly suppressed. The bitter legacy of the colonial period was not easily forgotten. A professor at a university in Seoul who conducted research on Japanese politics once told me, 'The attitudes towards Japan in this country are terrible'. It would not be hard to find similar derogatory views about Koreans in Japan.

Travelling annually to Japan over several years, I was able to witness the emergence of fundamental changes in the nature of the South Korean regime. The first time I visited, President Park Chung-Hee, who had pioneered the Korean 'economic miracle' but ran a harsh dictatorship, had been assassinated five years earlier by his chief of security in a safe house on 26 October 1979. But his successor, the similarly autocratic President Chun Doo-Hwan, was now in power. Ground-level entrances to metro stations were guarded by soldiers, and at five o'clock in the evening the national anthem was played over loud speakers (at least in central Seoul). When this happened, people would stand still until the anthem was over. This of course reflected the semi-militarisation of the country in the face of what was seen as an imminent threat from the North Korean regime.

Over the years that followed I could trace a gradual relaxation, and during the 1990s the development of democratic institutions, under the transitional President Rho Tae-Woo (President 1988-93). The first presidents to preside over substantially democratic regimes were Kim Young-Sam (President 1993-8) and Kim Dae-Jung (1998-2003). Kim Dae-Jung was a charismatic and radical leader, the only Korean ever to be awarded the Nobel peace prize. He had been kidnapped from Tokyo by South Korean agents in 1973, and later condemned to death in 1980 in a Korean court. In response, however, to a wave of international protests (including from Pope Paul VI – Kim was a Catholic), his sentence was commuted to a long term of imprisonment, from which he was eventually released. As President, he made vigorous attempts at dialogue with the North Korean regime, which were not met by equivalent flexibility by Pyongyang.

Relations between South Korea and Japan remained difficult. A doctoral thesis that I supervised in Oxford was by the son of the principal Korean negotiator for a treaty of friendship between Japan and the Republic of Korea in 1965, and his thesis concerned those negotiations. The treaty normalised relations between the two states, but many issues remained. Koreans remember Japan's harsh colonial occupation of Korea between 1910 and 1945, and the insensitivity of successive Japanese governments since. Korean governments sometimes used Japan as a bogeyman for domestic political purposes. Relations between Japan and Taiwan (Japanese colony, 1895-1945) have been much easier.

The longstanding American military presence in Japan has also produced tangible political and atmospheric effects. On one occasion when I was in Seoul I was invited to a social meeting with the Director of Korean Airways. Early in our conversation he said to me, speaking forceful English with a strong American accent, 'Come and visit my ranch in Jejudo' (a tourist island off the south coast of Korea). Gradually, as he came to understand that, surprisingly, I did not talk much like an American general and was from an entirely different background, he toned down his manner – even his accent – and became a low-key and intellectually sophisticated commentator on the politics of his country. It left me wondering how many Koreans found it necessary to be social chameleons in this way. Perhaps they became chameleons without ever realising how they were behaving.

One year, when Audrey and I were together in Japan, I went with her to Seoul, unusually in January, for the scholarship interviews. The temperature was well beyond our experience of winter cold in Tokyo, and Audrey even sustained a frost-bitten ear that had to be treated after we returned to the UK. The British Embassy and

British Council offices in an elegant area of central Seoul were helpfully involved in organising the interview process, and one evening we were invited to dinner at the Embassy. The head of the British Council was Tom White, whom I had met on previous occasions. It so happened that Audrey was placed next to Tom's French wife, Danielle, and Audrey mentioned casually to her that we had been vaguely considering buying a property in France, preferably in a mountain area. 'Ah', said Danielle, 'we own a property in the Ardèche that we are trying to sell, so might you be interested?'. Next summer when we were back in the UK after sabbatical, we travelled to the tiny hamlet of La Davalade, near a village called Rocher. We came across the farmer who was our contact walking along the road. He did not need to find a key to enter the house because there was no front door. The house was full of bats, the barn had no roof and the neighbour was refusing access across his land. We quickly resolved that this was not for us. The farmer told us. 'Ils l'ont acheté en regardant par les lunettes fumées' (They bought it looking through smoked glasses).

Our first attempt to find a *résidence secondaire* in France was a spectacular failure, but it set us on a path that we pursued for the next three summer breaks. In the summers of 1992 and 1993, we stayed at Argentat, on the upper reaches of the Dordogne, where Audrey had a stall in a pottery fair on the banks of the river. While there we contacted an estate agency and viewed a number of properties, though none of them fulfilled our requirements for adequate living accommodation and somewhere where Audrey could make pottery. One property had been a farm and was now owned by an elderly man who had worked in the nuclear industry in an eastern European country. It contained amazing antique furniture, including a number of huge dressers. The estate agent took us into an undeveloped area under the roof, where we discovered an ancient fridge, nearly six foot tall. When we opened it, we found it was crammed full of ammunition. The estate agent was of the opinion that if it had gone off it could have destroyed all the buildings in the area, including the church (though we didn't see a church nearby). But this property was far too big for us, so we did not pursue the matter further.

It was not until the summer of 1994 that Audrey discovered in a France-related magazine an advertisement placed by an English estate agent who had just set up his business in the cheese-making town of Ambert, This was some distance to the east of the area we had been exploring, and was located roughly midway between the cities of Clermont-Ferrand and Lyon, at the extreme eastern edge of the Massif Central, in a mountain area known as the Livradois Forez. We were shown several properties and finally bought a former thatched dwelling where years ago cattle and farmers had lived together in the annual spring cattle migration from the valley to the high country in what was known as 'transhumance'. We were in a tiny settlement of about twenty houses in the commune of Valcivières. The height above sea level was over 1,000 metres. From our house we sometimes looked out over an apparent ocean of cloud, with high ground on the other side of the valley resembling islands in that same ocean. It did not take us long to make good friends among the local inhabitants of the area.

I will tell a story of some political interest at this point. Audrey set up her pottery in the *cave de la maison* (cellar), but in order to be allowed to exhibit in local fairs and markets, she was required to join the *Chambre de Métiers* (an kind of Chamber of Commerce catering for craftspeople and small businesses). This did, however, involve her in some complicated bureaucracy. In discussing this problem with our friends in the village, we were advised to consult the *Conseiller Général* for the local region, a man called André Chassagne. So one day, Audrey being unwell, I drove alone across the valley to see him at a school of which he was headmaster. After I had explained the problem to him, he made two telephone calls to relevant sections of the local bureaucracy, and the problem was sorted out. The next year, in the spring, national elections were held in France. Back in England, I checked in *Le Monde* to learn who had been elected from our local area. To my surprise I found that the new member of the National Assembly for our area was this self-same André Chassagne. I was even more surprised when I read of his affiliation with the French Communist Party.

This was an election in which the national seat total for the FCP had nearly halved from forty-seven to twenty-five. M. Chassagne was the only Communist Party member in the whole of France who had been *newly* elected. It was true that the area had been dirt poor before the war and into the post-war period. But today it was reasonably prosperous, based on cheese, agricultural production more generally, and tourism. How was it then that a Communist could have won in the national elections from this area – and indeed, continued to increase his majority in later elections? When I talked around I found that his secret was that he made it his business to understand the economic circumstances and problems of every small business and many individuals in his electoral district, and to help people when they were in difficulties. Even devout Catholics voted Communist, not because they were voting for the Communist Party, but because they were voting for André Chassagne. As we would say in the UK, he was above all a constituency MP.

I was reminded of the politics of Japan at the time this was happening in France. Though, as we shall see, this aspect of Japanese politics has changed significantly, at that time it was the candidate, rather than his or her party, that was seen as crucial. This was particularly true of the long period up to 1994 in which the House of Representatives electoral system was based on multi-member districts (normally between three and five in one district). That meant that candidates standing for election appealed on local rather than national issues, and emphasised candidate name recognition rather than party recognition. This was very evident from campaign literature. The system also encouraged corruption, in the sense that a candidate was expected to be generous to his constituents, and this meant such things as donations to local associations and financing trips to visit the National Diet in Tokyo. Even after the election system changed, the localism of Japanese electoral campaigns took a long time to change. The early 1990s, however, saw the issue of corruption come to the fore in the reform agenda, with legislation introduced to crack down on 'money politics', while attempts were made to create a stable party system out of the complexities of the old.

If the 1960s had been our child-producing decade, the 1990s were our decade of grandchildren. Our first grandchild was born in 1990 and the last of six was born in 2000. Meanwhile, Jane had married Russell in 1985, Rupert had married Maggy in 1989 and in 1990 Kate had married Michael, after which Kate and Michael stayed with us for a week or two in Tokyo, visiting Tokyo Disneyland among other attractions including the Akihabara electronics market.

But even at the end of the decade the loss of Tim remained painful for all of us.

14

The Twenty-first Century

⅄

I NOW NEED to retrace my steps and record a few episodes that occurred in the 1990s and into the 2000s, all except the first one being Japan-related.

On the spring of 1990 I had been clearing out my parents' house in Birmingham before selling it. My mother had died in August 1983 and my father had recently gone into a nursing home. Neither of my parents had been good at throwing things away. I had been aware of a wooden chest under one of the beds, but it was locked and I had no key. But there were keys in drawers all over the house, and eventually I found the right one. What I discovered was my mother's treasure chest, and among her treasures was a humble cardboard box tied up with rough string. It contained letters between my mother and a young lieutenant in the British forces, called Geoffrey Boothby. My mother was living in Birmingham, and Geoffrey was first at a training camp in Dorset and then, via northern France and into Belgium, fighting around the town of Ypres. Although I had known of Geoffrey's existence, that he had been killed in the First World War and that my mother remained in touch with his family, it had never remotely occurred to me that there was anything romantic between them. At my discovery, so many years after the events, I was shocked, but also immensely moved.

Nearly a decade and a half later I found a niche publisher willing to publish the letters, under the title *Thirty-Odd Feet under Belgium: An Affair of Letters in the First World War, 1915-1916.* (copies of the second revised edition available from me at arthur.stockwin@sant. ox.ac.uk). The letters tell the story of a love affair developed almost entirely through letters, while Geoff was experiencing appalling conditions in tunnels under the trenches in the notorious Ypres

Salient, between two highly intelligent, humorous and literate individuals. Geoff was killed when the Germans blew a 'camouflet' into his tunnel on 28 April 1916. They had never met again after his departure to training camp in February 1915.

Much later still, I came in touch with a wonderful theatrical group – the Glow Company – which has performed a dramatized version of the story, with both acting and animation, in various towns and villages of the United Kingdom.

The other episodes, In subtle and not always obvious ways, suggest insights into the nature of Japanese society, interactions among Japanese people and interactions between Japanese people and foreigners.

The first of these episodes might be titled 'The Caravan', since it involved structured meandering through northern Honshū in September 1986 by a largish group composed in roughly equal numbers of Germans and British, with a smaller number of Japanese (the organisers) – mostly academics with an interest in local and regional government. The Caravan began with a conference at Tōhoku University in the city of Sendai, in effect the 'capital' of the Tōhoku (Northeast) region. This was the region of which the eastern part was to be devastated by the triple disaster of earthquake, tsunami and nuclear meltdown in March 2011.

The conference, which had a broad-brush title concerning the future of the Tōhoku region, was organised by two social science professors at Tōhoku University, Abe Shirō and Okamoto Tomotaka – both good friends of mine. Professor Abe conducted research at St Antony's College, Oxford at various periods. The most obvious difference between them was that Abe was a political scientist whereas Okamoto was an economist. A more subtle difference was that Abe would have probably described himself as a moderate conservative, whereas Okamoto still used some Marxist vocabulary (for instance, 'monopoly capital') in his discussions. Both, however, were deeply committed to the development of the Tōhoku region, which they regarded as seriously disadvantaged in relation to other parts of the country.

They had been instrumental in setting up an organisation titled 'Tohoku Intelligent Cosmos' (title in English), with extensive participation from local businesses, academia, and interest also from local government. In 1986 it had already been in existence for ten years. It sought to promote development in R&D, information networks, infrastructure, improvements in rice production, and so on. Even though the Intelligent Cosmos had its headquarters in Sendai, an important part of its approach was to involve, in a co-ordinated fashion, the various prefectural centres of the region in its activities. During the subsequent 'caravan' it became evident to me that this was no easy task, with local rivalries being a serious obstacle in some instances. I am pretty sure that the Abe/Okamoto strategy in inviting a mixed European group to tour the region with them was in part connected with this attempt to make local authorities and businesses understand the need for forward-looking thought in the region as a whole.

After the conference was over, the three groups together set off on the 'caravan', travelling mainly by train, and we toured all seven prefectures of the Tōhoku region. We visited local mayors, business-people, labour union leaders, farming groups, sections of the media and others. In places we were treated with amazing hospitality, and this was particularly true of the smaller, more rural, places we visited. Naturally, we saw mostly farmers at such meetings, and some of the Europeans questioned whether they were genuine farmers because they wore dark suits at the meetings. The leader of the German team was Park Sung-Jo (a Korean long resident in Berlin) and I led the British team. Another very interesting member of the German team was Ulrich Jürgens. One problem we had was that the Japanese organisers tended to assume that British and Germans would find each other hard to stomach, and therefore they tried to separate the two national groups. We assured them that we all got on well together, as indeed we did. Accommodation varied between good hotels and dormitories. One member of the British team was seriously upset that he had to sleep alongside a whole lot of others, in a dormitory. Nobody else complained. This reminds me that, in a sign of the times (not only in Japan), there were no women in any of the groups. I cannot remember anybody remarking on this. Wherever we went, we left carrying piles of often book-length propaganda material, mostly in Japanese, that we had to carry, until arrangements could be made to transport it to Sendai.

Occasionally, there were discussions about Japan-UK trade. We visited the offices of a local radio station, where the station chief told us that the British Ambassador (at that time Sir Hugh

Cortazzi) had visited the previous week, and told him that Japan should buy British aircraft. The station chief was incredulous, replying, 'We like buying Scotch whisky, but aircraft???'

We visited an industrial estate, at the entrance to which was an *arch* on which was written in enormous letters:

RYOBAN INDUSTRIAL PLAZA (RIP)

Examples of JAPanese EngLISH furnished the Europeans among us with many laughs.

Another problem we had was that while in most places interpreters had been arranged, some of them were not trained to a sufficient level for the task at hand. One of the British participants would sharply criticise interpreters (who were mainly young women in their twenties) if ever he found he had been misinterpreted. Another was not happy when he found that his rendering of the popular song "She was poor, but she was honest" at a party we were taken to, had not been translated at all. A few times, there was no interpretation, so that either I or Park Sung-Jo had to step in and exercise our interpreting skills. On one embarrassing occasion we were visiting the fisheries town of Shiogama on the Pacific coast to the north-east of Sendai. Nobody was available to interpret for the town mayor, so I had to step in. Since the principal industry of the town was fishing, not surprisingly he devoted a good part of the speech to the fishing industry. As part of this, he uttered the world 'tororu' several times. Not having heard the word before I assumed it must be some species of fish. So I think I made something up about the spawning habits of the 'tororu'. But if I had followed first principles I would have realised that it was in fact a katakana-isation (japanisation) of the English word 'trawl'. In other words he was talking about trawling.

Interpreting is a highly skilled occupation, requiring rigorous training, and is often under-appreciated. Given that English and Japanese have contrasting word order and a very different grammar, interpreting between those languages creates particular pitfalls. Let me throw in just one interpreting joke: a British and a Japanese businessman are negotiating a deal. The Japanese says what I will translate as, 'We are not making a profit at present, but we soon shall be.' The interpreter puts it into English as, 'We are now in the red, but the future is black.'

We gained a useful insight at a small town (more like a village) somewhere north of Sendai, where we visited an incredibly lavish community centre next to the rice paddy. While we were there we listened to a concert by the strings of the Berlin Symphony Orchestra, followed by an acrobatic display by the local fire brigade. For obvious political reasons a great deal of funding was poured into local facilities in rural areas where LDP voters predominated.

One place we visited was a village called Nagai, too much off the map for easy access to such development resources. During our visit we were right royally entertained with an amazing display of hospitality, and subsequently Park Sung-Jo made it his business to stay in touch with that community and help it along its way.

Professor Okamoto Tomotaka was one of the two principal organisers of the trip. He was an economist, who still retained some remnants of his early Marxism, which had inspired so many Japanese intellectuals soon after the war. He once told me the following story: When the atom bomb fell on Hiroshima on 6 August 1945, he was a boy of twelve evacuated along with women and children on an island of the Inland Sea not far from Hiroshima. Some hours after the bomb fell, bodies started washing up on the shore of the island, so that the women and children had to dig trenches and bury them. All those living on the island had been issued with sharpened poles, with which to repel the Americans when they came to invade, as everybody expected. After the bomb fell, and the war ended, the women *en masse* took these same sharpened poles and in a frenzy attacked inanimate objects, shouting 'Kill the Emperor'. But the next year, 1946, the Emperor visited the island in person, and these same women bowed reverentially before him.

Okamoto-sensei was a lateral-thinking intellectual deeply affected by his childhood experiences, which had convinced him that economic development was essential if descent into war was to be averted. The Tōhoku region, after all, had been in the 1930s a poverty-stricken area from which many had been recruited into far right and militarist causes. As an economist at the region's principal university, he put his organisational skills to use in setting up what he saw as the wherewithal to impel the region to embrace high technology in a coordinated fashion. In that enterprise, he had the able support of Abe Shirō-sensei, a more cautious and moderate individual, so that they made a good team. But in the end the enterprise made far less impact than was required. Politicians were not interested, some businesses were signed up and some relatively minor projects went well, but they lacked really powerful backers, or remotely enough power to make much of a difference.

In 1990, Okamoto-sensei, a heavy smoker like many of his colleagues, died of lung cancer at the age of fifty-six. His colleague Professor Abe Shirō and the President of the University – himself a medical doctor – after much discussion decided not to tell him that he had cancer. This seems to have been normal medical practice in Japan at the time, though I believe things have now changed to some extent. I find it difficult to understand, however, how Okamoto, a highly intelligent man, could have accepted (if indeed he did accept) an assurance that he was cancer-free, when his symptoms must have suggested otherwise. The argument about whether or not to tell cancer patients the nature of their illness raged for many years in Japan, and may say something about the preference for indirect communication in society generally – itself a reflection of the extreme concern with subtleties of human relationships.

My next episode concerns the problem of deaths that occur overseas, without normal cultural supports.

One Saturday morning in January 1992, I received an unexpected telephone call at home from a Japanese professor who was staying for several months in Oxford studying Roman history, updating his knowledge of the subject that he taught at his home university in Japan. Around the time that the previous academic year began this professor had visited the Nissan Institute to pay his respects. I had then seen him occasionally when he came to attend some of our seminars, but had not had much contact with him until I received his telephone call on that Saturday morning.

He phoned to tell me that his wife, with whom he had travelled to Oxford, had been taken ill in mid-December, had been diagnosed with a rare form of stomach cancer, and by the time the diagnosis was made was too ill to be flown back to Japan. She had died just before he phoned me. As I wrote in my diary at the time. '...the two of them had to face tragedy far from home, in a country where they had only been staying for a few months'. I went to his flat, where I found him deeply upset but stoically calm, and we discussed ways of arranging her funeral.

I had no experience in this area, but I phoned quite a number of people in an attempt to find a Buddhist priest to conduct the funeral. I was told of a Buddhist Peace Pagoda in Milton Keynes, and arranged for a priest from the Pagoda to officiate at the funeral, which would be held at the Oxford crematorium. Less than a week later, on a day that I characterised in the diary as 'a cold day, characterised by a clinging fog appropriate, no doubt, for a Buddhist funeral', I collected the professor from his flat, together with his brother, who had flown over from Japan, bringing some sutras from the Pure Land sect liturgy.

The priest arrived from Milton Keynes. Dressed in white and saffron, head shaved, he seemed surprisingly young. Talking with him later I learned that he had been involved in the Japanese movement against nuclear weapons. His Peace Pagoda was affiliated with the Nichiren sect, named after a Buddhist priest of the thirteenth century, but not connected with the Sōka Gakkai (also from the Nichiren tradition, but with its own political party, the *Kōmeitō*). The professor and his brother, by contrast, belonged to the Pure Land sect of Buddhism, which many in Japan would see as more 'orthodox' than the more 'radical' Nichiren sect.

I was initially worried that this divergence might cause problems for the professor, and indeed for the priest. This, however, proved not to be the case at all. The priest chanted sutras from his tradition, but also read the sutras from the Pure Land tradition brought by the professor's brother. My colleagues and about 40 people attended the service, and the Roman historian with whom the professor had been working, together with his wife, held a reception for participants at his own home.

If relations between the two sects did not pose a real problem, the question of how to handle the cremated remains was more problematic. In British cremations, what remains is ash, but in Japanese cremations what is required by the bereaved is bones. There also seemed to be a legal issue about taking cremated remains out of the country. It became clear to me that these issues were beyond the experience of the undertaker, and with the professor helping me, I had to explain with some persistence what was required. In the end the professor received a sample his late wife's burned but not pulverised bones, all the fees were paid, and the professor could return to Japan taking with him the Buddhist requirements for the interment of cremated remains.

A couple of weeks later I received a formal letter from the undertaker, asking whether the bones would be taken out of the country, and if so when. By this time the professor was back in Japan, together with the remains. I did not reply, and heard no more.

Some eight years later the professor returned to Oxford, and came to see me. He had remarried, seemed happy, and was getting on with his life.

During the second half of the 1990s matters relating to St Antony's College began to take up more of my time. In 1997 Ralf Dahrendorf (by now Lord Dahrendorf), came to the end of his ten-year term as Warden. In his running of the College he had actively promoted St Antony's as *the* centre of postgraduate studies in the social sciences, in particular, where empirical research into specific areas of the world (rather than pure theory) was concerned. Almost from its foundation in 1950, the College had fostered within itself several 'area centres' (European, Middle Eastern, Latin American, Russian, Asian, with the Nissan Institute of Japanese Studies functioning as a *de facto* area centre separate from the Asia Centre). The University itself later institutionalised area studies within its own structures under the title of the 'School of International Area Studies', whereby discipline and area could be combined in a rational fashion. Ralf's glory days as Warden had continued over the period 1989-90, when the Soviet Union was approaching collapse, Eastern European countries were detaching themselves from Soviet control, and his home country of Germany was being reunited. During that period, and its aftermath which included the civil war in Yugoslavia and its break-up into mini-states (even 'mini-states' within mini-states), he was immensely active in organising all kinds of high-level research and teaching activity to understand and propagate the understanding of the dramatic events in contemporary history that were occurring all around. He had also become politically involved with the Liberal Democrats, so that it was the Lib-Dem whip that he took on entering the House of Lords.

His final two years as Warden were less happy. The College had to face financial difficulties, and Ralf Dahrendorf was a developer, not a retrencher. But in a broad perspective he had been central in fostering a new intellectual dynamism in the College and the University, as well as the wider community.

He was succeeded by Sir Marrack Goulding, a former diplomat who had also spent some years working for the United Nations, organising peace keeping operations in various parts of the world under Secretary-General Boutros Boutros-Ghali over the period comprising the ending of the Cold War in Europe. By the early 1990s Marrack was in charge of fifteen UN peacekeeping missions in various parts of the world, including parts of Africa, and Yugoslavia.

Following appointment as Warden of St Antony's, Marrack set out to simplify the College committee system, at times commenting ironically 'this is a not very efficient small embassy'.

In 1999, it was my turn for a two-year stint as Sub-Warden of the College. I found that there was some truth in Marrack's ironic stricture, and that in particular the College administration faced serious problems of internal conflict. Nevertheless, during this period St Antony's found the wherewithal to construct a large new student accommodation block. As Chair of the building committee, I learned something about building techniques, and enjoyed talking with builders.

Returning to the study of Japan, the British Association for Japanese Studies held annual conferences at various university campuses in the United Kingdom, where more or less the full gamut of the topics scholars of Japan were concerned with were discussed, from language teaching to economics. The BAJS, or 'badgers' as it was often called, ran at that period, and still runs, a scholarly journal of Japanese Studies titled *Japan Forum*. This is a prestigious, well run journal, one of the best Japanese studies journals in the world. In the mid-1990s, however, a dispute broke out involving its editor on the one side and publisher on the other. The BAJS as the responsible body was called in to sort out the dispute, and since I was serving a one-year term as President of the organisation at the time, in 1994-5 I was right in the middle of this process. The dispute, involving legal action, dragged on through my presidency and through that of my two successors, and was eventually brought to an end by an agreement that financially favoured neither party over the other. It did, however, cost both parties a good deal in solicitors' fees. I still retain a bas-relief that my maternal grandfather, a Birmingham GP, used to keep on his surgery wall. It depicts a dispute over a cow. One man is pulling the cow by its horns and another by its tail. In between is a man in a cloak – clearly a lawyer – milking the cow.

The European Association of Japanese Studies was set up in 1973 and holds conferences every three years. Since the opening up of Eastern Europe in the 1990s the geographic scope of these conferences has widened, both in terms of where the conferences are held and (in the 1990s) by the discovery of excellent centres of Japan scholarship that were previously little known in Western Europe. After the fall of the Ceausescu regime in Romania in 1989, The Nissan Institute received a letter from students in a university Japanese studies department in Bucharest, telling us that their library had burned down in the revolution, and asking for books to replace those lost in the fire. We did our best to help, though it was not much in the broader picture.

Sometime in the 1990s, following a casual conversation between two or three political scientists, I was involved in organising what we called the 'Japanese Politics Colloquium', planning to meet annually as a group of those with a special interest in the politics of Japan that we felt was inadequately represented in conferences of the BAJS (mostly because of sheer lack of space and time available). Once we were able to get this new group started, we held annual colloquia at different universities prepared to host it: that is universities having a continuing interest in Japanese studies. One permanent feature we established was that a speaker would be chosen each time to give us a rundown on developments in Japanese politics and foreign policy over the previous year.

The need to raise funds for each colloquium meant that we had to apply for funding to various grant-giving bodies, in particular the Japan Foundation Endowment Committee, set up in the 1970s on the basis of a lump sum given by the Government of Tanaka Kakuei towards the study of Japan in the United Kingdom. Since I was a member of that committee, it meant regular journeys to the city of Sheffield, where the committee normally sat, and which was about the largest centre of Japanese studies in the United Kingdom. This was where our first-year students had been taught during most of the 1980s, as I described earlier, and a city I came to know reasonably well.

In September 2001, we held the annual Colloquium at the Nissan Institute. Enrolments well exceeded our expectations, and I had not set up a system for sifting potential participants, so that we found ourselves with more than forty attending, including a US Navy seal, fired up by a course on Japan at a university in California, and thus our organisational and even financial resources came under some strain. Nevertheless, it was a brilliant conference, and showed us that interest in Japanese politics seemed to be greater than we had expected. This rather surprised us, given the continuing failure of the Japanese economy to recover from the stagnation into which it had fallen during the 1990s.

A likely reason for this was that in Tokyo there was a new kid on the block, whose name was Koizumi Jun'ichirō. He had become Prime Minister in April 2001, promising to end the banking indebtedness crisis and bring in reforms that would help reinvigorate the economy. In a lecture I gave at the International House of Japan later in the decade, I made a facetious comparison between Prime Minister Koizumi and Prime Minister Tony Blair. My comparison went along the following lines:

If you examine photographs of Blair a few years before he became prime minister, you will see that he had hair considerably longer than the regulation business length. But the photos of him once he was prime minister show that his hair length was fully in conformity with business regulations. With Koizumi, however, it was the other way round. Both businessmen and politicians in Japan are in general highly conformist in matters of bearing and attire, and photos of Koizumi two or three years before he graduated to the top political job reveal that he was no exception to the rule of boring uniformity. But once he was in charge of the country, he stood out for his magnificent mane of greying hair.

His hirsute image became his calling card, domestically and to some extent internationally, of a prime minister happy to break the rules and design his own idiosyncratic persona. This was so unusual in elite circles in Japan that it gave him a remarkable publicity advantage.

Koizumi was a determined reformer from a neo-liberal perspective. He was particularly concerned with postal services, wishing to eliminate what he regarded as the gigantic slush fund available to politicians for their pet causes provided by the widely used post office savings bank. He appointed a vigorous and personable economist, Takenaka Heizō, as Minister for Economic and Fiscal Affairs with a brief to overcome the longstanding problem of unrepayable debt impeding the business viability of much of the banking sector. Takenaka dealt vigorously and with substantial success with this problem, and the economy began to register significant growth.

In August 2005, the Koizumi Government was defeated in the upper house (House of Councillors) over a bill to privatise postal services, including the savings bank. Directors of local post offices constituted a powerful national lobby, and had their sympathisers in both houses of the National Diet. Koizumi reacted immediately, dissolving the House of Representatives (the upper house has fixed terms), and declaring new lower house elections. He de-selected LDP members that favoured the postal lobby and promoted other candidates (known in the media as "Koizumi's children") in their stead. This led to an unprecedented stand-off between the Government and the postal lobby, but the LDP under Koizumi won the subsequent elections handsomely, and Koizumi was able to go ahead with his privatisation agenda.

In September 2002, Koizumi made an important international *démarche* by paying a visit to Pyongyang, the capital of North Korea. Two results emerged. One was that the North Korean leader, Kim Jong-Il, admitted for the first time that a number of Japanese had been kidnapped several years earlier by Korean agents and taken to North Korea. The other was that that the two leaders signed a joint agreement on relations between the two countries. Unfortunately, however, Kim also admitted (or claimed – the facts were later disputed in Japan) that a majority of those kidnapped had subsequently died. This led to a long-running series of disputes about the abductees among Japanese politicians and others. Moreover, the impetus towards improved relations created by the joint agreement were short-lived, for a variety of reasons.

Koizumi decided to resign in September 2006, a resignation leading to a period of instability that lasted until the election of the Abe Government in December 2012. He was criticised in some quarters for permitting this to happen by resigning prematurely.

Meanwhile, I myself retired as Nissan Professor of Modern Japanese Studies on 30 September 2003, and was succeeded by Roger Goodman, a social anthropologist who had been on the staff of the Nissan Institute for a decade or so. In practical terms, retirement was a gradual process, since several of my graduate students had yet to finish their theses, and I continued to supervise them until they completed.

Within a few short weeks after retirement, I found myself leading a three-person review committee of the Sainsbury Institute for the Study of Japanese Arts and Cultures, at the University of East Anglia in Norwich (with a branch within the School of Oriental and African Studies in London). It was universally known as SIS-JAC. Apart from me, the committee was made up of a professor of Japanese traditional graphic arts from Tokyo, and an American lady in the same field at a university in California. SISJAC, a very recent foundation, occupied a big old house in the grounds of Norwich Cathedral. We uncovered a number of problems, which in retrospect may be seen as the teething pains of a recently established institution, and its somewhat reluctant acceptance by the university authorities. I had not visited Norwich before, and found it a charming city. Researching the situation, and compiling the report turned out to be a fascinating exercise, and SISJAC has subsequently gone from strength to strength, while the UEA has now introduced Japanese studies as a standard university discipline for its students.

With retirement came more free time to engage in research and writing, and to do more of things I enjoyed. From early in the new millennium, however, a small but gradually expanding cloud was beginning to overshadow our lives. Audrey's health was gradually deteriorating, and after more than a decade, she was prey to the horrors of inexorably, if slowly, advancing dementia (Alzheimer's disease). I had begun to notice problems with her memory from around 2002, one of the curious manifestations of which was that she was forgetting that people had died, and was talking about them as if they were still alive. But although she was suffering from memory loss, and had other medical problems, she was still able to function on many fronts, and in particular, she could still make her beloved pottery.

In 2009, I was recruited by a local tourist agency working for Oxford University, to give lectures on an alumni tour of Japan. My task was not to act as a guide, since we had both a tour guide who was with us for the whole trip, and also local guides, but rather to give a series of lectures at places we stayed on aspects of Japan – mainly on its modern history and contemporary society and politics. Audrey, although she was beginning to develop mobility problems, was well enough to accompany me, and we had a fascinating time, travelling, mainly by train, between Tokyo, Kyoto, Nara, Hiroshima and various places in Kyūshū including Mount Asō, a still active volcano emitting sulphurous fumes that had an effect on the throat like tear gas. While we were in Kyūshū I managed to persuade the organisers to take us to the tiny pottery village of Onta that we had visited several years before. Audrey amazed me by giving an impromptu talk about the pottery made at Onta, and even though she was not entirely coherent, her audience loved her performance.

I have two observations about this trip. The first relates to the local English-speaking guides that accompanied us on parts of the journey. Most, though not all, were female. One example will suffice. We were on a long bus journey through countryside. Our guide talked about this and that, made jokes, and when she had no more to say, would play music. But as became clear to her audience, it was *de rigueur* for her to entertain us every moment of the trip. This became quite tedious, and after a while one imperious Englishwoman shouted out 'silence!', to which our guide asked whether we really wanted her to stop talking, and after a short break, continued talking.

Secondly, we visited the atom bomb museum in Hiroshima. This was where we encountered the first really excellent guide of the whole trip. She was relatively young, the daughter of a *hibakusha* (a person injured by the atom bomb), and was a committed peace activist, who knew the history of Hiroshima since the bomb in great depth. It so happened that I was scheduled to give a lecture about an hour after we had concluded our visit to the atom bomb museum. This was my second visit to the museum, having first visited it about two decades before, when I had witnessed the delivery of a large stone on which a person had been sitting when the bomb fell. The stone still retained the shadow of that person. On this second occasion, there was far more written explanation than before, including about the history leading up to the war, no doubt because of criticism in the intervening period about the impression that the museum reflected Japanese 'victim consciousness'. I found myself so affected by the horror of what the museum displayed (even though I had seen it before and read about it many times) that I had to return to our nearby hotel and compose myself before I could give a lecture. In the event, I gave up on what I was supposed to be talking about, and devoted the lecture entirely to the experience of Hiroshima and Nagasaki, and to the historical background.

Audrey's health continued to deteriorate slowly over the ensuing years. She made her last pots, in the pottery she had established in the 'cave' of our house in the Livradois Forez, in the summer of 2014. After that, she no longer possessed the necessary coordination of mind and body to practice her skill. For some while afterwards, however, with my help, she exhibited at various local exhibitions, especially at the Oxfordshire Museum in Woodstock, and St Barnabas Church in Oxford.

She lived the last six months of her life in a local care home, where she was safe and well looked after, and where I visited her nearly every evening to feed her. Audrey died on 4 September 2018, aged 82. We had been married for fifty-eight years.

After my retirement, I remained determined to continue with my academic work, and in particular, to carry on researching and writing about Japan. The fourth edition of my textbook was published in 2008, under the title *Governing Japan: Divided Politics in a Resurgent Economy.* (Whether it was resurgent at that point was moot). And then in 2017, my colleague and former graduate student Kweku Ampiah and I published *Rethinking Japan: The Politics of Contested Nationalism.* These two books together form a set of reflections, not only on the politics and political system of Japan, but also, by implication, on politics and political systems generally. In the next chapter I want to re-address the themes taken up in these books and see what they tell us about Japan as we approach the third decade of the twenty-first century.

But I must end this chapter on a bitter-sweet note. Near the end of August 2014 the European Association of Japanese Studies held its triennial conference at the University of Ljubljana in Slovenia. I was attracted by the prospect of spending some days in Slovenia in part because I had been there just after graduating from Oxford in 1959, when I hitch-hiked through what was then still Yugoslavia, as far as Dubrovnik further south on the coast. While I was in Ljubljana I took a detour past the lovely small town of Bled as far as Lake Bohinj, under the shadow of Mount Triglav (Three Peaks) – the highest mountain in former Yugoslavia. It was such a beautiful part of the world that I was keen to revisit it.

As usual, in the summer of 2014 we were spending our summer holidays at our place in south-central France. We decided that instead of returning to the UK and flying from London to Ljubljana, we would drive through the French Alps, across the top of Italy and into Slovenia through Trieste. But instead of simply crossing Italy, we would also call in on Italian friends who had a holiday home in the Italian part of Switzerland. These were Itala and Enrico, Itala having been a friend of mine from undergraduate days in Oxford, who had later taught post-colonial literature at the University of Milan. When we looked at an atlas of Europe, it was clear that this was going to be a marathon trip, but although we didn't talk about it, I think that Audrey knew as well as I did that this was likely to be our last adventure together. 2014 was, as I have mentioned, the last year in which she was able to make pottery.

Our family was apprehensive about such a long and complicated trip, and wrote us emails urging caution. But we were not to be deterred, and set off determined to enjoy the trip. Indeed, we made it from France to the village of Soglio, in the Engadine, part of Italian Switzerland, in a single day, even though we were very late. In the evening, Enrico, an architect with interests in East Africa, picked my brains on the prospects for the forthcoming Scottish referendum on the proposed separation of Scotland from the rest of the United Kingdom. I think I predicted the negative result with reasonable accuracy.

The next afternoon I negotiated the twenty-four tunnels (more tunnel than non-tunnel) back between the Swiss border and the motorway north of Milan, where I turned east towards the Slovenian border. We looked for a hotel in the town of Pordenone, north of Venice, which was celebrating a festival of blues music, but we could not find the hotel district. Eventually, I stopped the car, got out and asked a passer-by. He immediately said 'I will drive you there', jumped into the driver's seat, telling us he had never seen a wheel on the right hand side of a car before, and drove us to a quite attractive, and reasonable, hotel. He would then have had a long walk back to where we had found him. 'Could this happen in Japan?', I ask myself, or indeed, 'could it happen in the UK?' I suspect that answer is negative in both cases.

The next day, we drove into Slovenia, arrived in Ljubljana on the motorway, taking a while to find our bearings, so that at one point I once again asked the way of a passer-by. I asked in English, and she replied in Russian (which luckily I understood). We stayed at the Penzion pod Lipo (Inn under the lime tree), which was small and intimate, quite unlike the starred hotels where most of the conference delegates were staying. I had found it myself, but not from the officially recommended list of hotels.

As in all conferences, much of the purpose is to interact with fellow researchers and meet one's friends, but I could focus on several of the papers whose writers were thinking much along the ways I was myself, or indeed sometimes more stimulating, where their research was pointing in the opposite direction.

Before pointing the car in the direction of France, we travelled north-west, into the Triglavski National Park, where we stood on the banks of the lovely lakes Bled and Bohinj, where I had stood myself as a student all those years ago. We then took two days to return to the Livradois Forez, staying at a quite swish hotel at Piacenza, south of Milan, and crossing the French Alps in a westerly direction, among innumerable cyclists. And a day or two later, we were back in Oxfordshire.

15

What Future for Japan?

⅄

IN THIS CHAPTER I want to put together my thoughts on Japanese politics and the political system, focusing on the underlying factors driving or inhibiting change. I have chosen a title for the chapter suggesting the possibility of prediction, in the full knowledge that in matters of politics, prediction is a dangerous exercise.

As I write this, the thirty-year reign of the Heisei Emperor (Akihito) has just ended with his retirement, and a new Emperor (Naruhito), whose era name is Reiwa, has ascended the Chrysanthemum Throne. It used to be thought that Popes in Rome and Emperors of Japan did not retire, but now one of each has done so, not without controversy in both cases.

According to the 1947 Constitution, Article 1:

The Emperor shall be the symbol of the State and of the unity of the people, deriving his position from the will of the people with whom resides sovereign power.

Articles 3 and 4 read as follows:

Article 3: The advice and approval of the Cabinet shall be required for all acts of the Emperor in matters of state, and the Cabinet shall be responsible therefor.

Article 4: The Emperor shall perform only such acts as are provided for in this Constitution and he shall not have powers related to Government.

The notion of a 'symbolic' Emperor has put down roots in Japan since 1947, even though substantial elements of the far right dislike it.

But this does not mean that the Emperor is insignificant. Symbols are important in politics, and even though the Emperor's formal acts are confined to ceremonial activities, what the Emperor says and does – and more importantly, perhaps, what the Emperor does *not* say and do, can have significant implications for politics. The most famous example of such deliberate non-action has been the decision of the Shōwa Emperor (Hirohito) in 1978, followed consistently by his son the Heisei Emperor throughout the thirty years of his reign, not to pay homage to the war dead at the Yasukuni Shrine in Tokyo.

The Yasukuni Shrine was established in the aftermath of the Meiji Restoration of 1868, originally to commemorate the dead of the wars that followed that transition, but later to recognise the Japanese dead of later wars (of which there were many up to 1945). There are no human remains at the Shrine, but it remains a place of pilgrimage at which a strongly nationalistic message is propagated about the justification for past wars, including the Asia-Pacific War between 1937 and 1945.

The proximate cause of the decision of the Shōwa Emperor no longer to visit the Shrine was the decision of its then Abbot Matsudaira Nagayoshi in 1978 secretly to enshrine the 'souls' of fourteen individuals who had been arraigned as war criminals at the Tokyo trials after the war. Strongly right-wing elements in Japan still regard the Tokyo trials as 'victor's justice', and revere the memory of Justice Pal, the Indian judge on the panel who opposed the majority verdict.

If we look back at the Meiji Constitution of 1889, we see that the roles it attributes to the Emperor contrast strikingly with those in the 1947 Constitution. Articles 1 to 17 of the 1889 Constitution enumerate the overtly political, and indeed also military, functions of the Emperor within the functioning of the State. Does this therefore mean that that the Emperor was all-powerful between 1889 and 1945, but merely 'symbolic' since 1945? The matter remains controversial as to the extent of the Emperor's power up to 1945, but an absolutely crucial distinction needs to be made between the power of the Emperor *Institution*, and the personal decision-making power of the Emperor himself. The power of the Imperial institution was major (though it fluctuated over time), but from all the evidence historians now have it seems reasonable to conclude that the Emperor only exercised significant personal power on very few occasions. He did indeed personally concede defeat in war in August 1945, but this was in extreme circumstances where the exercise of coherent power had broken down.

A long succession of Emperors before the Meiji Restoration, resident in Kyoto, had in effect ceded power to the Shōgun, a military man who ruled from Edo (later Tokyo), and those emperors exercised a religious, not a political, role. So it may not be stretching historical reality too far to say that the 'norm' for the Emperor institution in Japan is to be symbolic rather than involved in running the country. Such a view, of course would be vigorously contested by contemporary right wing advocates. Even during the period between 1889 and 1945 when the Emperor-centred Meiji Constitution was in force, the personal political power of the Emperor was very limited, despite the fact that the power of the Emperor *institution* was central.

To enjoy a constitutional position as 'Symbol of the State and of the unity of the people' in today's world makes it not impossible for an Emperor to exert a stabilising influence also on the politics of the State, although of course it does not entirely eliminate the possibility of capture by destabilising or extremist forces, and Japan is by no means lacking in such forces. On the other hand, the essentially moderate character of the new Emperor, as well as of his modernising father, makes 'capture' appear unlikely at the present time.

During the mid-1980s the Crown Prince's son, whom we knew as Prince Hiro, was taking a Masters course in Oxford, and although I was not involved in teaching him I met him on a number of occasions. Indeed, in January 1985 we invited him and his bodyguard to dinner at our home in Wootton. A brief diary entry records the event as follows:

> In the evening we had Prince Hiro and his bodyguard for dinner. All the culinary resources of the family were put to work. There was lively conversation. When asked what he appreciated about his life in Oxford, he replied unhesitatingly 'freedom'.

And on 1 May 2019, this same Prince, now using the name 'Naruhito', became Emperor of Japan, the first to have been educated abroad. He later wrote a book in Japanese about his experiences in Oxford, translated into English as *The Thames and I: A Memoir of two Years at Oxford*, Global Oriental, 2006.

In the fourth edition of my textbook *Governing Japan*, published in 2008, I set out six areas of ongoing 'crisis' that seemed likely to remain problematic for the foreseeable future (pp 8-11). I wrote this at a time when prime ministers were succeeding each other on a more or less annual basis, and a year before the LDP would be heavily defeated in a general election, to be succeeded by a government based on the Democratic Party of Japan (DPJ), which proved even more unstable.

I want to recapitulate the arguments I made in relation to these 'crises' in order to assess the state of these issues in 2019. The 'crises' I identified were as follows:

1. A crisis of political power and democratic accountability.
2. A crisis of political participation and non-involvement in politics.
3. A crisis of the Constitution and political fundamentals.
4. A crisis of liberal and illiberal ideas.
5. A crisis of ageing society and diverging life-chances.
6. A crisis of national status and role.

I was not arguing was that these crises were all peculiar to Japan, but rather that this particular combination characterised the problems faced by Japanese politics.

I subsumed two particular issues under the first crisis. On the one hand there was the dominant role of the LDP, to that point almost always in power since its foundation in 1955, and on the other there was the weakness of Cabinet and the power of unelected civil servants in decision-making. I also mentioned the problem of some ministries apparently becoming too politicised.

A decade later, the LDP is even more embedded in power than it was at the time I wrote, partly as a result of the poor performance of the DPJ when it was in power between 2009 and 2012. On the other side of the political divide, opposition parties are much weaker, and the opposition as a whole more divided, than they were in 2008. On the other hand, under the long-running Government of Abe Shinzō, Cabinet is plainly more unified, more entrenched, and probably also more clearly goal-oriented, than it was a decade earlier. As for politicising of ministries, the Abe Government has been more activist than most of its predecessors in controlling appointments to senior public service positions.

The second crisis that I identified was of political participation and non-involvement in politics. Today, towards the end of the twenty-tens, the electorate shows relatively little interest in, or passion about, politics, and gives every indication of complacency in relation to political realities, and specifically to the actions of the Abe Government. In my 2008 book I noted that

> ...the bundle of activities referred to as 'civil society' showed few signs of life until participation in non-profit organisations (NPOs) increased after the experience of helping victims of the Kobe earthquake of the mid-1990s (p.9).

In the intervening period the terrible disasters of a magnitude 9 earthquake, up to 40-metre tsunami, and nuclear meltdown occurred, causing approximately 18,000 deaths, huge numbers of displaced persons, disruption to industry and to energy supply, as well as political disruption. This gave a further boost to civil society, particularly in opposition to the government's policy of reactivating nuclear power stations, after they had all been closed down following the meltdown at the Fukushima No. 1 nuclear plant resulting from the tsunami. Even so, popular movements in Japan in recent years have proved hard to sustain, although volunteering now has a much better image, especially among younger people, than it used to have.

My third crisis concerns the 1947 Constitution and political fundamentals. The Constitution has been controversial ever since it came into force, but paradoxically (as some might see it), it has never been revised in any particular. Every word and punctuation mark remains in place since the beginning. No other contemporary constitution has survived over such a long period entirely intact, and it is now one of the world's oldest constitutions. The LDP since its inception in 1955 has proclaimed constitutional revision as a major party objective, but most LDP-based governments have done little towards realising this aim. This, however, changed with the first Abe administration in 2006-7, which set up the procedures for a referendum of the people on constitutional revision, as required by article 96 of the 1947 Constitution. The other requirements of the article are a two-thirds majority of the members of each chamber of the National Diet, taken separately, prior to a national referendum.

The election of the second Abe Government in December 2012, which remains in power at this time of writing in 2019, led to a concerted governmental campaign to revise the constitution. This, however, remains unrealised, despite the degree of commitment invested in it by the Abe Government and by Abe Shinzō personally. I will explore the reasons for this later in this chapter.

The fourth crisis, as I saw it in 2008, was a crisis of liberal versus illiberal ideas. As I expressed it in the fourth edition of *Governing Japan*:

> There has long been a division between liberal and democratic ideas, resting on the primacy of the individual as the fundamental political unit, and collectivist ideas, centred on the family, the quasi-family group and the state. This of course reflects the juxtaposition of the collectivist policies, prescribed by the state, that were dominant in the period up to 1945, and the liberalising reforms of the Occupation between 1945 and 1952.

Now, although the introduction of values based on liberal individualism after 1945 were widely popular, they also provided a powerful rhetorical weapon to right wing conservatives nostalgic for pre-war values because the new order had been introduced, not by Japanese, but by Americans. (in fact, the issues were not quite so simple: there had been significant Japanese involvement in the rolling out of the new order).

Until the Abe Government came to power and was able to establish stable long-term government from 2012, something of a balance could be struck between liberal and democratic values on the one hand, and communitarianism embedded in Japanese culture on the other. Thus, Japanese society did not entirely assimilate rip-roaring individualism sometimes attributed to American society. At the same time, communal values were adapted to fit the more liberal and individualist society that gradually emerged after the war. To take one example, as has been widely documented in literature on Japanese education, schools exhibit a culture that combines individual striving for success with a sense of the school as a community, with pupils encouraged to help one another, and a widespread requirement that pupils combine together regularly to clean the school premises. We should not be naïve about this. What used to be called the Ministry of Education (now MEXT: Ministry of Education, Culture, Sports, Science and Technology), from early in the post-Occupation period replaced a highly 'progressive' American-influenced regime in schools with a regime that emphasised both intensive work and a communal ideology.

During the twenty-tens government policy has striven to shift the balance in favour of the authoritarian values of top-down decision making, curbs on free expression and on the mass media, and intolerance of political opposition (admittedly the opposition parties have done themselves no favours by failing to unite or declare convincing policies). To a disturbing extent, the long-established balance between liberal individualist values and communalism has been breaking down.

The fifth crisis that I identified in 2008 was a crisis of ageing society and diverging life-chances. According to the 2010 census, the Japanese population had just touched a peak of 128 million, but by 2018 it had declined to slightly less than 126 and a half million. The birth rate, especially in big cities, remains among the lowest in the world, whereas expectation of life at birth is among the highest in the world for both females and males. The result is a declining workforce and an increasing population of the elderly. An industry that flourishes at present is the manufacture of robots designed to aid the daily tasks of the old and infirm. Japan, unlike most advanced countries with very low birth rates, admits very small numbers of immigrants as permanent residents. There are now some signs of this policy relaxing, but it would require far greater levels of immigration than would be politically or socially acceptable before a significant impact would be felt upon population decline. Long-range projections of population growth or decline far into the future are highly speculative, but some current projections suggest that the total population of Japan could be as low as 100 million by around 2050, and continue to decline thereafter.

The economic consequences of such a rate of population decline are serious, although it may have a positive effect on the environment. It makes the funding of pension schemes difficult, and is already creating widespread rural depopulation. With the exception of the Tokyo region, Nagoya, and Okinawa (which has special circumstances), all prefectures are currently suffering net population decline. This in the long term shifts the regional balance of power in favour of the capital and its periphery, and may partly explain the emergence of new political movements (parties) based in the Kansai region, especially Japan's second city of Ōsaka, whose population continues to decline.

The sixth and final crisis I identified in 2008 was a crisis of national status and role. At that time it was already evident that the Chinese economy was growing much faster than that of Japan, and that Japan was going to formulate very carefully its policies towards its giant neighbour. For several decades the Japanese economy, in terms of its gross domestic product (GDP), was second largest in the world after that of the United States of America. But in 2011 Chinese GDP overtook that of Japan, relegating Japanese GDP to third place. We may say that China was replicating the spectacular recovery and growth of the Japanese economy from the post-war period up to the collapse of the asset bubble around 1990. But a key difference is that the population of China remains more than ten times the population of Japan, so that in global terms the impact of growth in China is much greater than that of Japan.

At the end of the twenty-tens China looms large indeed over the foreign policies of Japan. There are two fundamental reasons for this. The one, most importantly and obviously, is the continued rapid growth and sophistication of the Chinese economy. Even though growth has slowed, the economy still registered a growth rate of 6.6 per cent in 2017. In the same year, Japanese GDP stood at US$4.87 trillion, while Chinese GDP was now $12.4 trillion. The GDP of the United States was still a long way ahead at $19.39 trillion, but if current trends followed predictions, the Chinese GDP seemed likely to overtake that of the US by 2030. We surely have to acknowledge the extraordinary achievement of China in lifting more than 500 million people out of poverty during its years of spectacular economic growth (World Bank statistics). Between 1990 and 2005 some three quarters of global poverty reduction was accounted for by the reduction or elimination of poverty in China. By 2018 a mere 2 per cent of the Chinese population lived in conditions defined as poverty-stricken.

The second reason is more problematic. The Chinese economic 'miracle' was pioneered after the death of Mao Zedong in 1976 by Deng Xiaoping, who put an end to the chaos of the Maoist years and became the architect of 'Socialism with Chinese characteristics' from the late 1970s. Deng freed up economic activity in a radical fashion, while maintaining the commanding role of the Chinese Communist Party (CCP). In 2013, a new and ambitious leader, Xi Jinping, became the supreme leader of China, following his predecessor (Hu Jintao), who had broadly speaking followed Deng's example in allowing a moderate degree of personal freedom to individuals and to businesses.

The advent of President Xi marked a radical shift in the politics of China. His new regime was determined to reinforce discipline in the CCP, and to model society so far as possible along Leninist lines. This did not mean to say that China was under a regime that inhibited economic growth in the name of Marxist-Leninist or Maoist ideals. Far from it: The Chinese economy is developing across the board, determined to conquer world markets in the most sophisticated areas of technology. This would appear to be the aim of the so-called 'Belt and Road' strategy, modelled romantically on the ancient silk route between Asia and Europe. A central part of Xi's objectives, however, is to establish the supremacy of the CCP over businesses and other types of institution in China (even if CCP might now stand for 'Chinese Capitalist Party' rather better than for 'Chinese Communist Party'). This creates grave concerns within China, but also serious implications for neighbouring countries, including Japan. In 2012-13, not long after Xi became President of China, a long-running dispute broke out between the two countries over some uninhabited rocky islets called *Senkaku* in Japan and *Diaoyu* in China. The historical origins of the dispute are obscure, but for some years it seriously threatened the peace between them.

Meanwhile the Abe administration has been reasonably adept at handling relations with the hard-to-predict President of the United States, Mr Donald Trump. Early in his administration, Trump pulled the US out of the Trans-Pacific Partnership (TPP), whereupon Abe acted with other signatories to rescue the project despite the withdrawal of its trans-Pacific partner. Abe was also able to capitalise on Trump's own trade disputes with China in order to keep reasonable relations with the American President, and also to strengthen the defence relationship between Japan and the US.

On surveying these six areas of crisis in the politics of Japan in 2008 from the perspective of 2019, it seems sensible to analyse the trends that have emerged in the meantime, first from a domestic standpoint, and secondly by examining how far Japan's situation has changed in the international arena. There is, obviously, important interaction between the two categories.

The domestic political system, and thus the ways in which Japanese politics operates, has undergone profound changes since the 1990s. In broad brush terms, the system has changed from a developmental system to a system based on consolidation and protection of the status quo. But secondly, and rather in contrast to the first, the system has altered from one in which the practice of politics was pluralist and in part at least 'bottom up' to one in which it is unipolar and 'top-down'. Also, and crucially, since the 1990s, the balance of the political system has moved substantially towards the right.

This evolution stems from developments in the 1990s following the sudden ending of rapid economic growth at the beginning of that decade. Abstracting from the shifting and even chaotic character of politics during the 1990s, it seems evident that the psychological effect on politicians, public servants and others in the public and private domains then and into the twenty-first century, was to retrench public spending and search around for ways of bringing stability back into the system, rather than embarking on new ventures or seriously trying to reignite the rapid economic growth that had made the economy seem unstoppable until the collapse of 1990. Viewing Japan with extraordinary prescience, Bill Emmott, later to be editor of the *Economist*, coined the pithy phrase a year or so before the collapse, 'The Sun also Sets' (*The Sun Also Sets: Why Japan Will Not be Number One*, Simon and Schuster, 1989). His book's subtitle reflects critically upon Ezra Vogel's *Japan as Number One*, published exactly a decade earlier, when the Japanese economy seemed to be sweeping all before it. (*Japan as Number One: Lessons for America*, Harvard UP, 1979).

In the politics of consolidation that followed the unstable politics of the 1990s, Prime Minister Koizumi Jun'ichirō played a pivotal part. As we have seen, he was able to stabilise the banking system, apply market principles to the running of postal services, and even preside over some return of economic growth. His resignation in 2006 was followed by a loss of direction, with frequent changes of prime minister, and the emergence in 2009 of the first non-LDP administration to be elected as the result of a general election since 1955. The DPJ-led Government, however, was in the unfortunate position of putting in place welfare-state provision without sufficient funding to pay for it. Undermined by inexperience, battered by contingent events (most notably the disasters of 3/11), divided by internal conflict and changes of leader, that government came to an ignominious end in December 2012 and was replaced by a right-wing administration led by Abe Shinzō. (Funabashi Yoichi and Nakano Koichi, *The Democratic Party of Japan in Power*, Routledge, 2017.)

Over the five years between Abe's resignation as LDP President in 2007 (citing health issues) his regaining the LDP presidency in September 2012, and then resuming the post of prime minister in December 2012, he worked hard behind the scenes in the party and elsewhere to gather support. Aiding him in that endeavour were two organisations of the far right: the *Nippon Kaigi* (Japan Association) and the *Shintō Seiji Renmei* (Shintō Political Alliance). Most members of the successive Abe cabinets since 2012 have belonged to one or both of these organisations. When intra-LDP elections have been held in which Abe has sought to renew his mandate, potential challengers have found it extremely difficult to gather sufficient supporters to validate their challenge. In a country that obsesses over public opinion polls, Abe has retained reasonably high support in the polls compared with the poll ratings of most of his predecessors. His administrations have been adversely affected by two scandals involving alleged cronyism, both in the field of educational institutions. When such corruption happens, support dips into the thirty-forty per-cent range, but when things are going well in the eyes of the electorate, ratings tend to rise to a little more than fifty per cent. Plainly, Abe continues to receive support because he appears to have provided stability, principally political stability, but also stability in foreign policy and the economy. This being a widely accepted perception, political scandals appear to many voters less important than maintenance of stability. To some extent also, the same may be said of restrictions on freedom of speech and human rights. That does not, however, translate into a secure majority for revising the Constitution.

As suggested above, the domestic political system has also changed from one in which elements of pluralist democracy were important if not always dominant, to one in which a long-serving prime minister with authoritarian instincts was in charge of a cabinet that, impolitely, might be described as a cabinet of clones. This is an extremely important point, in the sense that up to the 1990s the structure of the ruling LDP was dominated by discrete and durable factions, each having its own distinctive character based on the character and policy orientation of its leader, but in the twenty-first century this gradually morphed into a monolithic body occupying policy positions on the far right of the political spectrum. This does not mean that factionalism in the former, pork-barrelling, sense has disappeared, but that ideologically, nearly all factions and faction leaders adhere to a deeply conservative set of attitudes.

In our book *Rethinking Japan: The Politics of Contested National-ism* (Lexington Books, 2017) Kweku Ampiah and I analysed various policy initiatives of the successive Abe governments, including constitutional revision, the Designated Secrets Law and freedom of speech, war apology issues, collective self-defence, and Abenomics. Now Abenomics was the name given to Abe's economic policies which, to oversimplify, he had used as a sweetener to impress the electorate at the outset of his regime, in the hope that they would accept his more radical policies as the price to pay for the economic recovery that Abenomics was supposed to bring. Opinions differ widely over how far Abenomics has succeeded in reviving the economy, but it is difficult to regard it as having had more than a modest success. It is also important not to forget demographic decline in this context.

The defence and foreign policies of the Abe Government are closely interlinked. Defence policy also relates closely to the issue of constitutional revision. Abe's longstanding ambition has been to revise the 'peace clause' of the 1947 Constitution in such a way as fully to legitimise the 'Self-Defence Forces' that in all but name constitute conventional armed forces. He knows, however, that a substantial part (probably a majority) of the electorate regards the 'peace clause' as a necessary bastion against a return to militarism, so that he risks losing a referendum of the people that would require him already to have won two-thirds majorities of each house of the Diet voting separately. Therefore he has turned to the device of 'rearmament by constitutional reinterpretation'. The key example of this was the passage through the National Diet in 2015 of the highly contentious 'Collective Defence' bill, which legitimised actions by the Self-Defence Forces to cooperate with the forces of an allied power in situations of military conflict. Previously, the legal position had been that the mission of the Self-Defence Forces was the defence of Japanese territory. In practical terms an 'allied power' means The United States.

The foreign policy of Japan towards the end of the second decade of the twenty-first century is necessarily dominated by relations towards and between China and the US. When Donald Trump was elected President of the United States in 2016, Abe was quick to meet him and attempt to establish a certain rapport with the Trump regime. With President Trump attempting to counter what he sees as unfair Chinese trading practices, it makes some sense for Abe to cultivate good relations with the American regime, given Japan's own difficulties with a resurgent China.

The resurgence of China should be seen as the most important and far-reaching development in contemporary world politics. As I have suggested earlier, the nature of the Chinese regime has radically changed since Xi Jinping took over in 2013. China is far more oppressive, nationalist and expansionist than it was under his recent predecessors. But the nature of the 'China problem' is quite different from what it was under Mao. Whereas Mao was economically illiterate and ruined the economy, the Xi regime is economically sophisticated and presides over an economy at the cutting edge of innovation in many fields. In this sense also it is very different from Putin's Russia, which runs an oil-dependent economy with only modest efforts to modernise its economy. In other words, China represents a new phenomenon in international affairs: a regime that is radically anti-democratic and illiberal, combining high levels of domestic oppression and wide-ranging expansionist ambitions with the kinds of Enlightenment attitudes to science and technical innovation that are normally associated with open, liberal and democratic societies.

The issue for Japan, therefore, and for many other countries is how to react to this new phenomenon. At first glance, two essentially opposite strategies suggest themselves. One would be to resist Chinese expansionism and refuse to engage with China on the grounds that it is controlled by an undesirable, repressive and dangerous regime. The other would be to ignore the repressive and anti-democratic aspects of the regime and engage actively with the rapidly advancing and innovating Chinese economy to the potential advantage of one's own economy. In other words, jump onto the Chinese economic bandwagon.

The problem with the first option is that is most unlikely to work. The only country in the world today with the economic clout to curb China's expansion in a definitive fashion is the United States. In April 2019 two US naval vessels were sent through the strait between China proper and Taiwan as a gesture to deter a possible military takeover of Taiwan by mainland China. But China is massively rearming, and although the United States still retains naval superiority, it seems unlikely that the effect of such a deterrent would last for long. It would also bring with it the danger of a destructive war between two nuclear powers.

But the second option entails even more serious issues of principle and practice. Recent media reports tell of outrageous discrimination against the Muslim Uighur population in Xinjiang Province of western China, claiming that large numbers of Uighurs are being corralled into 're-education camps' where they are being indoctrinated into stereotyped Chinese values and behaviour, so that they may be forced into a common mould quite incompatible with their religious and cultural beliefs. This is a small part of a wider policy on the part of the regime, whereby the control exercised by the CCP is more and more pervasive. For foreign countries to ignore such issues in order to profit from the Chinese economic bonanza hardly seems worthy of states based on liberal and democratic values. In addition to that, national interest considerations dictate that Chinese proposals to other countries be treated with careful scrutiny, based on good understanding of how the current Chinese regime makes decisions in practice. Italy, now under a government of the far right, is the first European country to sign up to a Chinese proposal, in this case for China to manage the port of Trieste. Even if this does not infringe international trading rules, it is the kind of arrangement that deserved meticulous prior examination. The 2019 issue of the Huawei Company being allowed to develop part of the British 5G network, is subject to the same concerns.

There is no simple answer to this question, but any strategy in relation to China should attempt to combine a readiness to engage, together with extreme care over the implications of agreements being entered into. So far as Japanese China policy is concerned, some stability at least seems now to have been reached in the Japan-China dispute over the Senkaku/Diaoyu islets. The complex disputes between China and various littoral countries bordering the South China Sea do not concern Japan in a territorial sense, but may be seen as threatening the Japanese interest in maintaining freedom of the seas in a maritime area across which much Japanese trade passes.

A final point to be made about Japan's relations with her enormous neighbour is that events suggesting a 'China threat' tend to increase popular support for hard-line Japanese governments that appear to be tough on China.

Another 'threat' that is often perceived, rightly or wrongly, in Japan, relates to the Korean peninsula. The North Korean nuclear weapons programme since the 1990s has regularly raised alarm in Japan, but Japan has few realistic means of influencing it. In addition, a series of kidnappings, mostly of young people, from Japanese shores that occurred in the late 1970s and early 1980s became a major polarising issue in Japan in later years, especially following Koizumi's visit to Pyongyang in 2002. More recent meetings between President Trump and the North Korean leader Kim Jong-un followed on from contacts between Kim and the recently elected South Korean President, Moon Jae-in. But the aim of persuading North Korea to abandon its nuclear weapons programme in the foreseeable future seems remote. When I asked a retired British diplomat, familiar with North Korea, whether Kim Jong-un was likely to abandon his nuclear programme, he replied in two words, 'Would **you**?' Indeed, North Korean nuclear weapons should be seen as a deterrent, largely against possible American attempts to force regime change in the north. North Korea, though it is slowly modernising, remains an economic midget, and should be far less of a concern to Japan than China.

Between Japan and its northern neighbour, Russia, there a long-standing territorial dispute over islands taken from Japan at the end of the war. The best that can now be said about this, however, is that while Putin remains in power, the prospects of their return to Japan is minuscule. The Russian regime has its sights focused much more on Europe than on Japan.

Let me now attempt to answer the question posed by the title of this chapter, 'What future for Japan?'

Any prediction has to begin with present reality. Japan in 2019 is prosperous and civilised, while its citizens enjoy a standard of living that is high by international standards, as well as an expectation of life that is practically the highest of any country in the world. The Japanese economy is the third largest in the world, though it lags well behind the first two. Japan, in the proud words of the recently retired Heisei Emperor (Akihito), 'has been at peace throughout my reign'. On the other hand, pluralism in the political system has been giving way to a much more monolithic regime, where dissident views are closely controlled. What the Australian scholar Gavan McCormack calls 'The Construction State' encapsulates a system where building anything, anywhere becomes the norm, including even the concreting of river beds throughout the nation. McCormack also writes of 'The Client State', meaning that Japan is a client of the United States. One sad manifestation of this is the overwhelming presence of US military bases on the small south-western island of Okinawa, to which McCormack has devoted a great deal of time and research. (Gavan McCormack, *The State of the Japanese State: Contested Identity, Direction and Role*, Renaissance Books, 2018; and [with Satoko Oka Norimatsu) *Resistant Islands: Okinawa Confronts Japan and the United States*, Rowman and Littlefield, 2nd edn., 2012). It is arguable, however, that the Security Treaty with the United States has at least slowed down the development of military potential by Japan itself.

What, then, of the future? I leave aside 'black swans', meaning unpredictable events (though in Australia most swans are indeed black, not white). It is true that the possibility of a major seismic event devastating the Tokyo region, which is the centre of the Japanese economy, should not be ignored, but it raises so many possible scenarios that a reasonable prediction would require another book. A 'black swan' called 'Covid-19' comes too late for this book.

I see two sorts of likely development over the next few decades: Japanese aspects of world-wide trends, and trends more or less specific to Japan. Most serious among worldwide developments is clearly climate change, which will affect Japan just like everywhere else. Second is fragmentation, especially social and political. The impact of the Internet and particularly of social media, though having many positive advantages of facilitating communication, inevitably fragments societies and removes many established inhibitions on irresponsible speech and behaviour. So-called 'hate speech', whereby individuals feel freed from restraints on violent, racist and insulting expression, is already a serious issue in Japan. Social media companies worldwide, despite their huge resources and technological expertise (but low contribution to employment) are unable or unwilling to remove the most incendiary and damaging material from their networks. In too many cases, they are the inadvertent facilitators of terrorist acts. Unless the manifold problems created by social media are addressed, Japan and many other countries will suffer greatly.

One area where Japan provides a magnificent example to the rest of the world, including especially the United States, is gun control. Whether a safe society with a low crime rate can be maintained in the face of rampant extremist expression, remains to be seen.

Among trends specific to Japan, I am inclined to include population decline and the closely connected phenomenon of deindustrialisation in areas of the country outside the metropolitan megalopolis. It is true that this is not entirely unmatched elsewhere, especially in parts of southern Europe, but it is at its most extreme in Japan (and in South Korea, where the birth rate is also very low). In terms of global over-population this may not be entirely bad, but in narrow Japanese terms it is already causing serious economic and social problems. It is hard to persuade people to have children if they don't want to, but children in Japan are more expensive and difficult to rear and to educate than in many other countries, which suggests a series of measures that should be taken to mitigate the problem. Moreover, government reluctance to permit even quite manageable levels of immigration does nothing to alleviate the problem. Recent easing of immigration restrictions need to be further developed, along with appropriate measures to integrate those moving to Japan.

The final problem I want to discuss is Japan's incomplete (and I would argue retreating) democracy. The greatest tragedy of Japanese politics since the war has been the poor performance and ultimate collapse of the DPJ-based government in office between September 2009 and December 2012. It was a government launched amidst high hopes for the emergence of genuine political alternatives that would give the electorate a genuine choice, instead of voters knowing that only one party – the LDP – had a serious chance of being elected to government. A good part of the reason for LDP dominance was the strength and sophistication of its organisational structure, which traced its roots back to conservative parties in the period before the Asia-Pacific War. Though far less monolithic than the Chinese Communist Party, the LDP was a growth under the shade of which other plants were hard put to grow and prosper. In its brief periods out of power, first in the mid-1990s and more recently between 2009 and 2012, it was able to reorganise itself effectively, without the distraction of having to run the country, so that by the time Abe began his second government, he could rely upon a fully functioning and well organised structure. In addition, it now had a leader able and willing to shape the party in his own image, favouring those whose base lay in organisations of the far right.

Abe has been elected to a term as President of the LDP that ends in 2021, when presumably a new party leader will be elected. It is to be hoped that a new leader may emerge, of a different stamp from Abe, recognising that Japan needs a pluralist political system, in which genuine competition between different competent and well organised parties becomes possible. This will require also competence and good organisation on the part of a party or parties challenging the LDP. Only if a balanced system comes about will it be possible for moderate but decisive political activity to flourish.

And finally, the new Emperor, 'symbol of the state and of the unity of the people' will have an important role to play in ensuring the health of Japanese democracy.

16

By Way of a Conclusion

ᚼ

AUDREY AND I had our first sight of Japan from a ship moored offshore from the Port of Yokkaichi early in the morning on a day not far into 1962. We were young, adventurous, new parents, with our adult lives ahead of us, journeying to a strange country that became our home for fifteen months, and which we got to know over many subsequent visits and occasional longer periods of residence.

For me, Japan became a place where I could study politics without having to fit in with preconceptions based on what most textbooks regarded as a normal state of affairs, but which was a reality specific to Europe and North America. Japanese politics appeared to work along familiar lines, but under close analysis turned out to follow pragmatic rules reflecting cultural assumptions contrasting with those of Europe or North America. For Audrey Japan inspired and educated her in her developing talent for pottery. In our tours of Japanese pottery regions, we encountered an amazing variety of local traditions (some in south-western areas derived from Korea), where potters belong to 'dynasties' that could be traced back for many generations. At the same time, tradition was not incompatible with modernity, and we met younger potters who were quick to experiment with new techniques. Audrey studied with various potters in the metropolitan region (including the woman who started on the whisky at 11.00 in the morning), and absorbed much of what, perhaps pretentiously, might be called 'the Japanese aesthetic'.

I think it was significant that we came to Japan, not directly from our native England, but from Australia where we were relatively new residents. Australian culture is obviously closely derived from that of the United Kingdom, but it was not long into our life in Australia that we realised that Australia was different from what we had been used to while growing up in the UK. I can only put in fanciful terms, but there was for us something in the air of Australia that was liberating and relatively uncluttered with preconceptions. When we travelled within Australia, not just by plane to other cities, but to outback locations such as the mining town of Broken Hill and the awe-inspiring emptiness of Wilpena Pound in South Australia, we breathed that air of liberation. In her wonderful book titled *The Road from Coorain*, Jill Ker Conway tells graphically how utterly tragic life in the outback can be for those who live there during droughts that can last for years, but the book is infused by a sense of the possibilities of liberation as well as the challenges of an unforgiving environment.

Much in Australia contrasts with much in Japan, and such similarities as there are have different causes. Australia is a large island continent most of whose population lives in cities round the coast, leaving the empty centre to marsupials and desert winds. Japan is a chain of islands off the coast of Asia, densely populated to an extent unimaginable in Australia. The Japanese population is also concentrated around the coast, because most of the interior consists of high mountain ranges. Japan experiences some twenty per cent of the world's earthquakes, whereas almost all of Australia has stable geology.

For Audrey and me, going from Australia to Japan was the second stage in a two-stage transition, from an old established European cultural environment, to a closely related but more liberated society, and then to a country where ancient traditions of a non-European, non-Christian provenance coexisted with institutions and practices typical of the modern world. The past century has seen a gradual retreat from religious commitment in most of the modern world, including Japan, but it is far from dead. One of the things that has fascinated me about Japan is the difficulties involved in attempting a comparison between religion in Japan and religion in the Christian – or indeed Jewish or Islamic – worlds. Those 'Abrahamic' religions are as one in worshipping a single all-pervasive God, whereas religion in Japan hovers between polytheistic and essentially non-theistic belief systems.

There are, it is true, those in Japan who profess the Christian faith, but they do not amount to much more than one per cent of the population, even though indirect influence from Christian-derived morality is substantially greater. The three principal religious traditions are Confucianism, Buddhism and Shintō. Confucianism is a philosophy with a religious patina, concerned with the proper (hierarchical) ordering of society. Japanese Buddhism is part of an Asia-wide religious tradition, but reverence for the Buddha, who was a historical person, is hard to compare with reverence for a super-natural God. Japanese people today adhere to Buddhism principally as the religion of death and funerals. Shintō is derived from polythe-istic folk religion, was developed by the State after the Meiji Restora-tion of 1868 as a system for legitimising of the regime ruled by an Emperor seen as 'father' of the people, but after the war it reverted to something closer to folk religion, having a strong concern with purification rituals. Buddhism and Shintō are closely intertwined today, and it is common to find a Buddhist temple and a Shintō shrine cheek by jowl in the same compound. There is also a variety of 'new religions' or even 'new new religions' that have emerged in recent times, some of which have given religion in general a bad name. There was something of a religious boom in the 1980s, but the release of poison gas on the Tokyo Metro in 1994 by a bizarre sect resulted in a *general* discrediting of religions.

One problem with any attempt to compare Japanese and Chris-tian religious practice is that in Japan there is no easily quantifiable indicator of religious commitment such as regular church atten-dance. Large numbers of Japanese visit shrines and temples at fes-tivals such as that of New Year, and many affix written prayers to sacred trees. Some families have shrines within their own homes. But how far this represents serious religious involvement is ques-tionable. Contact with Japan raises in acute form the question, 'what is religion?'

My purpose in introducing religion here is that in Japan I found a society where one could not make the assumptions about a famil-iar religious-cultural background such as would be normal in most European countries. So in analysing Japanese politics, what differ-ence did it make that 'normal' (i.e. European) assumptions could not be relied upon? The only serious party in Japan based on a religious movement is the *Kōmeitō* (sometimes translated as 'Clean Government Party'), based on the *Sōka Gakkai* sect of Nichiren Buddhism. It is currently part of a coalition government with the LDP. The LDP itself has links with various religious groups at local level, but more significantly relies for support on the right wing *Shintō Seiji Renmei* mentioned above. This represents a nostalgic link with the pre-war period, in which *Shintō* was put into service as an ideological bastion of the regime. In my research on the LDP and other political parties, however, I found only partial evidence that religion played a major role in their ideology or support strategies.

In the United Kingdom, the Church of England used to be referred to as 'the Conservative Party at prayer', while the Labour Party in its early days took seriously its roots in Methodism. Such links have since declined. But if we are looking for political links with religion, we need look no further than to Northern Ireland, where the religious divide between Catholicism and Protestantism also defines a fundamental political cleavage about the division or unity of the island of Ireland.

In both Japan and the UK, religious observance has tended to be associated with broadly conservative political attitudes. In Japan between the Meiji period and 1945 this took an extreme form in the shape of State Shintō, used by the political regime to legitimise the Emperor-centred regime. There is no close correlation with this in the UK, but the once dominant Church of England was indeed a broadly conservative institution.

One of the most important developments in both countries since the 1990s has been the development of the Internet and in particular the growth of social media as a principal means of communication. If the Internet is a million encyclopaedias rolled into one, social media make it possible for anybody, of whatever social status or level of education, to express opinions or disseminate material, with hardly any discipline or curbs on what is presented airily as free speech. Free speech it may indeed be, but a disturbing amount of it is either 'hate speech' or 'fake news'. Moreover, hate speech exhibits a disturbing tendency to be translated into action. Ms Jo Cox, Labour MP for the Yorkshire constituency of Batley and Spen and a 'remainer' in the Brexit debates, was murdered by a white supremacist during the campaign for the June 2016 referendum on whether to leave the European Union. When the referendum delivered a narrow majority for 'leave', this gave the green light for even more hate speech and seems to have influenced, through social media, later instances of violence against those seen as 'not like us'.

For some perpetrators of hate speech the target is believers in the Islamic faith, for others foreigners in general, particularly those arriving from European Union countries such as Poles.

It is true, of course that the European Union is far from a perfect organisation. In Africa, for instance, it attracts resentment over EU trading policies that many Africans regard as damaging their own efforts to trade with Europe. Greeks, Italians and Spaniards (especially Greeks) see Brussels, aided by Paris and Berlin, as having bullied them over economic policies in defence of the euro. Previous Greek governments, on the other hand, were surely delinquent in their failure to manage their economy responsibly at an earlier stage. Power politics operates within Europe, as in other multinational communities, but the achievement of the EU in resuscitating Europe as a coherent entity is surely a major achievement to be balanced against this.

It is also disturbing to realise that a large number of individuals receive information on political and social matters from sources that are neither monitored nor checked against reality. Thus for instance it seems that many people actually believed the fake news that Pope Francis was supporting Donald Trump in the US presidential elections of 2016. It is of course true that the Internet has enormously expanded the amount of information available to ordinary people, and that social media make it easy for ordinary people to express their own opinions and interact with society, but hate speech and fake news are seriously malign side-effects of these otherwise beneficial technologies.

Japan, much like the UK, has experienced an epidemic of hate speech since social media became widely available, as well as being infected by fake news. Ever since the end of the war in 1945, there have been many nationalist organisations inhabiting the far reaches of the right wing. I remember several years ago standing near Roppongi crossing in central Tokyo and watching a long procession of sinister-looking trucks and vans, decked out with nationalist slogans and regalia and blaring out military music. They were going to a rally, perhaps in Hibiya Park, organised by the far right. As on previous occasions when I have seen such processions, I seemed to be the only bystander taking any notice of them. These organisations have run candidates in elections at various levels, but normally receive a negligible fraction of the vote. The arrival of social media, however, provides a potent tool for the propagation of ultra-nation-alist ideas. Before social media, ultra-nationalism, though associ-ated with occasional acts of violence, was basically kept in check. With social media pervasive, such checks are much reduced.

Both in Japan and in the United Kingdom, protest movements were most commonly associated with left-wing parties and organisations such as trade unions. In both countries also, there is now a strong tendency for protest to be channelled into far right movements. Electors seem to find little incongruity in jumping from one extreme to the other. In Japan, the decline of the political left is very marked, with union membership in sharp decline. Since, in the past, union backing has been crucial for left wing parties, the decline of unions is particularly serious for such parties. Moreover, the effect of an overtly nationalistic government, in power now for nearly a decade, has been to 'normalise' a political atmosphere that in previous decades would have been widely regarded as extreme. In the UK, unions still retain significant political clout, and are central to the politics of the Labour Party. But as in Japan the developing shape of employment makes it hard for unions to maintain their earlier numbers or level of influence.

The Brexit referendum was held on 23 June 2016. When I heard the results on the radio at seven o'clock in the morning of the 24th, I was so shocked that I felt physically ill for the rest of the day. The margin was narrow, but decisive. But I found it hard to accept that my country would no longer be a member of the European Union, an institution that had done so much (along with NATO) to reunite the European continent after two bloody wars costing tens of millions of deaths, followed by the Cold War that had divided Europe in two on a line stretching from the Baltic and the Adriatic, called by Churchill the 'Iron Curtain'. My parents were both born around the beginning of the twentieth century, and it was their generation that bore the brunt of 'the war that ended peace', to cite the title of Margaret MacMillan's fine study of the origins of the First World War (*The War that Ended Peace*, Profile Books, 2013). Whatever the faults of the European Union, its achievements have been extraordinary, but all too often neglected and underestimated, including by its advocates. Brexit represents a threat to its achievements in the current atmosphere of narrow nationalism that infects much of Europe as well as other parts of the world including the United States.

In May 2019, the British Conservative Party elected Boris Johnson as its new leader to succeed Theresa May, and thus as Prime Minister. Some months later, Johnson was able to negotiate a new 'leave' agreement with Brussels, much like the previous agreement negotiated by Theresa May but with a more flexible set of conditions concerning the border between the Irish Republic and Northern Ireland designed to avoid a 'hard border' (that is, a border including checks on merchandise and produce crossing the border in either direction). This was not to the liking of the Democratic Unionist Party in Northern Ireland (the principal party representing the Protestant community there), because it implied some kind of hard border in the Irish Sea between Northern Ireland and the United Kingdom. Even so, the agreement was finally accepted by the House of Commons, which had rejected the May agreement on three separate occasions.

The new Prime Minister dissolved the House of Commons and held new elections in December, which resulted in a clear majority of eighty seats for Johnson's Conservatives. A salient feature of the elections was the drastic loss of support by the main opposition Labour Party, under its far-left leader Jeremy Corbyn. The most surprising aspect of this was the conversion of many formerly safe Labour seats in the north of England and elsewhere (many had never elected a Conservative before) into seats with a Conservative majority. This dramatic shift in support from left to right seems explicable by a predominance of 'leave' voters in those constituencies, disillusion with the Labour leadership, resentment at London political dominance, and a desire to end the political paralysis of the past three and a half years.

The Prime Minister declared that the UK would leave the European Union on 31 January 2020, leaving a further eleven months to negotiate a trade deal with the European Union. It remained to be seen whether such a trade deal was feasible within such a tight timetable.

The period between June 2016 and December 2019 were a profoundly difficult and frustrating period in British politics. So how does the current British dilemma over Brexit compare with the political situation in Japan? At first sight British and Japanese political reality appear to be far apart. Japan does not belong to a multinational organisation such as the EU, although it has close defence and economic links with the USA. Regional bodies such as APEC are much narrower in scope. Whereas what among Brexiteers in the UK was regarded as uncontrolled immigration affecting local services and disadvantaging local people, in Japan immigration is strictly controlled at low levels (despite some recent relaxation). In the Brexit debates, 'return of full sovereignty', and 'give us our country back' were a powerful slogans, whereas national sovereignty is a much less salient issue in Japan. Largely because of the Brexit impasse, politics in the UK has recently gone through a prolonged period of unstable and divisive politics, in Japan it appears to be more stable than it has been for a long time.

Such stability, however, does not, necessarily mean a healthy political system. The Abe Government is democratic in the sense of accepting the results of elections, but is both authoritarian in many of its policies and nostalgic for the pre-war authoritarian state. Since the general failure of the DPJ Government over the 2009-2012 period, opposition has been weak, divided and ineffectual. Meanwhile, opposition *within the LDP*, in the shape of articulate factions with their own policy positions, has largely given way to factions that are ideological clones engaged in pork-barrel politics with each other and with many other interest groups. Corruption scandals still infect those involved in government. The system is surely awaiting radical reconstruction, which may start to occur assuming Abe steps down in 2021 and concludes his fourth term as LDP leader.

Revision of the 'Peace Clause' of the 1947 Constitution is a key ambition of Prime Minister Abe Shinzō. Many of those who agree with him point to the increasing gap between the wording of the article and the reality of increasingly capable and sophisticated Japanese military forces (albeit retaining the euphemistic name of 'Self-Defence Forces'). On the other hand, I believe that there is an analogy here with the Brexit debates in the United Kingdom. In the UK, membership of the European Union to a significant extent acted to legitimise internationalism and the value of having different cultures able to coexist and cooperate towards common goals.

Similarly, the 'Peace Clause' of the Japanese Constitution has legitimised the idea that a peaceful society and a peaceful world is a value that should be pursued, despite all the manifest obstacles to its realisation. Thus, to get rid of the clause – or even to modify it – risks opening the floodgates to promoting nationalism of a kind even reminiscent of Japan's 'sacred wartime mission', a key aspect of propaganda that infected relations between government and people in the pre-war and wartime periods.

Brexit in the United Kingdom, President Trump's hostility to multinational agreements in trade, the environment and other matters, as well as 'Peace Clause' revision and authoritarian tendencies in Japanese government, are aspects of a much broader shift in the balance of political movements and ideas in favour of narrow nationalism and derisory attitudes towards international conventions and practices in trade, diplomacy and many other areas of necessary regulation that have promoted reasonable sanity in a difficult world since 1945.

Despite my criticisms of how Japanese politics now works in practice, I think that in the longer term it has delivered many benefits for the Japanese people. Japan is prosperous and has been free from war for over seven decades. Some argue that such a long period of peace is despite, rather than because of, government action, but it defines Japan today. The country is technologically advanced, culturally sophisticated and infused with modernising energy, especially among highly educated young people. Equality of opportunity and reward between men and women is much less advanced than in other comparable countries, but the ability and drive of many women is impressive. Demographic decline is serious and has complex causes, but not all aspects of it are necessarily negative in an overcrowded world. The Okinawan base issue, however, continues to fester.

The rise of China over recent decades has cast a shadow over Japan, which used to be regarded as the brightest economic light of East Asia. But to re-coin a phrase that was used in Japan, perhaps prematurely, in the 2000s, 'Japan is back'. This is true, not only in the world of cultural artefacts such as cartoons and animation films (manga and anime) but also in areas of high tech such as robotics. Japan is now the world leader in the construction of robots that can perform many domestic tasks, such as providing daily assistance for elderly and handicapped people. In the field of artificial intelligence (AI) Japanese research and development is among the most advanced. In the automotive industries many of the best known international names (Toyota, Nissan, Honda, Mazda and so on) are Japanese.

When Audrey and I, with our baby daughter, travelled *towards Japan* by ship early in 1962, we were on a *personal journey* in which Japan was to play a major part. We had many things to learn. From the ship we went by local train to Nagoya, the nearest big city. The train was full of what at first we took to be very young postmen. In fact they were schoolchildren in standard issue uniform. We learned many other things about that extraordinary country in years to come. At the outset of the Reiwa era, the future of Japan, despite many problems, looks hopeful.

In this book, I have tried to splice together my own life with the modern reality of Japan. I would love to see what has become of Japan in fifty years' time, but by then my brief period of 'frenetic activity' will have ended and I shall have returned to a state of 'eternal idleness'. That is wholly natural, but what really matters is that the world should come to terms with what is required for the survival and stability not only of mankind but also of the planet as a whole. I believe that Japan will play its part in that.

A 'black swan event' known as 'Covid-19 arrived early in 2020 too late to be discussed in this book. Japan has been rather less seriously affected than the US and Europe, even though the Tokyo Olympics have been postponed to 2021. But it is the worst global crisis since 1945 and will change all our societies in ways hard to predict.

Index

⊼

For Product Safety Concerns and Information please contact our EU
representative GPSR@taylorandfrancis.com
Taylor & Francis Verlag GmbH, Kaufingerstraße 24, 80331 München, Germany